Engaging Young Engineers

Engaging Young Engineers

Teaching Problem-Solving Skills Through STEM

by

Angi Stone-MacDonald, Ph.D.

Kristen Wendell, Ph.D.

Anne Douglass, Ph.D.

and

Mary Lu Love, M.S.

University of Massachusetts Boston

Baltimore • London • Sydney

KH

Paul H. Brookes Publishing Co.
Post Office Box 10624
Baltimore, Maryland 21285–0624

www.brookespublishing.com

Typeset by Scribe Inc., Philadelphia, Pennsylvania.
Manufactured in the United States of America by
Sheridan Books, Inc., Chelsea, Michigan.

The individuals described in this book are composites or real people whose situations are masked and are based on
the authors' experiences. In all instances, names and identifying details have been changed to protect confidentiality.

Photographs are used by permission of the individuals pictured and/or their parents/guardians.

Cover image © istockphoto/CEFutcher
Photographs in Figures 3.3, 3.4, 4.4, 6.3 and on pages 126 and 155 by Kristen Wendell. All other photographs by K.A. MacDonald
(www.kamacdonaldphoto.com).

Library of Congress Cataloging-in-Publication Data

The Library of Congress has cataloged the print edition as follows:

Library of Congress Cataloging-in-Publication Data
Stone-MacDonald, Angela
    Engaging young engineers : teaching problem solving skills through stem / Angi Stone-MacDonald, Ph.D., Kristen Wendell,
Ph.D., Anne Douglass, Ph.D. and Mary Lu Love, M.S., University of Massachusetts Boston.
        pages cm
    Summary: "This title provides instruction on how to teach problem solving and critical thinking to young children (birth to 5)
using engineering, science, and routines as a framework. The engineering process is an ideal framework for designing learning
experiences that support science, technology, engineering, and mathematics (STEM) learning and cognitive development for
young children. Young children problem-solve in their daily play, and teachers and caregivers can promote the development of
problem solving and critical thinking skills through intentional activities that support young children's brain development and
prepare them for kindergarten. Key activities are outlined for each age group, with information on how each activity teaches young
children to be curious, persistent, flexible, reflective, and collaborative. This title also provides specific guidance for supporting
problem solving and science learning in inclusive classrooms using the universal design for learning (UDL) model, and it helps
teachers to prepare children to work towards the Common Core State Standards (CCSS) for kindergarten math and the Next
Generation Science Standards (NGSS) for kindergarten science. This title can serve as a supplemental text for early childhood
curriculum or instructional methods courses" —Provided by publisher.
    ISBN 978-1-59857-653-5 (paperback) — ISBN 978-1-59857-849-2 (retail pdf) — ISBN 978-1-59857-846-1 (retail epub)
    1. Science—Study and teaching (Early childhood)—United States. 2. Technology—Study and teaching (Early childhood)—
United States. 3. Engineering—Study and teaching (Early childhood)—United States. 4. Mathematics—Study and teaching
(Early childhood)—United States. I. Stone-MacDonald, Angela II. Title.
    LB1139.5.S35S86 2015
    507.1—dc23   2015000368

British Library Cataloguing in Publication data are available from the British Library.

2019   2018   2017   2016   2015

10   9   8   7   6   5   4   3   2   1

8/19/16

Contents

About the Forms

Purchasers of this book have permission to photocopy Appendixes A–G for educational use. These materials are also available for download. Please visit **http://www.brookespublishing.com/ stone-macdonald/materials** to access them.

About the Authors

Angi Stone-MacDonald, Ph.D., is an assistant professor at the University of Massachusetts Boston in the Early Education and Care in Inclusive Settings program. She received her doctorate from Indiana University in special education and African studies. Dr. Stone-MacDonald has worked with children with disabilities and their families since 1997 as a paraprofessional, teacher, consultant, and researcher. She has taught courses in assistive technology and technology for young children. Her areas of research include early intervention, international special education for children with developmental disabilities, and teacher preparation for early intervention. She published two articles on the use of technology in professional development and early childhood education. Her current research agenda includes work on immigrant family experiences in the early intervention system and early intervention personnel preparation and inclusive education in Tanzania. She has several grants to support her research from her university; the Massachusetts Department of Early Education and Care; and the Office of Special Education Programs, U.S. Department of Education.

Dr. Stone-MacDonald serves her field and children and families with disabilities at the local, state, and national levels on a variety of committees and projects. She has been actively involved in state and local committees, organizations, and grant work with the state government to promote inclusion and adequate teacher preparation to work with children with disabilities in early childhood. Most recently, she served on the Higher Education Early Intervention Task Force and Personnel Preparation Committee and the board of the Massachusetts Association of Early Childhood Teacher Educators.

Kristen Wendell, Ph.D., is an assistant professor of elementary science education at the University of Massachusetts Boston. She received a B.S. in mechanical and aerospace engineering from Princeton University, an M.S. in aeronautics and astronautics from Massachusetts Institute of Technology (MIT), and a Ph.D. in science education from Tufts University.

Dr. Wendell's teaching and research interests include preservice and in-service teacher education in science and engineering and the integration of engineering design into children's science, reading, and writing experiences. A recipient of the National Science Foundation CAREER Award for early career faculty members, she investigates recommended practices for the introduction of engineering in pre-K–12 school settings and introduces future educators to the discipline of engineering as a key component of science education and a context for mathematical thinking, scientific reasoning, and language development.

Dr. Wendell previously worked at the Center for Engineering Education and Outreach at Tufts University, where she helped conduct a National Science Foundation–funded project on the impact of engineering-based curricula on elementary students' science content knowledge. While at Tufts, she worked with elementary teachers and students in the urban rim of Boston. Dr. Wendell is also an engineer. She was a graduate policy fellow at the National Academy of Engineering in Washington, D.C., and a research assistant in aerospace engineering at the Man-Vehicle Lab at MIT.

Anne Douglass, Ph.D., is an assistant professor of early childhood education in the College of Education and Human Development at the University of Massachusetts Boston, where she directs the bachelor's degree program in early education and care in inclusive settings. Dr. Douglass received her Ph.D. from the Heller School for Social Policy at Brandeis University, her master's degree in education from the Harvard University Graduate School of Education, and her bachelor's degree in political science from Wellesley College. She has taught graduate and undergraduate courses in early childhood STEM education and served as the principal investigator on a professional development project to promote STEM teaching and learning with children from birth to age 5. Through these experiences, she found that educators of children from birth to age 5 had very little access to professional development opportunities focused on STEM education.

Dr. Douglass's research focuses on early childhood policy, professional development, quality improvement, and leadership. She studies relational organizational practices and how they contribute to early educators' capacity to apply new knowledge to improve their teaching practices and their partnerships with families. Dr. Douglass brings almost 20 years of expertise as an early educator to this work, enabling strong connections among research, practice, and policy. She worked in the early childhood field in Boston as a teacher of children from birth to age 5, a program director, a family child care provider, a trainer, and an organizational consultant. Most notably, she developed and directed an early childhood program at a shelter for homeless families in Boston for 8 years.

Mary Lu Love, M.S., is a lecturer/director of early childhood services at the Institute for Community Inclusion at the University of Massachusetts Boston, where she manages grants, evaluation projects, and a variety of grant work in the early childhood field. Her undergraduate degree is from the State University of New York, Potsdam, where she graduated with a major in interdisciplinary social science and elementary education certification. She holds a master's degree in child care administration and has worked in early childhood education for 40 years as a teacher and administrator in public schools, Head Start, and private and nonprofit early childhood programs. She was a part of the 2011 Department of Early Education and Care–funded project *Focusing a New Lens: STEM Professional Development for Early Education and Care Educators and Programs*.

Ms. Love has taught in higher education part time since 1986, teaching ethics, science, and mathematics for all young children and supervising internships. Her two adult children are a particle physicist and an architect.

Foreword

ENGINEERING? REALLY? YES.

My initial reaction to *Engaging Young Engineers: Teaching Problem-Solving Skills Through STEM* was a mixture of astonishment and delight: astonishment at the very idea of organizing a book around "emergent engineering" (engineering for babies, really?) followed by delight at the book's insights and practical relevance. STEM (science, technology, engineering, and mathematics) is now a weighty presence in early childhood as in K–12 education. Yet many teachers and teacher educators have anxieties about this domain and struggle with how to address STEM concepts in developmentally appropriate ways.

"Engineers use problem-solving methods to find solutions to our everyday problems." With the book's first sentence, the authors make a natural connection between engineering and the things that children birth to age 5 love to do, whether they're unrolling the toilet paper in the bathroom, making the tallest block tower *ever*, or stirring up the ingredients for a class pancake feast. "Think about it. Try it. Fix it. Share it." This is the authors' easy-to-remember version of the cyclical process that engineers use in their work, fitting neatly with how young children learn. As you will see, Stone-MacDonald, Wendell, Douglass, and Love view emergent engineering activities as a promising way to promote five core thinking skills: curious thinking, persistent thinking, flexible thinking, reflective thinking, and collaborative thinking. Each thinking skill is reflected in engineers' work but is also essential for success in school and in life, and each can be promoted in developmentally appropriate ways from infancy onward.

A DREAM TEAM

There couldn't be a better team of authors to develop the ideas in this book. Angi Stone-MacDonald, Kristen Wendell, Anne Douglass, and Mary Lu Love have diverse yet complementary professional backgrounds. Together, they bring deep knowledge of early childhood development and learning; special education and inclusive programming; assistive technology; early childhood professional development; STEM education; science education; and even engineering—one of the authors is, in fact, an engineer, among her other areas of expertise. Members of the team have led funded projects and implemented seminars, professional development workshops, and conference presentations to help educators promote STEM-related outcomes for young children. The book is a logical outgrowth of that collective knowledge base.

FIVE REASONS TO VALUE THIS BOOK

Engaging Young Engineers has many features that make it valuable for teachers, future teachers, and professional development providers. Here are five of the most important.

1. *Combining the "Why" with the "What."* Books that only provide theories and research findings can be frustrating to practitioners. But equally frustrating are books with a simplistic, cookbook approach. In contrast, here you will find an engaging discussion of the evidence behind the authors' conceptual framework combined with concrete

classroom suggestions and detailed activity plans. This combination builds educators' capacity to fine-tune their own strategies, using the book as a starting point.

2. *Addressing standards-related outcomes through a focus on problem solving.* The authors illustrate how each of the five problem-solving skills is aligned with and supports national, state, and professional standards whether the standards address mathematics, science, cognition, or approaches to learning (Hyson, 2008). Teachers and teacher educators can implement the book's proposed activities with confidence that important outcomes are being supported.

3. *Identifying universal design for learning supports to create access and participation for all children.* UDL (universal design for learning) is a concept that still needs to be better understood and more widely used. Here it is not just an add-on; UDL supports are suggested in every chapter and for every activity, using profiles of real children to illustrate how to scaffold and support children with disabilities and delays as well as those who are dual language learners.

4. *Using "emergent engineering" and STEM to support competencies across multiple domains.* Teachers often worry, and rightly, about the fragmentation of the early childhood curriculum. This book takes a very different approach. Throughout, engineering activities are used not only to integrate STEM competencies across the curriculum but also to promote children's language, literacy, and social-emotional development through engagement with relevant books, pretend play, and multiple means of representation.

5. *Providing practical resources for planning, assessment, and reflection.* Teachers will be delighted with the easy-to-use planning and assessment forms, including rubrics tied to activities. Self-reflection checklists are a great professional development tool to help readers track their progress in applying the book's ideas. I could see these and other resources being used collaboratively by professional communities of learners.

A UNIVERSAL WRENCH FOR EARLY CHILDHOOD PROFESSIONALS

A "universal wrench" is a handy sort of tool, able to be used in many different ways, adjusting the fit for different tasks and needs. It occurred to me that *Engaging Young Engineers* is a kind of universal wrench. With the powerful concept of emergent engineering, teachers have a tool that makes it possible (and enjoyable and easy) to address many different, distinct, yet connected problem-solving skills and to support development across multiple domains. In addition, the book's suggested activities are not one-size-fits-all; each can readily be adapted to respond to children's unique characteristics and needs, including their developmental level, culture and language, and abilities and disabilities.

In so many ways, this is the right book at the right time for the right purposes. The authors should be commended for offering readers an eye-opening, thought-provoking, and eminently practical resource.

Marilou Hyson, Ph.D.
Adjunct Professor
College of Education and Human Development
University of Massachusetts Boston

REFERENCE

Hyson, M. (2008). *Enthusiastic and engaged learners: Approaches to learning in the early childhood classroom.* New York: Teachers College Press; and Washington, DC: NAEYC.

A Note to the Reader

Engineers use problem-solving methods to find solutions to our everyday problems. The engineering process is an ideal problem-solving framework for designing learning experiences that support science, technology, engineering, and math (STEM) learning and cognitive development with young children. Young children problem-solve in their daily play. As teachers and caregivers, we can promote the development of problem-solving and critical thinking skills through intentional activities that support young children's brain development. The concepts and methods of universal design for learning (UDL) provide a structure for planning lessons to meet the needs of a range of children.

This book came out of several years of work with early childhood educators through different projects to promote STEM-related learning outcomes. Some of these individuals and projects are discussed in the Acknowledgments. After completing a seminar with early educators on improving STEM education for children from birth to age 8, the authors presented the results of that seminar and the recommendation report at two national conferences: the Division for Early Childhood Conference and the National Association for the Education of Young Children Conference. We were approached by Paul H. Brookes Publishing Co. to write a book about using engineering in early childhood inclusive classrooms and jumped at the idea. We devoted substantial time working together to deepen our theoretical foundation and think about what messages we wanted to convey. We were especially interested in demonstrating how educators and caregivers can intentionally teach problem solving and STEM through engineering with children from birth to age 3. After research and activity development, we piloted the activities in infant, toddler, and preschool classrooms.

We also interviewed the teachers about what worked and what changes were necessary to implement the engineering experiences most effectively. The teachers gave us lots of substantive feedback on the activities, materials, and presentation of activities, and we incorporated that feedback into the chapters. The activities in this book can be taught in isolation or as a complete unit. Table I.1 provides an overview of all the lessons in the book sorted by age group and thinking skill. For these learning experiences, we have suggested several books to use in conjunction with the activities. Other books can be used to teach the same concepts, but we chose these books because they are high-quality examples of children's literature and easily accessible to early childhood educators and parents.

This book is divided into two sections. Section I explains the theory and evidence base behind the proposed framework. Section II includes the activity chapters where we show educators and caregivers how to use the problem-solving framework to participate in engineering learning experiences with infants, toddlers, and preschoolers. In the beginning of this book, we provide a foundation for the book's content by describing the engineering design process, engineering design in early childhood, and the five foundational thinking skills critical to developing young and adult problem solvers: curious thinking, persistent thinking, flexible thinking, reflective thinking, and collaborative thinking. Each thinking skill is discussed in a chapter. Table I.2 provides examples of each thinking skill for each of the three age groups. These thinking skills prepare young children to be successful in STEM activities and to learn to think as problem solvers. Finally, these skills support positive social-emotional development, self-regulation, and the development of executive functioning.

Chapter 1 begins by unpacking engineering design, engineering design for young children, and the five foundational thinking skills (as listed in Table I.2) for engineering and STEM. The premise of this book is twofold: First, young children can engage in a type of complex problem-solving called *engineering design*, and second, children's engagement with engineering design can

Table I.1. Thinking experiences by age group

	Infants	Toddlers	Preschoolers
Curious thinkers	With *Where's Spot?* by Eric Hill (2003), infants are provided with Hide-and-Seek experiences.	With *One Duck Stuck*, written by Phyllis Root (1998), toddlers explore what mud feels and looks like and compare and contrast it to water and dirt.	Preschoolers engage in "garden engineering" alongside Mr. McGreely, the main character of *Muncha! Muncha! Muncha!* by Candace Fleming (2002). They investigate sturdy garden walls by asking questions, making predictions, and building and testing.
Flexible thinkers	Through *Have You Seen My Cat?* by Eric Carle (2009), infants participate in a story and a game in which they must react to the problem of a missing cat.	Using *One Duck Stuck*, toddlers focus on the process of finding and excavating for objects stuck in dried mud.	Preschoolers consider all the ways that Mr. McGreely tries to solve his problem in the book *Muncha! Muncha! Muncha!* and they have the opportunity to plan at least two of their own solutions.
Persistent thinkers	*Baby Says Peekaboo!* by DK Publishing (2006) provides infants with large flaps that can be opened to reveal a hidden picture. Manipulating these flaps and searching to find a hidden object both require persistence.	With *Ten Dirty Pigs, Ten Clean Pigs*, written by Carol Roth (1999), toddlers focus on getting all 10 pigs clean and the process of scrubbing and cleaning to get the pig toys clean after mud play.	After more reading from *Muncha! Muncha! Muncha!*, preschoolers have the opportunity to build and persistently improve their own designs for protecting Mr. McGreely's vegetables.
Collaborative thinkers	Using the class-made *Find a Friend Book,* infants have the opportunity to strengthen positive and trusting relationships with others.	Using *One Duck Stuck,* toddlers focus on the process of finding objects stuck in wet mud using teamwork.	Using *The Tale of Peter Rabbit* by Beatrix Potter (2002), preschoolers consider the feelings that different individuals have in different situations and have an opportunity to work with a friend on a vegetable-carrier design challenge.
Reflective thinkers	Using a homemade baby faces game, infants have the opportunity to find a friend's picture.	With *One Duck Stuck,* toddlers have the opportunity to recall the story, retell it, and create a new ending.	Preschoolers have the opportunity to remember how they planned to solve a problem, how they created their initial solution, and what happened when they tried it out.

support their higher order thinking skills and, at the same time, provide an exciting context for integrated STEM learning in the early years.

Chapter 2 discusses the UDL principles because we strongly believe that all children should have access through the application of UDL principles to high-quality STEM activities in an

Table I.2. Developmental continuum of thinking skills

	Infants	Toddlers	Preschoolers
Curious thinkers wonder and actively explore people and things, especially the new and novel, and eventually abstract ideas.	• Use senses to explore the immediate environment • Explore and investigate ways to make something happen	• Show eagerness and interest in people, objects, and experiences • Use senses to explore and manipulate the environment • Investigate ways to make things happen in the environment	• Show interest in learning new things and trying new experiences • Ask questions to get information • Increasingly make independent choices
Persistent thinkers engage consistently in a challenging task and attempt multiple tries.	• Show interest in and excitement with familiar objects, people, and events • Repeat actions many times to achieve similar results	• Show interest in favorite activities over and over again • Find pleasure in causing things to happen • Try several times until successful	• Attend for extended periods of time when engaged, despite distractions or interruptions • Seek help when encountering a problem • Create and carry out a plan to solve a problem
Flexible thinkers adjust to changing information and goals, anticipate and plan for future scenarios, and consider new or different perspectives to "think outside the box."	• React differently to people, events, and settings • Try several ways to reach simple goals	• With adult support, make transitions between different tasks or activities • Use different ways of completing a task • Shift attention as needed • Observe and imitate how other people solve problems	• Try different ways to solve a problem • Adjust to new settings and people with minimal assistance • Exhibit adaptability, imagination, and inventiveness when attempting to solve a problem • Draw on different resources to solve a problem
Collaborative thinkers coordinate two or more people's actions in order to achieve a common goal.	• Engage in joint attention • Imitate the physical actions of others • Play simple games • Anticipate predictable interactions • Develop secure attachments with trusted adults	• Use adults as a safety point to explore and return to • Engage in parallel play with peers • Use trusted adults as a secure base from which to explore the world • Show concern about the feelings of others	• Recognize basic emotional reactions of others and their causes • Notice and accept that others' feelings about a situation might be different from their own
Reflective thinkers recall an object or event in their minds, remember it later, analyze it, and then plan to carry out next steps.	• Recognize familiar people, places, and objects • Look for hidden objects based on their previous location • Recognize familiar people and objects by name	• Look for familiar people and recognize names • Make connections between objects and events • Recall familiar people • Know familiar routines	• Try different ways to solve a problem • Talk about experiences to evaluate and understand them • Draw on daily experiences and apply this knowledge to similar situations

inclusive setting. After highlighting the evidence base for these principles for creating inclusive classrooms and lessons, we look at how the principles can help early childhood education teachers support young children with disabilities or delays as they engage in the engineering design process with their peers. We then discuss how we adapt the UDL principles to support children from birth to age 5 in inclusive settings. Finally, we discuss the templates we use in our engineering experiences to support young children using the UDL supports to make the problem-solving framework accessible to all young children.

In Section II (Chapters 3–8), we demonstrate how to use the early childhood UDL-focused problem-solving framework to teach the five thinking skills to infants, toddlers, and preschoolers. Each thinking-skill-based chapter in this section includes three activities (one at each age group: infant, toddler, and preschooler) to illustrate how to design activities for that thinking skill within the problem-solving framework. All the activities also incorporate UDL supports so that all children in the classroom can participate in these engineering experiences. Each chapter follows the same sequence. In the thinking skill chapters, we do the following:

- Briefly revisit the applicable thinking skill for that chapter and why it is foundational to STEM readiness for young children

- Explain a routine or activity that can be used at each age level (infant, toddler, or preschooler) to teach the thinking skill, providing planning forms and templates to support educators in these activities and to plan additional activities

- Highlight UDL practices for six children described in the "Profile Children" section that follows (two at each age level) and offer modifications and suggestions for these children with special needs or who are English language learners (each chapter shows teachers how to plan intentionally to meet the needs of *all* children)

- Link all activities to standards/developmental milestones across domains

- Offer additional suggestions to support various learners in the class

In each chapter, we describe activities to teach specific thinking skills to each of the three age groups and provide the tools to implement these activities in an early childhood setting. We walk through the activities, the planning process, and the implementation of the activities. Each activity uses a portion of the engineering design process to teach problem-solving skills. These activities illustrate methods to teach the prerequisite problem-solving and thinking skills that young children need to be successful in STEM learning. In addition, the activities presented in this book are accessible to all young children in the classroom through the implementation of UDL guidelines that have been adapted for early childhood education (Center for Applied Special Technology [CAST], 2012). Each of these engineering experiences at a given age level uses the same template. The infant activities focus on the prerequisite skills for different aspects of problem solving, whereas the preschool activities take children through an entire step in the engineering process. All activities are linked to standards addressed in various infant-toddler and preschool curricula used in settings such as Head Start as well as the kindergarten Common Core standards and Next Generation Science Standards to support school readiness (see Table I.2).

Many of the activities presented in this book could be used to teach more than one or even all the thinking skills, but we have chosen to use the described activities in each chapter to highlight how to teach that specific skill. Using the templates, educators and caregivers can create customized lessons around an activity to teach children a different skill or focus on different outcomes depending on the goals and standards for the lesson. For example, in Chapter 7, the toddler collaborative thinking activity "Mud Excavations" is a great activity for teaching flexible thinking, but this activity can also be used with preschoolers and can teach persistent and curious thinking. We have chosen to use the activity for collaborative thinking and with toddlers to show very intentional ways to teach that skill with that age group.

Chapters 3–7 highlight UDL supports for six children, two at each age level, who need additional supports to maximize their learning. The following "Profile Children" section provides more information about these children before ways to address their unique learning needs during the STEM activities are discussed. As we demonstrate the various activities, we emphasize strategies within the UDL framework to support all children in your setting. Finally, we will provide blank planning and UDL forms as appendixes to help educators plan additional activities to teach the specific thinking skills using the UDL and problem-solving framework. The completed planning materials are embedded in the chapters and appear as blank forms in the appendixes.

Chapter 8 discusses how to help educators apply this framework to their practice and adult learning and how to model problem solving as adults in their classroom and with their students.

PROFILE CHILDREN

The children described in this section represent real children we have worked with who are members of inclusive early childhood settings in the United States. These children are featured in the following chapters to help illustrate specifically and generally how to use early childhood UDL principles to support young children of all abilities. The examples include children who have different special needs and some who are English language learners. We hope the profile children will be similar to children you have in your own classroom who can learn problem solving and practice the five thinking skills through the activities in the book. In the templates, look for the UDL supports included specifically for one of these children and the supports that will help all children in the classroom develop problem-solving and complex thinking skills.

Julia, Infant

Julia is a 12-month-old girl who was born at 29 weeks and spent parts of her first 6 months in the hospital due to underdeveloped lungs and low birth weight. Despite these health challenges, Julia is doing very well. She lives at home with her mother, father, two older brothers (6 and 8), one sister (9), and her grandmother. She is babbling, can pull herself up, and is taking some steps with the support of an adult or a railing. She crawls all around the house and is very excited to explore the living room and kitchen. She is very excited to point to things and ask for them. Her parents have taught her some sign language that she uses, such as MORE, JUICE, ALL DONE, and MILK. She is eating finger foods and has a good appetite. Julia sleeps through the night most of the time. Julia loves to imitate what her mother and siblings are doing. She plays well with her brothers and sister, but they do not always want to play with her. She likes to shake her head no, point to something out of reach, or wave bye-bye. She is starting to show inflection when she is babbling and has almost said "mama" and "dada." She enjoys hearing books, and her favorites are those by Eric Carle and Dr. Seuss. She thinks they are very funny. She also likes books with soft and crinkly parts.

Julia attends a child care center during the day while her parents are at work. She goes to the center Monday through Thursday and is at home with her grandmother most Fridays. On the weekends and in the evenings, she often tags along to sports and lessons with one of her older siblings.

David, Infant

David is 14 months old and was born with Down syndrome and a congenital heart defect. He had open heart surgery when he was 6 months old. In his first year, David often got ear infections and has recently had a set of pressure-equalizing (PE) ear tubes placed in his ears. David lives at home with his parents and is an only child. Currently, David is not crawling or walking, but he can sit up on his own and scoots himself along the floor. He has good head control and enjoys tummy time. He is a poor sleeper at night but can take long naps. This results in crankiness and an uncertain progress at times for his various therapies because he is so tired during sessions.

David is working with a speech-language pathologist through the early intervention program and is working on oral stimulation, oral-motor awareness, and multiple experiences with oral sensory stimulation. In speech therapy visits, the therapist has used short descriptive sentences to describe toys David picked up. After 2–3 weeks of speech therapy, David's mother became adept at these techniques and began describing his activities as he did them so that he could hear them and associate the object he had with the words he heard. David is making a few sounds, and his parents have taught him some sign language. At this time, his mother is a stay-at-home parent and works with him every day on therapy goals. She takes him to a mommy-and-me playgroup at the early intervention site and also to the children's hospital each week for his physical therapy appointment. He enjoys going to the pool and floating in the water with his parents. His parents want to enroll him in a child care center when he is 18 months old but are concerned about his many therapies and if the center will be able to handle all his needs.

Tam, Toddler

Tam, a 20-month-old girl, was referred to the early intervention program for a developmental delay 6 months ago because she was failing to thrive and had some heart issues. She has been receiving services for early intervention for 4 months. Tam's parents and grandparents are from Vietnam, but Tam was born in the United States. At home, they speak Vietnamese. Tam lives with her mother, father, and 4-year-old sister, and her maternal grandparents live nearby and often care for the children. Tam and her mother see an early intervention specialist and an occupational therapist in the home once a week.

With the support of the of the occupational therapist, Tam is learning to eat baby food, hold an adapted spoon, and drink small amounts of liquid from a sippy cup. Her mother reports that Tam needs assistance with dressing but enjoys bath time. Tam plays by reaching for and batting toys, using Picture Communication Symbols the family has been given by the early intervention specialist, and making sounds or gestures. The symbols have the words in both English and Vietnamese so her parents and grandparents can understand what each picture means from both the picture and the word. Tam is very interactive with those around her and tries to join in imitative sound play by making her own sounds following sounds made by others. She is starting to speak in syllables. Her mother told the early intervention specialists that Tam will use gestures and sounds to let her mom and dad know when she wants something, such as when she wants to be picked up, when she is full, or if she does not like a particular food. Tam will cry and fuss when she is not understood. She is motivated to move to get her toys, although she is not able to move far without assistance. Tam appears to enjoy being with adults and other children and likes to be read to. When with other children, especially her sister, Tam watches them, laughs, and attempts to imitate sounds they make. She loves toys that make sounds and is more motivated to be happy when given one of these toys. She especially likes toys that play tunes.

Jessie, Toddler

Jessie is 2 years, 5 months old. Her mother is from India and her father is an American of Swedish heritage. After a full term of 9 months, her mother gave birth to her via normal delivery. As an infant, she was healthy and breastfed by her mother. They would like to raise her as a bilingual child who can also speak Hindi. Both parents speak Hindi and English. Her father is a real-estate agent and her mother is a professor. They met in India. Jessie met her early developmental milestones and started walking at 10 months and talking at 13 months but was struggling with social-emotional development. She did not like to separate from her family and had tantrums easily. Jessie does not have a diagnosed disability but has been assessed for early intervention based on social-emotional concerns from both the family and the child care center. She started speaking mostly in English but then shifted to using both languages for single words to two-word phrases. She seems to already recognize that she speaks Hindi at home mostly but English at school, and her vocabulary in both languages is growing.

When she was 1 year old, her mother decided to go back to work, and Jessie started going to a family child care center in the neighborhood. At first she had difficulty adjusting to the setting, because Jessie would cry every time her mother left the house or left her at the child care center.

It seemed that she was very attached to her mother, but gradually she stopped crying and started to play with the other children. Her motor and cognitive development are typical, and she has excellent visual-spatial skills and hand—eye coordination. Jessie has several playmates at her family child care center. She talks with the other children and initiates games and conversations, but she can lose her temper very quickly if she does not get what she wants. She can engage in violent temper tantrums in which she kicks and screams and throws herself to the floor. She does not hurt her peers during her tantrums, but the other children usually go to another part of the room or another room if there are several adults. She particularly likes playing with the older children. Her favorite toys are building blocks, balls, and her veterinarian kit. She likes to build large structures but gets upset when the boys knock them down, purposely or accidentally. She likes to play with the family dog and cat. She is also fond of scribbling and asks for crayons.

Brandon, Preschooler

Brandon is a 3-year-old child with autism. He participates in an inclusive preschool classroom with 18 typically developing children and 3 other children with various disabilities. Brandon lives with his mother and two older sisters at home: Sara, who is in second grade, and Hilary, who is in sixth grade. Brandon uses a communication device to help him communicate and likes electronic toys and games, as well as playing with his toy trains. He has approximately 15 words to communicate verbally and uses signs or his communication device for more complex messages. He understands many picture symbols and recently started to use an iPad with all his symbols on it. His mother is happy to have a device that is easier to program with his communication boards and often asks Brandon's sisters to help her program new words from school or new menus of choices related to a community outing. Brandon loves his new iPad and is more interested in using it to communicate and showing his skills to his classmates than he had been with his old basic electronic communicator.

Brandon likes to go to school and enjoys free play and gym. He is more engaged in his reading activities when they involve a train, electronics, or his iPad, because these are his favorite things. Brandon has slightly delayed cognitive development, but his teachers and family hope that his cognitive development will improve as his communication and language improve. He seeks interaction from his peers, but sometimes he is frustrated when they cannot understand what he wants or he does not get a turn in a game, and he will hit or scream as a result. His inclusive preschool teacher is working with Brandon to find more positive ways for him to interact with his peers and to ask to be part of their activities. When outside on the playground, Brandon sometimes has trouble interacting with his peers appropriately because he does not use a device when outside and therefore is more limited in his communication capabilities. Because he is good at kicking and throwing, his peers like to play games with him and ride tricycles together.

José, Preschooler

José is a 4 ½-year-old boy who attends a preschool program in his city. He is friendly and cooperative and follows the rules and routines of his preschool program. He enjoys playing with toys and outdoor play equipment. He plays cooperatively with his peers, shares, and takes turns. José initiates hands-on activities independently and sustains attention until they are completed. He demonstrates curiosity through physical exploration. His favorite place to play is the dramatic play center.

José can draw shapes and simple pictures. His fine and gross motor skills and social-emotional development are age appropriate. José can follow two- to three-step directions. He enjoys looking at books and sitting with his teacher listening to stories, particularly ones that have pictures. However, listening to a story in a group and responding appropriately to related questions are difficult tasks for José. Attention in these tasks is variable. After 4–5 minutes, he tends to wander visually or get up and start walking around the classroom. At home with his family, José speaks Spanish, and his English expressive vocabulary is limited. His Spanish vocabulary and language skills seem more developed. None of his teachers speak Spanish. He will respond to adult questions but prefers to speak in Spanish and will interact with peers in the classroom in Spanish if other Spanish-speaking children are in the same area. He communicates frequently during free play and center time. When faced with a problem, he typically gives up, gives in, or walks away instead of using language to express himself. He generally describes objects by using color words. He asks questions infrequently, voicing them with inflection (e.g., "Mommy work?").

José can sort objects by shape, size, and color. He can name colors and identify shapes by pointing. José names simple objects and pictures in his classroom and can address his classmates by name. He demonstrates an emerging interest in letters and words, as evidenced by his journal writing. José can count by rote to 5 but is still working on his understanding of patterns.

Each of these children has unique circumstances but also strengths and needs educators will recognize in children in their own inclusive classrooms. The UDL planning sheets and completed templates will help teachers plan for children with similar needs in their own classrooms and develop ideas to support all children so they can fully participate in the STEM activities.

UNIVERSAL DESIGN FOR LEARNING SUPPORTS UNIT PLANNING SHEETS

A summary of the UDL supports used across the unit for each age group is included in the appendixes on a form called the Early Childhood UDL Planning Sheet. The Early Childhood UDL Planning Sheet summarizes the supports across the different activities based on the type of support (e.g., materials, methods of assessment) and whether the support is designed for an individual profile child or can be made available to any child who needs that additional scaffolding.

REFERENCES

Carle, E. (2009). *Have you seen my cat?* New York, NY: Little Simon.

Center for Applied Special Technology. (2012). *Research evidence: National design on universal design for learning.* Retrieved from http://www.udlcenter.org/research/researchevidence

DK Publishing. (2006). *Baby says Peekaboo!* New York, NY: Dorling Kindersley.

Fleming, C. (2002). *Muncha! Muncha! Muncha!* New York, NY: Atheneum Books.

Hill, E. (2003). *Where's Spot?* New York, NY: Putnam.

Potter, B. (2002/1902). *The tale of Peter Rabbit.* London, England: Warne.

Root, P. (1998). *One duck stuck.* Cambridge, MA: Candlewick Press.

Roth, C. (1999). *Ten dirty pigs, ten clean pigs.* New York, NY: North-South Books.

Acknowledgments

This book developed over the last several years, starting with a state professional development system grant in 2011 to fund a graduate seminar course in early childhood science, technology, engineering, and math (STEM) education. The purpose of this project was to bring together a cohort of early childhood STEM fellows to work with STEM experts. The team was to develop a report with recommendations to the state for improving professional development for early childhood educators and, in turn, outcomes for children in the areas of STEM. Anne Douglass was the principal investigator (PI) on the grant, Angi Stone-MacDonald was a co-PI on the grant and taught/facilitated the graduate seminar, and Mary Lu Love worked on the grant staff. Kristen Wendell participated in the seminar as an expert, taught us all about engineering design, and sparked our thinking about how to develop children as young engineers and problem solvers.

The seminar engaged participants in understanding and discussing the state of the field in STEM education for children from birth to 5 years old and in after-school care and the state of professional development for early childhood educators in STEM education. Participants examined what gaps and needs existed and offered suggestions to strengthen STEM education. Together with experts in the field, participants developed a set of recommendations for improved professional development for early childhood educators in STEM education (see Stone-MacDonald, Bartolini, Douglass, & Love, 2011).

We would like to thank the Region 6 Educator and Provider Support Collaborative and Region 4 Professional Development Partnership of the Child Care Resource Center in Massachusetts for the opportunity to work with early educators across our state to advance the field in the area of STEM education. We would also like to thank the experts and early educators who participated in the seminar, from whom we learned so much. We would also like to thank the participants in our conference presentations at the National Association for the Education of Young Children and Division for Early Childhood in 2012 for their thoughtful feedback about our work, which generated some of the initial ideas in the book.

Our learning experiences for infants, toddlers, and preschoolers would not be so rich without the dedicated teaching and comments from the educators at the Mission Hill School and Ellis Memorial Early Childhood Center. They graciously offered us their classrooms to pilot the activities and provided advice for improving the activities. Both places welcomed us and played with us while we introduced their children to the engineering activities.

For the idea to use the book *Muncha! Muncha! Muncha!* (Fleming, 2002) to launch engineering challenges, we are indebted to Brandon Lee. We are also grateful to the Center for Engineering

Education and Outreach at Tufts University for modeling so effectively how to integrate children's literature and engineering. We thank Marylin Bennett and her early childhood colleagues at Marlborough Public Schools for inspiring the four-part emergent engineering cycle. Kathy Clunis D'Andrea awed us with her talent for posing thoughtful question to nudge children to the next level of problem-solving.

We would like the thank Keith MacDonald for the wonderful and engaging pictures in this book. We all have a greater appreciation for the hard work it takes to create an excellent photograph that captures the moment of excitement and learning, particularly with young children who are always on the go.

Finally, we would like to thank Paul H. Brookes Publishing Co., particularly our acquisitions editor, Johanna Schmitter, for giving us the opportunity to write this book and for her support, and Sarah Zerofsky for all her guidance throughout the process. We hope our readers will benefit from reading this book as much as we have from writing it. Every project is a chance to grow as an educator, and we feel privileged to have had this opportunity.

REFERENCES

Fleming, C. (2002). *Muncha! Muncha! Muncha!* New York, NY: Atheneum Books.

Stone-MacDonald, A., Bartolini, V.L., Douglass, A., Love, M.L. (2011). *Focusing a new lens: STEM professional development for early education and care educators and programs.* Retrieved from http://www.communityinclusion.org/ecs/stem

I   Why Engineering and Problem Solving Are Important in Early Childhood Inclusive Classrooms

1

Young Children Are Natural Problem Solvers

A Framework Overview

There are two big ideas behind this book. The first is that young children can be *emergent engineers*. By that we mean that preschoolers, toddlers, and even infants exhibit many of the foundational skills used in the complex problem-solving activity of engineering design. The second big idea behind this book is that children's emergent engineering activities can develop their higher order thinking skills and at the same time provide an exciting context for integrated science, technology, engineering, and mathematics (STEM) learning in the early years. When we talk about STEM, we are not referring to stand-alone science, technology, engineering, or math activities that are isolated by subject area. Instead, we mean *integrated* STEM learning, where multifaceted experiences provide opportunities for children to participate in scientific and mathematical reasoning, computer and other technology use, and engineering design—all together within the same activity.

This book proposes a framework for children's STEM problem solving. This problem-solving framework is based on engineering design: It uses engineering design problems as content and context for all four STEM disciplines to be practiced simultaneously. Although engineering is one of the distinct STEM fields (it is the E in STEM), it can also be an activity in which knowledge, skills, and habits of mind from all four STEM disciplines are woven together. Of the four words represented by the acronym STEM, the word *engineering* is often perceived by educators, parents, and caregivers as representing something more daunting or unattainable than science, math, or technology. But really, at its core, engineering is the systematic solving of human problems by applying science, math, technology, and creativity. Engineers and engineering are all around, every day, and everyone engages in many engineering-like problem-solving activities. One of the goals of this book is to demystify engineering design and the skills that contribute to it.

In the problem-solving framework featured in this book, children and adults work together through four phases of engineering design that are appropriate for young children. These phases are as follows:

1.   Think about it

2.   Try it

3.   Fix it

4.   Share it

This chapter describes what children and adults do in each of these phases. It also describes five important higher order thinking skills that are essential for engineering designers and for young problem solvers. These thinking skills are as follows:

1.   Curious thinking

2.   Persistent thinking

3.   Flexible thinking

4.   Reflective thinking

5.   Collaborative thinking

The enhancement of these higher order thinking skills is the ultimate goal of engaging children in emergent engineering problem solving.

This introductory chapter begins with a summary of recent successful approaches to foster STEM learning among children from birth to age 5. Next we focus on the *E* in STEM and demystify engineering with some definitions of key terms and an overview of the engineering design process. We then turn to our problem-solving framework for emergent engineering. We describe its four main phases and its five foundational thinking skills. Finally, we set the problem-solving framework in the context of what we know about childhood development and standards for early education and care.

APPROACHES TO STEM LEARNING: BIRTH TO AGE 5

Recent developmental research tells us that preschoolers and some verbal toddlers can learn concepts in specific science domains (Gelman & Brenneman, 2004), exhibit reasoning skills for making sense of science investigations (Gopnik, 2012), use number sense to estimate and compare quantities (Clements & Sarama, 2003), and apply algorithmic thinking to create simple computer programs (Bers, 2008). Preverbal toddlers and infants also show early number sense and an understanding of relative quantity (Dehaene, 1997), and they demonstrate knowledge of important categories in physical science (e.g., which things stay up by themselves and which things need support; Hespos & Baillargeon, 2008) and life science (e.g., animal and nonanimal; Rakison & Poulin-Dubois, 2001). They can interact with and respond positively to developmentally appropriate computer technologies (e.g., digital photos of important people, videos of themselves solving problems; National Association for the Education of Young Children [NAEYC] & The Fred Rogers Center, 2012).

This body of knowledge about young children's abilities indicates that they have many resources to apply to activities that involve science, mathematics, and technology. We believe these resources also equip children for the engineering-based problem-solving framework used throughout this book. Many other early childhood educators and researchers have laid the groundwork for our particular approach to engaging young children in inclusive STEM learning activities. This section describes the work of some key contributors to early childhood science, math, technology, or engineering education. Their approaches give children opportunities to construct and represent their own knowledge through hands-on experiences facilitated by responsive adults. These contributions form much of the basis of what educators know about children's potential for STEM learning in the preschool years. Less is known about what it looks like when infants and toddlers are included in early STEM activities, and for that reason, we intentionally include those younger age groups in our work.

In the area of mathematics education, the *Building Blocks* program by Doug Clements and Julie Sarama is a federally funded, nationally tested preschool mathematics curriculum based on extensive research about the learning trajectories that children can follow in mathematics if ideally supported by research-based learning experiences. *Building Blocks* curriculum materials, manipulative kits, and software applications focus on finding mathematics in children's everyday activities, from art to songs to building blocks (Clements & Sarama, 2003). The focus is in children "mathematizing" by representing their activities with mathematical actions such as counting and transforming shapes. The *Building Blocks* materials use computer technology as a platform for electronic tools for this mathematizing work. In support of children's progress along the learning trajectories developed by the *Building Blocks* researchers, early childhood math educator Greg Nelson (2007) has pioneered a Montessori-based method of providing structured manipulatives and activities that preschool children choose and use to guide their development of number sense.

In early childhood science education, one widely used and praised inquiry-based approach is the *Young Scientists Series* created by Karen Worth and Ingrid Chalufour and their colleagues. Successfully applied across many different early childhood settings, this curriculum emphasizes hands-on experiences in which children construct and record knowledge about nature (Chalufour & Worth, 2003), structures (Chalufour & Worth, 2004), and water (Chalufour & Worth, 2005) under the guidance of expert adult facilitation. Chalufour and Worth stress the importance of sustained time for children to explore the properties of physical objects and materials—both those in nature and those that they construct themselves. Adults play a key role in posing questions about children's explorations and documenting their work and their discoveries.

The *Ramps and Pathways* approach developed by Rheta deVries and Christina Sales (2011) has much in common with the explorations of physical structures in the *Young Scientists Series*. What differentiates *Ramps and Pathways* is its focus on balls in motion and its explicitly constructivist take on developing children's physical science knowledge, inquiry skills, and design strategies. Children explore the never-ending possibilities for making balls move along tracks.

The *Preschool Pathways to Science (PrePS™)* approach (Gelman, Brenneman, Macdonald, & Roman, 2009) is a method for structuring and implementing a preschool science curriculum that is based on domain-specific constructivist theories and cognitive scientists' findings about young children's mental development. It represents a synthesis of emphasizing science process skills, science language, and core science concepts around which a long (from several months to a full year) sequence of science explorations is organized.

Several other current approaches to young children's STEM learning have their roots in Seymour Papert's (1980) theory of constructionism; proponents of this theory believe that intellectual growth stems from working on personally meaningful ideas with personally meaningful objects (both on computers and in tangible 3-D). Extending Piaget's theory of constructivism, constructionists advocate for children to have access to rich learning environments and powerful tools that can lead them to construct powerful ideas. The child-friendly computer programming language Scratch Jr. (Bers & Resnick, 2014), intended for children as young as 4 years old, is an example of a constructionist tool for children's exploration of personally meaningful ideas. Available on the web (http://www.scratchjr.org) and as an app for tablet computers, Scratch Jr. consists of a set of icons that can be dragged and dropped into place to command an on-screen "sprite" to act out a story of the child's own creation. Explorations with Scratch Jr. encourage computational thinking, which involves applying mathematical and geometric reasoning to create an algorithm for a behavior. Scratch Jr. is reminiscent of Logo, an earlier constructionist computer programming platform designed for children. Early childhood activities with LEGO bricks (Portsmore, 2010), LEGO Mindstorms robotics sets (Bers, 2008), and even wooden unit blocks can also be examples of constructionist STEM experiences, when the child is the one generating the ideas about how to use the tools.

ENGINEERING DESIGN DEMYSTIFIED

The learning activities in this book provide opportunities for young children to engage in something that we call *emergent engineering*. These emergent engineering activities are inspired by the way that adults participate in more sophisticated engineering design efforts. Although the results of engineering design are all around us, many people have an incomplete understanding of what engineers do or a negative impression about what engineering is. Before describing what young children's emergent engineering looks like, let us take a moment to unpack engineering design from an adult's perspective.

What Is Design?

Design is a very common term used in many different ways, but we use it to talk about any human activity with the conscious goal of creating a product—or plans for a product—that will solve an open-ended problem (Dym, 1994; Fortus, Dershimer, Krajcik, Marx, & Mamlok-Naaman, 2004). An open-ended problem is one that has multiple acceptable solutions. Design involves bringing about change in the physical world and changing a situation from the way it is to the way one wishes it to be (Simon, 1996). Often, design requires responding to an ill-structured problem. This kind of problem lacks all the information and structure needed to solve it. People engage in design to solve many kinds of problems, such as expressing themselves in words and graphics, decorating their homes and workplaces, putting food on the table, and creating new organizations and communities. Design is a key part of many professional domains, ranging from organizational design to fashion design, interior design, artistic design, graphic design, and architectural design. Engineering design is one of many types of design activities.

What Is Engineering Design?

Engineering design can be defined more specifically than design in general. It is the organized development and testing—through the use of math, science, and creativity—of products or processes that perform a desired function within specified limits (Davis & Gibbin, 2002; Dym & Little, 2004). The results of engineering design can be three-dimensional, such as vehicles and water filters; two-dimensional, such as drawings and printed sets of instructions; or digital, such as computer software.

A well-known example of engineering design applied to an ill-structured problem is the "shopping cart challenge" taken on by the California-based design firm IDEO. For a television documentary on innovation, their team of designers was asked to take the familiar grocery store shopping cart and redesign it in just 5 days (Kelley & Littman, 2001). They were given no specific goals except to make a better shopping cart and no guidelines except to get it done within 5 days. The IDEO design team had to figure out whom to consult about the current shopping cart experience, what to focus on as the most frustrating and important problems of existing shopping carts, what level of safety to maintain, how much money to spend on materials, and whether to design and construct one or many prototypes to test out their ideas. There was no specified path to follow to create a better shopping cart. This lack of a pathway is the essence of ill-structured engineering design work. Not only did the engineers have to figure out a solution to the problem, but they had to figure out what steps to take to achieve that solution. View the ABC *Nightline* "Deep Dive" episode for details on the IDEO designers' approach to solving the ill-structured shopping cart problem (ABC News, 1999).

Engineering design can also be applied to more well-defined problems. For instance, consider the highway repairs that are occurring all across the United States as cities and states work to maintain their transportation infrastructure. Civil engineers are often tasked with designing the set of materials, equipment, and processes that will be needed to repair a road. But for many roads, this is a well-defined problem that involves choosing from among a set of options rather than charting a new course to invent something unique. When a road needs to be repaired, the engineers already know how much wear and tear the road has to sustain, how cold it gets in the winter, how hot it gets in the summer, how wide the road needs to be, what driving speeds it must support, and what materials the road surface currently contains. The engineering design task is to choose the correct combination of materials (e.g., gravel, asphalt, paint) to repair this particular road surface and to plan the right sequence of heavy machinery to apply those materials safely and reliably. Because other engineers have solved this same general problem of road repair many times before, there is already a problem-solving path to follow, and any single instance of road repair is more like a well-defined problem than an ill-structured one.

Defining *Engineering* and *Technology* in General

Engineering *design* is just one activity—though a central activity—within the enormous enterprise of engineering, which also includes activities of failure analysis, economics, aesthetics, communications, and quality control (Petroski, 1996). Engineering has been informally practiced throughout history, but in recent centuries it has been formalized into professions and academic disciplines that rely heavily on math and science understanding (Petroski, 1996). Modern professional engineering companies work to make problem-solving products, systems, and analyses available to the public. Engineers work on many types of problems of different levels of complexity, ranging from very well-defined tasks, such as specifying the material for road repair, to highly ill-structured problems, such as improving the common shopping cart. In general, an engineer is anyone who applies creativity and knowledge of mathematics and science to work on solutions to society's needs and wants (Wulf, 1998). These solutions are called *technologies*.

Technologies are the products that result from engineering work (Wulf, 1998). This means that everything from washable crayons to toothpaste to airplanes can be considered an example of technology. The early education and care field often uses the word *technology* as shorthand for "computer technology"—that is, when educators talk about children using technology, they tend to think of children and computers or some other digital device, such as a tablet computer, a smartphone, a television, or a camera. In this book, when we talk about the *T* in STEM, we are referring to both these examples of computer technology *and* technology in general (i.e., all the tools and products that result from engineering, from pencils to robots). When children engage in emergent engineering, they might participate in creating technologies such as block towers that protect a pretend vegetable garden from hungry rabbits. They might also make use of existing technologies to scaffold their engineering activities. For example, a tablet computer might help them keep records of their different design ideas, or a specially designed nonslip surface might help them build with blocks more easily.

The Engineering Design Process

Engineers typically work together to solve the problems that face society. As mentioned earlier, engineering design is the process of creating solutions to human problems through creativity and the application of math and science knowledge. The fundamental practices within any engineering design process include at least the following six elements (Atman, Adams, Mosborg, Cardella, Turns, & Saleem, 2007; Gibson, Scherer, & Gibson, 2007; National Research Council [NRC], 2012; WGBH Educational Foundation, 2011):

1. *Defining a problem:* Observing a problem, seeing a need for a solution, and identifying criteria and constraints

2. *Researching possible solutions:* Gathering information and coming up with ideas to address the problem

3. *Choosing and planning the best solution:* Conducting an analysis of plans and data to determine which idea might best address the problem

4. *Building and testing a prototype:* Constructing a working model of the chosen solution and investigating the working model to find out if it solves the problem, holds up to any important tests, and follows any limits or rules imposed on the problem

5. *Improving the design:* Using evidence, comparing alternatives, and evaluating the ideas of peers to make adjustments until the working model solves the problem in a satisfactory way

6. *Communicating the solution:* Using oral and written language as well as tables, graphs, drawings, and models to express the solution to the problem and the advantages of the chosen solution

When engineering educators talk about engineering design practices, they are referring to ways of thinking and acting that are typical of adult engineers and that are productive for accomplishing engineering tasks (NRC, 2012). These practices do not occur in a regimented, consistent sequence of steps. They occur to different degrees and at different times within different engineering design processes. There is no single engineering design method (Lawson, 1997).

Even though there is no single engineering design method, there are commonalities across most expert engineers (Cross, 2003). Engineers continuously formulate and test hypotheses about the optimal solution to the problem they are trying to solve. They analyze and build models of potential solutions and clarify their understanding of the problem along the way. A strategy called *predictive analysis* is a tool used by engineers who are developing solutions that cannot be immediately built or tested due to budget constraints, complexity of design, lack of information about the client's needs, or human safety, for example.

Predictive analysis involves projecting how a proposed solution will behave before building and testing the solution itself. During predictive analysis, engineers estimate how many resources (e.g., time, money, fuel, raw materials) will be required to produce the solution, how successful it will be at solving the problem, and how long it will last. Once actually constructed or brought to the *prototype* stage, solutions often require further testing and experimentation to meet the criteria for success defined previously, and even the criteria for success may be amended as engineers progress through solving a problem.

The results of engineering design processes literally surround people in their everyday lives. Industrial, mechanical, and electrical engineers design the structures, systems, and machines that fill peoples' homes—including kitchen appliances, some furniture, heating and cooling systems, home lighting, televisions, music players, and computers. Every day, people use numerous substances perfected by chemical and biomedical engineers, including toothpaste, shampoo and conditioner, detergent, stain remover, plastics, Band-Aids, and medicines. Vehicles are designed by teams of engineers from many disciplines, including mechanical, electrical, aerospace, and manufacturing engineering. The infrastructures of cities and towns—including clean water, sanitation systems, roads, subways, bridges, tunnels, electricity delivery, traffic flow plans and traffic lights, skyscrapers, and  airports—were all designed with the help of civil and environmental engineers. And of course computer engineers and computer scientists are behind the computer technology that now affects almost every arena of daily life.

OUR PROBLEM-SOLVING FRAMEWORK FOR EMERGENT ENGINEERING

This book emphasizes four phases of engineering design that are most appropriate for structuring young children's problem-solving activities. These phases are *think about it, try it, fix it,* and *share it* (see Figure 1.1). Together with the five thinking skills (described in more detail later), the four phases make up our *problem-solving framework for emergent engineering.* Table 1.1 lists the tasks that children and adults carry out together in each phase and shows how those tasks correspond to the practices of professional engineers.

There are a few important caveats about the problem-solving framework. First of all, it is almost never developmentally appropriate—nor logistically feasible—for young children to conduct all four phases of the framework within a single sitting or activity. The phases are meant to help adults design units of learning rather than single experiences or lessons. However, by the same token, it is also typically not appropriate for young children to maintain focus on only a single phase of problem solving during any one particular activity. In fact, professional engineers often implement several engineering design practices at the same time. So it is not necessary to design learning experiences that limit themselves to only one of the four phases.

There are several other approaches to focusing early childhood learning environments around the activity of problem solving, and our emergent engineering framework builds on these. We differ in the idea that children can be competent emerging engineers, and their problem-solving work can be in response not just to problems they have identified

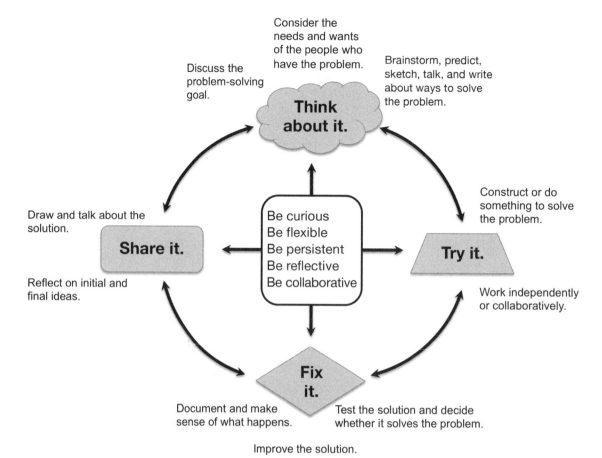

Consider the needs and wants of the people who have the problem.

Discuss the problem-solving goal.

Brainstorm, predict, sketch, talk, and write about ways to solve the problem.

Think about it.

Construct or do something to solve the problem.

Draw and talk about the solution.

Share it.

Be curious
Be flexible
Be persistent
Be reflective
Be collaborative

Try it.

Reflect on initial and final ideas.

Work independently or collaboratively.

Fix it.

Document and make sense of what happens.

Test the solution and decide whether it solves the problem.

Improve the solution.

Figure 1.1.   The phases and thinking skills of engineering design that make up this book's problem-solving framework for emergent engineering.

in their own daily activities but also to engineering problems that call for the application of creative thinking, mathematical reasoning, and scientific ideas. Our problem-solving approach using the emergent engineering framework could be incorporated into a Lillian Katz problem-based learning project or into a Reggio Emilia classroom, but the teacher would facilitate the children's enactment of an engineering design cycle to guide their work.

Thinking Skills for the Problem-Solving Framework

This book presents strategies for engaging young children in *emergent engineering*. To explain this idea of emergent engineering, it helps to draw an analogy to the field of emergent literacy. Early childhood educators and care providers know that most preschoolers and toddlers do not read entire books on their own from start to finish. However, even though young children do not often pick up a book and read it independently, adults do not wait until children are in first grade to start literacy learning experiences. Instead, from the infant stage on up, educators and care providers help children develop the book handling, phonological awareness, and letter knowledge skills that will help them become readers. Researchers have uncovered and clearly defined the skills that are foundational for reading, and educators and care providers work to develop these skills through early literacy initiatives and activities. Even though the children cannot yet read on their own, educators and care providers do many things to include young children in the act of

Table 1.1.   Phases and tasks within young children's engineering design

Phase of children's work	Tasks for children and adults	Engineering practices
Think about it	Talk, read, or listen about the problem. Discuss the goal for solving the problem. Identify the limits or "constraints" (e.g., number of materials, amount of time, size of structure) on solving the problem.	Identifying problems; unpacking requirements and constraints
	Look for similar problems and existing solutions. Discuss the needs and wants of the people who have the problem. Explore available materials. Make decisions about the problem-solving approach. ("We will build a boat instead of a bridge to solve the problem of crossing the river.")	Gathering information; revising the problem space
	Brainstorm. Design the solution to the problem. Model it. Predict how it will be carried out or built and how it will perform. Sketch, dictate sentences, and make other representations of how the solution might look and behave.	Modeling and analyzing potential solutions
Try it	Work collaboratively or independently with hands-on materials to "do" or "build." Take an action or construct an artifact that solves the problem. Materials can be blocks, recyclables, craft supplies, and so forth.	Prototyping
Fix it	Test out the action or artifact. Decide whether or not the action or artifact solves the problem. Document what happens during testing and what that means for the next version. Make changes to improve the solution.	Testing and analyzing prototype performance; iterating
Share it	Share the final action or artifact with children and adults. Draw and talk about it. Contribute to documentation panels. Reflect on initial ideas (brainstorms, sketches) and the final design and describe the differences between the two.	Representing and communicating about solution via multiple modes (e.g., drawings, text, speech)

reading: read aloud to babies, toddlers, and preschoolers; give infants books to feel and taste and gaze at; and help preschoolers retell stories as they view illustrations.

Just as infants, toddlers, and most preschoolers are not developmentally ready to pick up a book and read it independently from start to finish, they are not quite capable of independently tackling a complex engineering design problem using all the phases of the problem-solving framework. Also, just as young children can be considered emergent readers, they can be considered emergent engineers who have many of the precursor skills that will be necessary to engage in independent engineering design later on. In fact, just as certain skills are required for reading literacy, certain skills are required for STEM literacy, and appropriately designed learning experiences can help develop STEM literacy skills, just as appropriately designed learning experiences can develop prereading skills. This book focuses on five thinking skills that are important for adult engineering but that also are skills exhibited by young children and that can be extended and further developed through particular problem-solving experiences. The experiences presented in this book are designed to help children develop the foundational thinking skills for STEM problem solving; these skills also happen to be essential components of real-life engineering design. Infants are just acquiring these skills to begin to solve problems of reaching, grasping, and communicating nonverbally; toddlers are developing the thinking skills and applying them to many problems in the physical world; and preschoolers are nearing readiness for complex problem solving on their own.

So what are these foundational thinking skills for real-life engineering and young children's STEM problem solving? Studies of professional engineers have revealed that the enterprise of engineering draws upon individuals' cognitive, sociocultural, and affective resources and that substantial growth occurs as engineers shift from novice to expert practice in design (Atman et al., 2007; Cardella, Atman, Turns, & Adams, 2008; Cross, 2004). For instance, for engineers to plan possible solutions and revise solutions they have already tested, they need to engage in reflective decision making in collaboration with others (NRC, 2012; Schön, 1987). Rather than relying on random trial and error, engineers make decisions based on evidence about how well a design will work (NRC, 2012). To engage in reflective decision making in a collaborative way, people need tools for social interaction, including ways of communicating engineering ideas and ways of thinking like an engineer (Atman, Kilgore, & McKenna, 2008). Many of these ways of thinking overlap with the higher order thinking skills that should be fostered in young children. This book focuses on five thinking skills that overlap between engineering and young children's development: *curious thinking, persistent thinking, flexible thinking, reflective thinking,* and *collaborative thinking.* All the thinking skills come from our review of state standards for young children; they are the key skills that children from birth to age 5 need to learn at various levels of complexity. The following sections describe how engineers use each of these thinking skills and summarize the evidence of young children's development of each skill. This book's later chapters unpack each thinking skill in much more detail and describe what cognitive development research says about the thinking skills at each stage of growth from infancy to toddlerhood to the preschool years.

Curious Thinking

Engineers

When determining the goals and constraints of a design problem, engineers consider broad, contextual issues, including social, logistical, and environmental factors. For example, college engineering students working on a flood-control problem question the effects of possible design solutions on people and nature (Atman, Yasuhara, Adams, Barker, Turns, & Rhone, 2008). Expert engineers working on a playground design problem consider legal liability, neighborhood opinions, and maintenance concerns (Atman et al., 2007).

Before beginning to plan and build solutions to design problems, expert engineers spend a substantial amount of time asking questions and gathering information about the problem (Atman et al., 2007). When engineers conduct predictive analysis, they use curious thinking to anticipate how possible solutions to problems might actually perform.

Young Children

Anyone who has spent time with infants and young children knows that they love to explore new objects and environments. And when they encounter a puzzle about what makes something work, they attempt to solve that puzzle through play (Gopnik, 2012). However, their love of exploration and questions can be developed even further into a curious thinking habit of mind. For example, with encouragement to search and observe in the school garden for insects, toddlers can generate their own questions about insect behavior, such as how insects would respond to different surfaces and whether they sleep during the winter months when they cannot be found outside (Shaffer, Hall, & Lynch, 2009). In another example, when children are given a toy that only works one third of the time it is activated, they develop ideas about what hidden variables might be responsible for the failures (Schulz & Sommerville, 2006).

Flexible Thinking

Engineers

Experienced designers know how and when to use a range of design strategies (Daly, Adams, & Bodner, 2012). They are flexible in altering their approach when necessary to deal with limitations of time and resources (Crismond & Adams, 2012). They have to think creatively about how existing knowledge can be applied and combined in new ways (NRC, 2012). As they try out a prototype of a design solution, they find new information for how well it works, and they have to adjust their ideas according to this new information. Engineering problem-solving work requires great creativity and mental flexibility.

Young Children

Although young children sometimes perseverate on ideas and seem unlikely to ever relinquish their current thinking, cognitive science research has shown that young children can be quite flexible in their thinking when provided with enough evidence to accept new ideas (Gopnik, 2012). For example, in one study, 4-year-olds began by insisting that stomachaches could be not caused by psychological factors such as anxiety. However, as researchers presented the 4-year-olds with more and more evidence of psychologically caused illness, the children were more and more likely to give up their existing thinking and accept the new idea (Schulz, Bonawitz, & Griffiths, 2007).

Persistent Thinking

Engineers

Iterative redesign is a universal feature of engineering (Petroski, 1996). Engineers make tweaks and cycle through repeated attempts at each phase of the design process, from refining their statement of the problem, to constructing dozens of prototypes, to proposing several options for materials selection and final specifications.

Another way that engineering designers are persistent is by purposefully holding multiple sets of requirements in their minds all throughout a design process. They constantly refer back to the physical principles that govern the design scenario, the wishes that their clients have expressed for an acceptable solution, and their own personal experiences with similar problems (Cross, 2003). It takes persistence to keep all these elements in mind throughout a problem-solving process.

Young Children

Worth and Grollman (2003) document how classrooms of 3- and 4-year-olds can persist in solving the same problem (e.g., constructing ramps that keep cars from falling off, moving water from one container to another using pumps) for many days—even weeks. This persistent thinking is supported by their teacher's careful problem posing, provision of materials, and documentation (through photos, drawings, dictated text, and anecdotal records) of children's questions and findings.

Reflective Thinking

Engineers

Ahmed, Wallace, and Blessing (2003) found that recently graduated engineers utilized a systematic trial-and-error approach in which they implemented and evaluated each design idea through many iterations. By contrast, their experienced colleagues evaluated tentative design ideas before implementing them, thus engaging early in reflective decision making and spending their time implementing only potentially fruitful ideas. Daly, Adams, and Bodner (2012) similarly found that experienced engineers viewed evidence-based decision making as the cornerstone of engineering design. No matter what design process engineers follow, their activities always include analysis and testing of the work they are producing (Bucciarelli, 1994). When they have engaged in predictive analysis prior to prototyping and testing a solution, engineers use reflective thinking to compare their predictions to actual results.

Young Children

Reflection can be described as "remembering with analysis" (Epstein, 2003). For young children, remembering involves recalling both what they planned to do and what they did. Analysis by young children answers the question "How did it go?" When children are guided to plan, carry out, and reflect on their own learning activities, they show more purposeful behavior and more success on intellectual measures (Sylva, 1992).

Collaborative Thinking

Engineers

Informed engineering designers are effective group collaborators (Crismond & Adams, 2012). In fact, the ability to function well in teams is a requirement of college-level engineering education programs (ABET, 2012). Engineering professors often assign team design projects in order to help students improve their skills of teamwork, communication, and collective decision-making (Borrego, Karlin, McNair, & Beddoes, 2013). These professors know that engineering is a collaborative endeavor and that successful practicing engineers engage often in the communication tasks of translation, clarification, negotiation, and listening (Darling & Dannels, 2010).

Young Children

Worth and Grollman (2003) describe a preschool classroom where so many children were engaged in the challenge of making balls travel as far as possible down cardboard ramps that their teachers grouped them into teams of four children each; each team had either all 3-year-olds or all 4-year-olds. The teacher noted that although the 3-year-olds proceeded by carrying out trial-and-error methods together, the 4-year-olds truly collaborated by suggesting ideas to each other, trying them out, and communicating lessons learned to incorporate into their next ramp system. Being a contributing member of a team is a skill that can be learned. When encouraged to reflect on and listen to their peers' recommendations, elementary school students critiqued each others' engineering designs in ways that led to substantive changes in their products (Capobianco, Diefes-Dux, & Mena, 2011).

THE PROBLEM-SOLVING FRAMEWORK, CHILD DEVELOPMENT, AND STANDARDS OF EARLY EDUCATION AND CARE

Different theories of children's cognitive and social-emotional development call for different approaches to the creation of learning experiences. Our emergent engineering approach, grounded by the five thinking skills and the *think about it, try it, fix it,* and *share it* cycle, reflects the view that young children's development is a back-and-forth process in which the social and cultural context strongly influences a child's intellectual and emotional growth. Children's innate cognitive abilities, social-emotional skills, and perceptions all interact with the people and objects around them at any given time, and different areas of knowledge and different skills emerge in different contexts. This is why the different activities in this book foster different kinds of thinking skills and different parts of the engineering design cycle.

Our view of child development draws from several key theories of cognitive and social-emotional development. The first is Piaget's constructivist idea (1954) that children construct new knowledge through interactions with objects in their environment. For this reason, all our emergent engineering activities call for children to solve problems with physical objects and materials. Piaget's constructivist idea was elaborated by Vygotsky's theory that children's knowledge construction is influenced strongly by conversation with more knowledgeable adults (1962). With the tool of language, adults help children articulate the abstract concepts they are constructing in their minds through their play and exploration of the world. As a result, all of our emergent engineering activities place a strong emphasis on adults' use of language to interpret, elaborate on, and raise questions to children about their problem-solving work and play. We also propose activities that at times seem just beyond children's reach. We do this intentionally, because with the careful guidance of adults, children can stretch their skills to accomplish new tasks and then develop the skills needed to carry out those tasks on their own. This aspect of the emergent engineering framework relies on Vygotsky and Cole's (1978) notion that children have a zone of proximal development where adults can offer scaffolding to enable children to carry out higher mental processes that they would not be able to do alone. Of course, the zone of proximal development is only open when children trust the adult who is offering support, and so emergent engineering activities also call for adult caregivers to be responsive to young children's needs and to intentionally serve as a secure base from which children can explore. The notion that attachment networks (Howes, 1999) are essential to both intellectual and social-emotional development is important to the work in this book. Finally, to help children reach their potential as emergent engineers, we have designed activities that are inspired by Fischer et al.'s (1993) portrayal of children's competence not as a characteristic of an individual child but as an attribute of that child in context. The problem-solving experiences in Chapters 3 through 7 of this book provide rich, meaningful contexts in which children can explore big ideas and exercise higher order thinking skills to accomplish engaging tasks. These contexts allow children to demonstrate competence that often far exceeds what adults first thought possible for them.

Standards of early education and care also support this book's claim that young children can develop the five thinking skills of emergent engineering. In fact, the learning goal of becoming a curious, persistent, flexible, reflective, and collaborative thinker is reflected in the Next Generation Science Standards (NGSS Lead States, 2013) and the Common Core State Standards for Mathematics (National Governors Association Center for Best Practices & Council of Chief State School Officers, 2010), as well as in early childhood learning outcomes documents for several states, including California, Ohio, and Massachusetts. Table 1.2 shows how standards for early education and care from these national and state documents align with each of the five emergent engineering thinking skills. The learning activities in this book can help infants, toddlers, and preschoolers meet these standards and others as they take delight in becoming young engineering problem solvers.

Table 1.2. Alignment of the emergent engineering thinking skills with standards for early education and care

	Curious thinking	Persistent thinking	Flexible thinking	Reflective thinking	Collaborative thinking	Web link
Massachusetts Guidelines for Infants and Toddlers (Massachusetts Department of Early Education and Care, 2011)	SED19. The young infant explores the environment around them. SED22. The older infant more actively explores the environment.	CD12. The young infant repeats a pleasing sound or motion. CD13. The young infant discovers that repeated actions yield similar results. CD14. The older infant closely observes actions and discovers that repeated actions yield similar results. CD15. The older infant performs an action to get a resulting event to occur.	CD30. The young infant begins to learn how objects work by handling them and watching others use them. CD31. The older infant actively explores the environment to make new discoveries.	CD24. The young infant becomes aware of patterns in the environment. CD28. The older infant begins to recognize patterns.	LC8. The young infant understands and uses social communication. LC9. The older infant begins to comprehend and use social communication.	http://www.eec.state.ma.us/docs1/Workforce_Dev/Layout.pdf
California Infant Toddler Desired Results (Center for Child and Family Studies, 2010)	COG6: Curiosity	COG7: Attention maintenance	COG2: Problem solving	COG1: Cause and effect	SSD13: Social understanding	http://www.desiredresults.us/docs/Forms%20page/DRDP%20(2010)/IT%206_29_10F.pdf
Massachusetts Preschool Guidelines (Massachusetts Department of Education, 2003)	Science and technology, Inquiry Skills 1. Ask and seek out answers to questions about objects and events with the assistance of interested adults.			Science and Technology, Inquiry Skills 4. Record observations and share ideas through simple forms of representation such as drawings.	Science and Technology, Inquiry Skills 4. Record observations and share ideas through simple forms of representation such as drawings.	http://fcsn.org/pti/topics/earlychildhood/preschool_learning_eec.pdf
Massachusetts Preschool STEM Standards (Massachusetts Department of Elementary and Secondary Education, 2014)	Observe and ask questions about observable phenomena (objects, materials, organisms or events).		Construct theories based in experience about what might be going on. (PreK-LS2-2). Look for and describe patterns and relationships (PreK-LS1-2 PreK-LS1-3).	Support thinking with evidence. Engage in discussion before, during and after investigations.	Document experiences and thinking to communicate with others.	http://www.mass.gov/edu/docs/eec/2013/20131009-pk-sci-tech-standards.pdf

	COG4: Curiosity and initiative	COG5: Engagement and persistence	COG2: Problem solving	COG1: Cause and effect	LLD3: Expression of self through language	
California Preschool Learning (California Department of Education, 2010)					Expression of self through language	http://www.cde.ca.gov/sp/cd/ci/documents/drdp2010preschooleng.pdf
Ohio Early Learning Content Standards (Ohio Department of Education, 2012)	Approaches to Learning: Initiative and Curiosity	Approaches to Learning: Engagement and Persistence	Approaches to Learning: Innovation and Invention	Approaches to Learning: Planning, Action and Reflection	Social and Emotional Development; Peer interaction and relationships	http://education.ohio.gov/Topics/Early-Learning/Early-Learning-Content-Standards/The-Standards
Head Start Child Outcomes (Office of Head Start, 2011)	Approaches to Learning: Initiative and Curiosity	Approaches to Learning: Persistence and Attentiveness	Approaches to Learning: Reasoning and Problem Solving		Approaches to Learning: Cooperative	https://eclkc.ohs.acf.hhs.gov/hslc/tta-system/teaching/eecd/Assessment/Child%20Outcomes/HS_Revised_Child_Outcomes_Framework(rev-Sept2011).pdf
Common Core State Standards for Mathematics (National Governors Association Center for Best Practices & Council of Chief State School Officers, 2010)	Standards for Mathematical Practice, 1. Make sense of problems and persevere in solving them.	Standards for Mathematical Practice, 1. Make sense of problems and persevere in solving them.	Standards for Mathematical Practice, 2. Reason abstractly and quantitatively.	Standards for Mathematical Practice, 3. Construct viable arguments and critique the reasoning of others.	Standards for Mathematical Practice, 3. Construct viable arguments and critique the reasoning of others.	http://www.corestandards.org/assets/CCSSI_Math%20Standards.pdf
Next Generation Science Standards for Kindergarten (National Research Council, 2012)	With guidance, plan and conduct an investigation in collaboration with peers. (K-PS2-1)	Use observations (firsthand or from media) to describe patterns in the natural world in order to answer scientific questions. (K-LS1-1)	Use tools and materials provided to design and build a device that solves a specific problem or a solution to a specific problem. (K-PS3-2)	Analyze data from tests of an object or tool to determine if it works as intended. (K-PS2-2)	With guidance, plan and conduct an investigation in collaboration with peers. (K-PS2-1) Construct an argument with evidence to support a claim. (K-ESS2-2) Communicate solutions with others in oral and/or written forms using models and/or drawings that provide detail about scientific ideas. (K-ESS3-3)	http://www.nextgenscience.org/sites/ngss/files/k%20combined%20DCI%20standards%206.13.13_0.pdf

2

Universal Design for Learning to Support Engineering Experiences in Inclusive Early Childhood Settings

All children, regardless of ability or developmental status, have the right to partici-pate in rich learning experiences to develop their problem-solving skills and expe-rience fun and engaging learning through various STEM activities. Employing UDL principles is one way to ensure that this is the case. We have included the UDL principles in this book because we strongly believe that all children should have access through the application of UDL principles to high-quality STEM activities in an inclusive setting. These principles help teachers plan meaningful ways to actively engage all children—including those with disabilities, delays, and other learning needs—to participate in hands-on learn-ing experiences to increase their problem-solving skills. This chapter describes the UDL framework and guidelines and the evidence base for these guidelines for creating inclusive classrooms and lessons. Historically, the UDL framework has been applied to K–12 educa-tion, but we will explain how to apply the UDL principles to support children from birth to age 5 in inclusive settings when working on emergent engineering development. Finally, we incorporate UDL principles and supports into learning experiences for young children and provide examples using a sample lesson plan to show how to support young children using the adapted UDL framework. As mentioned in the Note to the Reader in the begin-ning of the book, each thinking skill–based chapter in Section II includes activities that incorporate UDL supports so that all children in the classroom can participate in these engineering experiences. The application of UDL provides access to the problem-solving framework described in this book for all young children.

HISTORY AND DEFINITIONS

The UDL concept originated in the architecture field, where it was determined to be more efficient and cost effective to plan and build a new building designed to meet the needs of multiple people, including individuals with disabilities, than to retrofit an older build-ing to allow access for everyone (Richardson, 2010). In addition, in planning the building design, individuals were provided choices for access, such as a closed captioning system for people who are deaf, ramps and elevators for people who use a wheelchair, and braille signs for people who are blind. The Building Inclusive Child Care program, an inclusive child care group in Pennsylvania that is committed to using UDL in its classrooms and teacher training program, provides the following definition: "The concept of Universal Design for Learning (UDL) facilitates an inclusive early childhood environment by ensuring equitable access and meaningful participation through flexible and creative approaches within a developmentally appropriate setting" (Cunconan-Lahr & Stifel, 2007, p. 1). UDL is a way to provide children with choices for what they are learning, how they are learning, and how they are showing what they know, as well as a variety of ways to be motivated and challenged. Children can show through both product and process what they have learned. Sometimes, offering children a different way to engage in the content helps adults understand what children know about the information.

The three primary principles of UDL state that educators should 1) provide multiple means of representation by providing choices for perception or using multiple modalities, provide options for language and symbols, and provide options for comprehension; 2) provide multiple means of action and expression, such as options for physical action, options for communication and expression, and options to develop and practice executive functions such as goal setting and self-monitoring; and 3) provide multiple means for engagement, such as providing options to support student interest, options to support students' persistence in the task, and options to develop and support self-regulation in learning and the classroom environment (CAST, 2012a).

When UDL was first proposed in education, technology was seen as a central concept and was the main method to address the three key principles. Since the recent revision of the UDL guidelines to version 2.0 in 2011, the Center for Applied Special Technology (CAST) acknowledges that technology is just one way to provide a UDL-designed classroom. This is especially true at the early childhood level, where young children should be engaged in play and screen time should be limited (Guernsey, 2007). Nevertheless, in pre-K–12 settings, "powerful digital technologies applied using UDL principles enable easier and more effective customization of curricula for learners" (CAST, 2012a). The key words in UDL are *flexibility* and *choices*, but flexibility and choices are not just given arbitrarily. UDL is a framework for removing barriers by anticipating the needs of students.

Children have choices, and *all* children should have access to the various options. When planning, educators may choose to include certain materials or assessments based on the needs of a few children in the class who will benefit from those options, but all

---

 When planning an activity or learning experience, educators must do the following:

- Identify objectives and standards that are being addressed
- Describe the strengths and needs of the children
- Provide choices and flexibility in what materials children use
- Highlight critical features
- Offer various levels of challenge
- Monitor how children interact with the materials and concepts
- Allow children choices in how they demonstrate what they learn
- Provide choices to motivate children to meet high expectations

children should be able to access those options and also will benefit from the flexibility. A UDL support is a material or choice of activity that helps a particular child better access the content being taught. For example, as a teacher, you may provide a center where children can listen to and follow along with a book that was part of a large-group activity to rein-

force reading skills and concepts taught in the book. This choice as a UDL support may have been included by the teacher to support a few children who need multiple readings of the book and who benefit from multiple means of representation (i.e., hearing it while looking at the words at the same time). Nevertheless, all children in the classroom can choose to go to the center and listen to the story again. A child whom the teacher did not think needed this extra support may choose to

attend the listening center and improve his or her vocabulary through the opportunity to listen to the book. Children learn differently: Some prefer auditory input, some visual input, and some kinesthetic input. Often, children benefit most from the opportunity to learn the same content in multiple ways—for example, both auditorily and visually. By providing multiple means of representation or different ways to take in the content, children who are auditory learners will benefit more from the listening station, whereas children who are visual learners will benefit more from seeing the words and pictures.

RESEARCH EVIDENCE FOR UNIVERSAL DESIGN FOR LEARNING

An established research base exists for UDL and its effectiveness for 1) supporting all learners and 2) creating inclusive settings where all students are successful. Most research has been done in K–12 classrooms, but researchers and policy makers advocate for its use in early childhood settings (Buysse & Hollingsworth, 2009; Odom, Buysse, & Soukakou, 2011). UDL helps address learner variability by suggesting flexible goals, methods, materials, and assessments that empower educators to meet these varied needs (Horn & Banerjee, 2009). Curricula that are created using UDL are designed from the outset to meet the needs of all learners (CAST, 2012b). Extensive research evidence supports the individual principles and subprinciples of UDL as well as the framework as a whole (CAST, 2012a). Research has shown that students with disabilities who have access to the general education curriculum are able to successfully address the state standards with UDL supports and careful lesson design and implementation by teachers (Browder, Spooner, Wakeman, Trela, & Baker, 2006; Spooner, Baker, Harris, Ahlgrim-Delzell, & Browder, 2007). Specific research on the role of UDL in teaching STEM concepts has been investigated at the elementary level (Basham & Marino, 2013; Howland, Baird, Pocock, Coy, & Arbuckle, 2013; Tinker, Zucker, & Staudt, 2009).

Limited research has been done on the use of UDL in early childhood, because the principles and strategies are specifically designed for the K–12 classroom. Nevertheless, UDL strategies are applicable to early childhood classrooms and help teachers support all children. This is especially true because children with and without delays or disabilities are often in the same inclusive early childhood classroom, and teachers need to prepare them for kindergarten. Much of the research on UDL in early childhood settings examines the use of particular types of technology or programs and their use in early childhood classrooms to support a variety of learners (Gillis, Luthin, Parette, & Blum, 2012; Gonzalez, 2014; Parette, Blum, & Luthin, 2013). In a recent dissertation study on the implementation of UDL in an early childhood inclusive classroom, Stone (2013) found that teachers were naturally inclined to implement the principles of UDL because they supported their inclusive classrooms, but they had limited time to intentionally plan and incorporate many aspects of the guidelines.

Universal Design for Learning Research and Applications in Early Childhood Settings

Given the increased diversity and inclusion in all early childhood settings, it is very important for early childhood educators to be prepared to teach a wide range of young children with many different strengths and needs, native languages, and cultural backgrounds. The Division for Early Childhood (DEC), as part of the Council for Exceptional Children (CEC) and the National Association for the Education of Young Children (NAEYC), published a joint position statement with a clear directive for inclusive early childhood settings where all children are provided access to the curriculum and provided multiple ways to promote learning and development (DEC/NAEYC, 2009; Odom, Buysse, & Soukakou, 2011). The universal design of early learning

> suggests that instead of creating a curriculum and then adapting it to meet the needs of individual children in the program, it is better to start off with an instructional design which provides learners with a variety of ways to access and process information and demonstrate what they have learned. (Blagojevic, Twomey, & Labas, 2002)

In early childhood classrooms, classroom environment and arrangement are as important as flexible methods and materials for children. Conn-Powers, Cross, Traub, and Hutter-Pishgahi argue that early childhood educators need to value the "importance of planning learning environments and activities for a diverse population—creating universally designed settings in which all children and their families can participate and learn" (2006, p. 2). In their framework for UDL for early childhood settings, all children and families are equal and valued members of the classroom community. They have access to all learning opportunities in the classroom, they are provided with meaningful ways to engage in the curriculum through choices and flexibility, they can learn and demonstrate what they are learning based on their strengths and interests, and specific children need minimal special assistance because supports are built into the planning from the beginning to support everyone.

Some children will need more intensive interventions or strategies for success in an inclusive classroom. Sandall and Schwartz's Building Blocks model (2008) incorporates the UDL model and builds on it to provide a multitiered support system for children with disabilities who need additional child-focused instructional strategies beyond the curriculum modifications and embedded learning opportunities that are part of the UDL planning curriculum.

The research-based Children's School Success Plus (CSS+) curriculum incorporates both UDL principles and the Building Blocks model to address preschool students' strengths and needs in designing a curriculum to address state and national standards but also allows for accommodations for individual students. The CSS+ research team found "the decision for when and what form the supports should take is determined through assessment and linking desired child outcomes to curriculum content and individualized child supports" (Butera et al., 2012). To meet the needs of all children in inclusive settings, it is important to combine the principles of UDL that address the base level and second level of a multitiered system, whereas the Building Blocks model adds additional supports and resources to address the needs of children at the second and third levels of the system, or the children needing the most intensive supports to be successful in the inclusive classroom (Lieber, Horn, Palmer, & Fleming, 2008; Moore, 2008; Sandall & Schwartz, 2008). UDL allows all children in a classroom to participate in the same lesson in a unique and personalized way to achieve the same objective (Stone, 2013).

UNIVERSAL DESIGN FOR LEARNING COMPONENTS DEFINED

In the UDL Guidelines 2.0, the three primary principles are as follows:

1. Provide Multiple Means of Representation
2. Provide Multiple Means of Action and Expression
3. Provide Multiple Means of Engagement (CAST, 2012b)

These principles correspond to 1) what children are learning (or the content), 2) how children are learning and demonstrating what they are learning (the process of learning and assessment), and 3) why they are learning and motivated to learn (the methods of engagement, levels of challenge, and self-regulation).

In the early childhood model for UDL, Conn-Powers, Cross, Traub, and Hutter-Pishgahi (2006) have added two additional concepts to address: accessible environments and a common, flexible curriculum. Cunconan-Lahr and Stifel (2013) have created a checklist for assessing early childhood environments for their compliance with UDL principles, which includes the following categories: teaching strategies, learning outcomes, physical layout, materials, and relationships. The Division for Early Childhood, with endorsements from the National Association for the Education of Young Children, developed a recommendation paper, which included recommendations and examples of the three core UDL principles as applied to the early childhood curriculum at three levels: 1) infant/toddler settings, 2) preschool settings, and 3) kindergarten/primary grade classrooms (Rous & Hyson, 2007). The recommendations focused on multiple means of representation, action and expression, and engagement for young children and ways to adapt curriculum for all children but specifically addressed some concerns for children with disabilities.

Let us look at what each UDL principle means and examples of its application in an early childhood setting. Because this book addresses lessons for children from birth to age 5, the examples will be limited to infants, toddlers, and preschoolers.

Multiple Means of Representation (What?)

In this principle, UDL focuses on what children are learning and the inputs or content provided to help children learn various concepts. Children are provided various options to engage in the content, including auditory, visual, tactile, and multimodal learning opportunities. In addition, children should be able to engage in the content in more than one modality for each lesson. This principle encourages educators to intentionally highlight key or critical features of the content and help children understand the most important parts to master. By purposely focusing on comprehension of learning outcomes, children are more likely to understand what they are learning and connect and generalize their learning to new ideas and settings.

For example, in an infant classroom, it is important to offer a variety of sensory toys and multiple sensory activities, as well as to incorporate language in a variety of activities and routines, including storytime, songs, diaper changing, and snack time (Rous & Hyson, 2007).

Multiple Means of Action and Expression (How?)

This principle of UDL centers on the process of learning. Children can gain information through a variety of learning activities, each of which highlights different learning modalities. Children can also show what they have learned and adults can assess the teaching and learning process in many different ways; these multiple learning formats and modes of assessment can be present in one classroom or caregiving environment. Simply put, not all children need to do the same thing to learn the same content, and we can assess their learning in different ways. In an early childhood classroom, it is expected that teaching and assessment are multimodal and do not reflect paper-and-pencil assessments; rather, this principle challenges educators to think further to use the children's strengths and interests as modes of learning and expression. Within this principle, it is critical for children to be physically involved (when able) in the action of learning in order to assess the content with peers. Children can also use various verbal, written, product-based, and experiential methods to demonstrate their knowledge and mastery of curricular concepts. In the final guideline for this principle, educators are to support executive functions in learning, such as goal setting, self-monitoring of learning, and planning and strategy use.

Young children can develop executive functioning skills through teacher scaffolding and support in recognizing strategies that help individual children with learning. Picture checklists or picture directions can be provided to help children complete tasks more independently and monitor their own learning. For example, preschoolers might demonstrate what they learned from a story by drawing, retelling the events of the story to an adult, acting the story out in the dramatic play area, or singing a song.

Multiple Means of Engagement (Why?)

In this final principle, children are engaged in the learning process through their interests, and teachers and caregivers must find the right level of challenge for each child. By tapping into children's natural interest areas, teachers can focus on the curriculum and learning objectives rather than using time to gain and sustain children's attention. Because young children are naturally curious problem solvers, using children's interests will help them to persist longer on a challenging task. Furthermore, finding a child's instructional level will help his or her learning process and stimulate his or her motivation to learn by avoiding frustration and failure. This process also places value on mastery learning of objectives, regardless of the child's current developmental level. Finally, children develop self-regulation skills through intrinsic motivation that increases through successful learning attempts and reflection on what and how they are learning. Opportunities for children to celebrate and recognize success will give them more confidence to try new challenging tasks in the future. For example, caregivers can offer infants toys with different levels of challenge or with different functions to learn which toys infants are interested in and which toys they find frustrating. In preschool, teachers who lay out a variety of building materials in the block area encourage children to plan and create their own designs rather than copy an adult model.

Accessible Environments

In an early childhood classroom, the environment should provide all children equal access to the curriculum and to classroom activities. Access can be obtained through the physical arrangement of the classroom for safety and access to all areas, as well as easily available materials to support learning. Materials and activities should be provided at a variety of challenge levels and address common areas of need for children, such as larger-handled pencils or crayons or left-handed or easy-grip scissors. Children must have a variety of seating options, and children who use wheelchairs need various seating or positioning options to work with and at the same level as their peers, including using a stander during some group activities. Early childhood classrooms should be welcoming, inclusive environments where children with various strengths, needs, and interests can participate safely and together in the curriculum (Conn-Powers et al., 2006; Cunconan-Lahr & Stifel, 2013).

A Common Flexible Curriculum

Finally, all children should be learning from the same curriculum with the same standards, but with flexible models of implementation supported by the UDL principles to address the needs of all children. For example, the Creative Curriculum is a popular preschool curriculum used in many classrooms around the country. In a UDL-based classroom, all children would be learning from this curriculum and all children would be working toward the learning goals. Within a set curriculum, there are multiple learning goals to accommodate children's multiple skill levels and interests. As children move through the essential indicators within curriculum frameworks to the more advanced learning indicators, all children achieve some level of mastery on the same curricular content. To address the various levels of learning in a classroom, different levels of support or scaffolding are provided using a variety of materials, peer and adult supports, and multiple learning and assessment activities.

UNIVERSAL DESIGN FOR LEARNING AND THE ENGINEERING DESIGN FRAMEWORK

Many elements within both UDL and the engineering framework complement each other and support the thinking skills we are trying to develop. Figure 1.1 in Chapter 1 examined the four steps in the engineering design process. Just like UDL, this process is flexible, and we do not follow each step in every activity but instead focus on one or two steps in the process to support the development of a specific thinking skill. In addition, although we aim to focus on a specific thinking skill in an activity, children are naturally working on several thinking skills at the same time by participating in a hands-on engineering experience. Looking at the four steps in the process, teachers can find other ways to offer options to support children's learning in each step.

For example, if the problem is how to get the ball down a ramp, the problem could be presented differently to different ages. At the infant level, a teacher could set up one or two ramps and put balls nearby. The infants could explore it with various levels of scaffolding and modeling or play with the materials provided. For toddlers, a teacher could set up the balls and ramps and ask the toddlers to predict what will happen or could put out specific materials and ask them to explore and see what will happen (but a model would help). With preschoolers, a teacher could discuss the problem, set out materials, and ask them to provide ideas and/or draw sketches of what a successful ramp would look like. A teacher could also extend the challenge with preschoolers by asking them to look at angles and different ball types to compare and contrast.

"Think About It" and Universal Design for Learning

In the "think about it" step, children and teachers are brainstorming together about the problem and what they can do to solve it, thinking about what they need, and making some predictions and possibly sketches of potential problem-solving ideas. In this step, they are thinking about options for materials and the process of solving the problem, addressing principles 1 and 2. Teachers are also offering children different ways to brainstorm their ideas: 1) They can talk about it, 2) they can simply try to experiment with materials provided, 3) they can draw out their ideas, and 4) they can work with a partner or group to think about the problem. For some children, thinking about the problem will mean talking and formulating ideas, but for others, it will be a more hands-on experience. Infants and young toddlers will be more hands-on when thinking about it, exploring the materials and then trying to explore the problem.

In looking at an engineering experience for each age level, teachers need to apply the UDL principles to maximize the experience for all children in their classrooms. For example, the infants "think about it" by looking at and touching the ball and ramp. A teacher could let infants try to put the ball on the ramp themselves or support them with a model appropriate to their ages and skill sets. As they learn about the properties of the ramp and the ball and see the model, infants will try to persist and do the action many times to see if the ball will

 actually fall down the ramp over and over. To support the various needs of children in the classroom at their current development levels (whether they are typically developing or demonstrating a delay or diagnosed disability), a teacher could offer different sizes and textures of balls to help infants explore their environment and think about how different sizes, weights, and textured balls go down a ramp differently. Infants' thinking is internal and increased through their experiences in the world, so when they are older and have the language to express their thoughts about balls and ramps, they will have had the scaffolded experiences with teachers and parents to understand what is happening in a ball-and-ramp engineering experience, and adults will have provided the language to infants for them to take in and use as they get older. Educators are making environmental changes to support engagement and motivation, such as using favorite balls or putting a favorite stuffed toy near the end of the ramp to encourage a child to crawl to the ramp and watch what is happening and develop a greater curiosity in the activity. The level of scaffolding and teacher interaction in the child's exploration is all part of applying the UDL principles. For toddlers and preschoolers, in the "think about it" phase, teachers need to support the thinking process and language to describe the children's thinking process. The goal is to plan and predict, which can be done with words or pictures or models. Children can be creative by acting out what they think will happen or by comparing it to other experiences they have had with similar activities or other experiences with balls. In planning, educators can use ideas, materials, and activities that they know are motivating to the children in the class to engage them in the lesson.

"Try It" and Universal Design for Learning

For infants, "think about it" and "try it" are similar because infants are thinking and processing through hands-on activities. It is difficult to separate the two processes for this age group because teachers are narrating the action for infants to support their thinking and planning. Therefore, we are using the same UDL supports as in the last step. For toddlers, we continue to scaffold language and the learning and building processes, providing children with hands-on experiences but also providing them with more opportunities to use prior knowledge to create their own ramps and test the balls of their choice. Teachers serve as facilitators to provide a variety of materials and give children language to describe their actions and support their thinking about the task. Educators and parents should provide a variety of choices for materials and picture supports and modeling to help children express what they are discovering. For toddlers and preschoolers, we encourage educators to start to look more at the barriers children may encounter as they attempt the hands-on exploration of balls and ramps and plan various ways to use materials, environmental adjustments, and teaching strategies to eliminate these barriers to the learning process so all children can take part in the lesson and improve their thinking skills. For preschoolers, we focus more on using UDL supports to make sure all children are actively building independently or with support and are able to work on their own thinking about the process.

"Fix It" and Universal Design for Learning

"Fix it" is also a hands-on experience within the engineering design framework, but in this step, children are testing their created design to see if it works and to make sense of what happens in the testing process. For infants, this step is very similar to the "try it" step, but adults may create a prototype for infants and young toddlers or make a model for them to copy, and then infants and toddlers can test the prototypes. Infants are very good at persistently testing an activity or function of a toy and repeating the action to see if the result is the same time after time. UDL supports can be used to help change the prototype or materials to keep the activity novel to the infants to help them test their theories of how it works with different materials, such as different balls or a higher or lower ramp. For older toddlers and preschoolers, "fix it" is the time when they can explore how their prototype or material choices work and think about how to redesign or change materials for a similar or different result. UDL supports can help children to further develop their thinking and maintain engagement through various material choices. Teachers can facilitate which materials or redesign processes children use by making suggestions based on the needs of the individual children and what options are given. Models can be provided through pictures or books. During the "fix it" phase, educators can assess how the children are working on the thinking skill and their thought processes in understanding the engineering design process using discussion, checklists, photographs, videos, and charts. Teachers can select the modes of assessment that are best for the children in the classroom based on strengths, needs, and the particular activity.

"Share It" and Universal Design for Learning

"Share it" is a perfect opportunity to incorporate photographs and videos of the activity into the classroom at all levels. Infants will enjoy looking at pictures of themselves doing the activity, and teachers can talk about what the child is doing in the picture. Pictures and videos can also be shared with families so that the activities can be practiced and reviewed at home with infants and toddlers. In the classroom, toddlers can use photographs, videos, and drawn pictures to discuss the activity and what they made and why they made it. Children can review media to discuss what worked, what did not, and why. Multiple forms of media are key UDL supports and can be incorporated into science or engineering journals for the class or individual children. Toddlers and preschoolers can use pictures to recall and reflect on the engineering activity, using the pictures as natural scaffolds to support language. Some children may need a communication board or picture board of key vocabulary to help them discuss their work. Children can also work together on pictures, an oral presentation, or a written journal to present their engineering project to the class,

Essential Questions to Consider in Universal Design for Learning for Early Childhood

- What materials will help children to understand the goal of the activity better and engage more in the activity?
- How can you design the work environment so that children are interested and have the freedom to explore and engage in the activity?
- What additional materials can you provide to scaffold individual children to use language and engage in the learning process?
- How can you authentically assess how well the children are engaging in the activity through different methods to assess the thinking and content?

their families, and/or the teachers. Looking at environmental supports, grouping is important, and some children may reflect individually with a teacher, whereas other children may present as a group or present to the whole class or a small group.

OUR UNIVERSAL DESIGN FOR LEARNING TEMPLATES

Chapter 1 presented the engineering design framework and the rationale behind the five thinking skills we will be showing you how to foster and grow using the engineering design framework in Section II. Because we believe strongly that *all* children need to learn these thinking skills and experience building and learning through the engineering design process, we are applying the UDL framework for early childhood classrooms to our engineering design process. In order to help educators plan how to use our lessons and plan their own lessons for inclusive early childhood settings, we have created a UDL Planning Sheet to help you understand how to provide UDL supports and individual accommodations to support children at each of the levels of support within a three-tier system. Some UDL supports will help all children be successful in these lessons and the classroom (level 1), some UDL supports combined with a few individual accommodations will facilitate learning for children with some additional needs (level 2), whereas others may need specific accommodations based on the Building Blocks model (level 3; Sandall & Schwartz, 2008). Our UDL Planning Sheet helps educators intentionally plan varied levels of support in their classroom for a single lesson or unit. Many of these supports may originate from the needs of a specific child in the classroom, but the material or assessment idea helps and is used with multiple children. Figure 2.1 shows a blank Early Childhoold UDL Planning Sheet. Figure 2.2 shows a completed Early Childhood UDL Planning Sheet so teachers can see how to use this tool in practice.

The UDL Planning Sheet is based on the three UDL principles, and the supports and accommodations are listed under each of those categories. To help make the principles and the guidelines under the principles early childhood–friendly and useful to teachers in the birth to age 5 classrooms, we have focused the UDL supports under "representation" (principle 1) on *materials* children are using to learn the content and practice the thinking skill and *multisensory opportunities* children have to engage with the content and engineering ideas. Under "action and expression" (principle 2), we focus on looking for supports for the different *activities* children are doing to learn the material or ways to differentiate the process and *multimodal* forms of assessment. In addition, we want to encourage preplanning of assessment when planning the lesson and multiple methods

Early Childhood UDL Planning Sheet

Age group: _____   Teacher: _____   Activity: _____

[All] = UDL suggestion for all students who need additional scaffolding; [Name] = UDL suggestion geared toward specific student based on strength/need; [Other] = UDL suggestion for children who have other needs, such as fine or gross motor challenges

UDL guidelines					
Representation (What are they learning?)		Action and expression (How do they learn and show what they know?)		Engagement (Why do they want to participate and be engaged?)	
Materials	Multisensory opportunities	Activities	Multimodal assessment	Environment	Preferences

Figure 2.1. Blank Early Childhood UDL Planning Sheet.

for understanding what children are learning using authentic, developmentally appropriate tasks, such as building, discussing their building, and thinking about their building. Finally, for "engagement" (principle 3), we focus on helping teachers think about ways the *environment* can support engagement in the classroom, as well as individual children's *preferences* for materials, activities, or themes. These preferences could be related to their developmental level or age, a theme, or simply a motivational tool the teacher has noticed that helps the children be more motivated in the activity. For example, many children will be very engaged in a hands-on activity such as digging in mud to find hidden objects, but a child with sensory needs may not want to get dirty and might be reluctant to become involved. By providing this child with a smock and gloves, he or she may be more likely to participate. This support is vital for that child's participation but may be desired by other children and support their active engagement in this lesson as well.

It is important to note that this UDL Planning Sheet can be used for a specific lesson or for an entire unit. At the preschool level, it might be better to use it lesson by lesson if the activities are very different, whereas at the infant level, we would likely use one UDL planning sheet for the whole unit. We want these sheets to be useful to educators and to encourage them to be thoughtful, intentional teachers as they plan and develop activities and lessons to support young children's problem-solving skills; work with these sheets so they are most helpful for this purpose. When teachers start with the goal for the lesson or unit, they know what they want all children to be able to know and do and think about during the lesson. Once they have that overarching goal in mind, they can think about the UDL supports needed for children in the classroom who may not reach that goal through direct engagement with the lesson or unit as it is written for the typical experience of a child in the classroom.

There are three steps to thinking about the useful UDL supports for a lesson or unit in your classroom: 1) Think about the lessons and how the children will engage in the lesson you have written and the typical experience for a child completing this activity; 2) think about each of the children in your classroom and decide if they will follow the general

Early Childhood UDL Planning Sheet

Age group: _Preschoolers_ **Teacher:** _Ms. T_ **Activity:** _Muncha! Muncha! Muncha! (Fleming, 2002) book/activity: wall building_

[All] = UDL suggestion for all students who need additional scaffolding; [Name] = UDL suggestion geared toward specific student based on strength/need; [Other] = UDL suggestion for children who have other needs, such as fine or gross motor challenges

UDL guidelines					
Representation (What are they learning?)		**Action and expression (How do they learn and show what they know?)**		**Engagement (Why do they want to participate and be engaged?)**	
Materials	**Multisensory opportunities**	**Activities**	**Multimodal assessment**	**Environment**	**Preferences**
Bristle Blocks [Brandon, All] Magnetic blocks [Brandon] Individual sticky work mats [José] Picture labels for materials (English and Spanish) [José] Communication board and story on iPad or tablet computer [Brandon]	Bristle Blocks [Brandon, All] Time Timer during storytime [José]	Have child tell other child how to build using communication device or words [Brandon, José] Provide picture directions and picture list of materials [Brandon, José]	Photographs [All] Explanation to students of steps and solution [Brandon] Explanation in Spanish and English [José]	Turn-taking stick [José]	Choice of building materials [All] Choice of assessment options [All]

Figure 2.2. Sample completed Early Childhood UDL Planning Sheet for preschoolers.

lesson you have written or which children need additional UDL supports and/or accommodations; and 3) plan using the UDL planning sheet the supports and accommodations for the lesson or unit based on the needs or interests of certain individual children, or based on the needs of all children, to provide choices in materials, assessment methods, and topics or engagement entry points (e.g., using cars as a topic or using an iPad or tablet computer for motivation).

Figure 2.2 is a sample completed template for the preschool *Muncha! Muncha! Muncha!* (Fleming, 2002) activity for persistent thinking. In this sample template, there are UDL supports that were designed for specific children and supports that were envisioned for all children in the classroom. It is important to remember that all children should have access to each of these supports if they express interest in them or would benefit from them. For example, the turn-taking stick is included to be used in the larger group lesson when brainstorming ideas because José needs to be reminded to talk when it is his turn and so that other children give him the wait time he needs to get his thoughts out. Nevertheless, all the children will benefit from wait time and clear markers of when it is their turn to speak in the group. In the lesson, the turn-taking stick is passed around as a motivator to have an idea to share with the group and practice patient listening skills. This strategy works in many classrooms to support children's engagement in the lesson.

It is essential to remember that UDL supports are usually chosen because of the needs or interest of a specific child in the classroom but should be available to all children if that support will help a different child. UDL requires planning for a lesson or unit and thinking about all the different ways children might have difficulty accessing the lesson and offering many types of choices to make sure that *all* children can access the thinking skill and the goal of the lesson (e.g., exploring balls and ramps). Flexibility is critical in a UDL classroom, where all children have the opportunity to participate in the same lesson and develop critical thinking skills but complete the activity in different ways and demonstrate their learning in different ways. Use the questions in Table 2.1 to plan the best UDL supports for your classroom.

The next several thinking skills chapters will present lessons using the engineering design framework to teach thinking and problem-solving skills to infants, toddlers, and preschoolers. In some cases, younger children are working on the prerequisite skills to problem solving, such as cause and effect, but all children are able to participate. Children in preschool are working on examining multiple solutions to a problem and discussing with their classmates why one solution is more effective or efficient than another. All children in these classrooms are able to participate regardless of development, disability, or other difference because the lessons are designed with UDL supports in mind and were planned from the beginning to offer choices for engagement. UDL is not just for children with disabilities; it also supports the diversity of learners found in early childhood classrooms today.

Table 2.1.   Universal design for learning key questions for completing the Early Childhood UDL Planning Sheet

Infants

1. Are you providing several different materials of the same type to explore the concept (e.g., several different thicknesses of balls, several different sizes and textures of balls)?
2. Do infants have several opportunities to try to repeat the activity?
3. Are infants able to use more than one sense to explore the activity or concept?
4. Are you using media to document the infants' learning? Are you showing the infants pictures of their participation and recalling the activities?
5. Are the materials accessible with scaffolds based on the mobility of the infants?
6. Are you incorporating preferred activities, toys, or adults?
7. Are you asking infants to complete the activities when they are well rested and fed?

Toddlers

1. Do toddlers have a choice of materials and activities?
2. Do toddlers have the necessary supports for communication about the activity?
3. Are you using media to document the toddlers' activities and sharing the media with them to recall and reflect?
4. Is the environment distraction free and set up with choices?
5. Are you using multiple modes of assessment, such as photographs, checklists, and discussion with the children?
6. Do toddlers have options for how to do the activity?
7. Are you incorporating preferred items, reinforcers, or adults to support the toddlers?

Preschoolers

1. Do children have a choice of materials and activities?
2. Do children have the necessary supports for communication about the activity?
3. Are you using media to document the preschoolers' activities and sharing the media with them to recall and reflect? Are they creating an ongoing journal to document their learning in multiple ways, including words, drawings, photographs, videos, and artifacts?
4. Is the environment set up with limited distractions and choices?
5. Are you using multiple modes of assessment to assess their products, processes, and thinking skill development?
6. Do preschoolers have options for how to do the activity and what they can create?
7. Are children given constraints or limits and asked to redesign to stretch their thinking or use a different material or method?
8. Are you incorporating preferred items, reinforcers, or adults to support the children?

II   Using the Problem-Solving Framework to Teach Thinking Skills in Inclusive Early Childhood Settings

3 | Curious Thinkers

Children are born curious about the world around them and actively explore and investigate all that they come in contact with. Children want to understand how the world works and if it will work that way all the time or what the rules or constraints are that dictate situations in which things change. Laura Shulz (Galinsky, 2011) argued that children become curious about objects, events, or people that are unfamiliar and do not fit in their current understanding of the world. Curious children are still figuring out what causes things to happen and only have partial information about the world.

What is curiosity, and how is it defined? This is a topic of debate in psychology and related fields, and several definitions have been offered that refer primarily to adult curiosity. Loewenstein's definition is widely used with adult curiosity but starts to explain children's curiosity as well. He viewed curiosity as "arising when attention becomes focused on a gap in one's knowledge" (Loewenstein, 1994, p. 75). According to the theory, this information gap exists when something is not known; people are motivated to fill this gap and therefore search for the missing information. For example, when children wonder why they see stars in the sky, they might ask an adult why there are stars in the sky to learn this information. Adults frequently use the Internet to search for information to answer their questions. Through extensive work on curiosity with children in science education, Jirout and Klahr (2012) found that when children are provided with novel objects, people, situations, and environments, they are motivated to explore to learn about these new things.

Curiosity requires two contrasting features: a concern for orderliness (or everything having its place) and openness to novel stimuli (or new people, objects, and experiences). When something new is encountered, the child's brain attempts to match the new concept with prior experiences or fit it into their previous knowledge and develop new brain connections. If the child cannot fit the new concept into his or her existing schema, the child will explore the concept and attempt to understand it to see how, in Piagetian terms, to accommodate or assimilate that concept. The child needs to have some cognitive awareness to notice the novel as just that: new and unexpected. These two qualities—the desire to seek out the novel, strange, or unusual and the desire for orderliness—are often not in balance in a person. Usually one desire is stronger than the other. Highly curious people tend to have high levels of both of these contrasting characteristics (Beswick & Tallmadge, 1971).

WHY IS CURIOUS THINKING IMPORTANT?

Curious thinkers actively explore people and things, especially the new and novel, and eventually abstract ideas. Humans are born curious, trying to make sense of their world by looking for patterns and noticing the new. Children wonder how things work, what things are called, and why things happen. Curiosity compels children of all ages to touch, taste, smell, and explore the world around them. Sometimes out of necessity, sometimes out of habit, or sometimes for no reason at all, adults discourage that innate curiosity in children, but without curiosity, there is little desire to discover or explore (Willingham, 2011). Conezio and French argued, "Real science begins with childhood curiosity" (2002b, p. 14).

The American Association for the Advancement of Science argues for the importance of curiosity in science education, including the need to "stimulate the curiosity children have for learning about the natural world" to increase their interest in science and develop their academic skills in all areas (Brewer & Smith, 2011, p. xiv). The National Association for the Education of Young Children (NAEYC) includes three separate "curiosity criteria" for assessing and accrediting preschool programs:

- *2.B.04:* Children have varied opportunities to develop a sense of competence and positive attitudes toward learning, such as persistence, engagement, curiosity, and mastery (all age groups).

- *3.E.03:* Teachers use children's interest in and curiosity about the world to engage them with new content and developmental skills.

- *3.G.02:* Teachers use multiple sources (including results of informal and formal assessments as well as children's initiations, questions, interests, and misunderstandings) to: a. identify what children have learned, b. adapt curriculum and teaching to meet children's needs and interests, c. foster children's curiosity, d. extend children's engagement and e. support self-initiated learning (NAEYC, 2014, pp. 12, 33, 35).

Children need curiosity to continue to learn and make sense of their world from the beginning of their lives to prepare them for their entire educational journey. The first goal set by the National Education Goals Panel (NEGP) includes "openness and curiosity about new tasks and challenges" as an indicator of school readiness (Kagan, Moore, & Bredekamp, 1995, p. 23). The NEGP suggests that "children who start school with . . . a lack of curiosity are at greater risk of subsequent school failure than other children" and reports that kindergarten teachers believe that curiosity is a more important predictor of school readiness than the ability to count or recite the alphabet (NEGP, 1993, p. 12).

Curiosity supports the development of creativity. Curiosity is creative thinking carried into action. The benefits of creative thinking are the abilities to see multiple possibilities and to think outside the box, or beyond the expected. Curiosity promotes initiative and fuels children to look at all the potential solutions to be tested. Children generate optimism and excitement from the challenge of finding a successful solution rather than being trapped by the solution that was unsuccessful. Initiative and optimism are both skills that are beneficial for people of all ages.

DEVELOPMENTAL CONTINUUM OF CURIOUS THINKING

Young children are naturally curious. As they learn about the world, they construct meaning by connecting actions, reactions, observations, and thoughts. The role of the adult becomes one of creating an environment that fosters creativity and curiosity. The ideal environment is created by emphasizing the process and engagement rather than the outcome or product and encouraging the child to continue his or her exploration. Play requires imagination.

Curiosity is the desire to learn, explore, investigate, and acquire knowledge about oneself and the world. Babies are born with a natural curiosity to explore the world. This curiosity fuels learning, serving as the internal motivation for lifelong learning. Adults can model, encourage, support, and scaffold babies' natural curiosity, which can foster learning.

Curiosity is the single most powerful ingredient to learning. If children seek information driven by their curiosity, they learn far more easily, remember things longer, and learn at a deeper level. Curiosity is the intrinsic motivation to learn. This is an approach to learning that is worth fostering because it helps the child learn more effectively throughout his or her life. A sense of wonder is the heart of curiosity and central to the higher order thinking skills of analysis and creation. Curiosity requires some key components: imagination, originality, self-confidence, divergent thinking, and making connections between areas of learning (Sharp, 2004).

Infants

Curious thinking is about recognizing that a problem exists and becoming motivated to pursue a solution to the problem. By providing experiences that engage infants, using the language of posing problems, describing the infant's attempts, and acknowledging the solutions, the educator creates the opportunity for infants to develop curious thinking.

An important cognitive development milestone is the concept of object permanence, which is the understanding that an object continues to exist even when it can no longer be seen or heard. Games of Hide-and-Seek, such as Peekaboo or searching for a hidden toy, can teach the concept of object permanence and promote the development of curious thinking in babies. Many educators already engage in Hide-and-Seek–type activities with babies, but by thinking about Hide-and-Seek games as a way to promote curious thinking, educators can increase the educational benefit of these activities.

Newborn infants initially respond to the world primarily with reflexes, blinking at bright lights or starling at unexpected sounds. Then they expand their responses by exploring the world with their senses, noticing new people, mouthing objects, and turning toward sounds. In the process, they are taking in enormous amounts of information, learning many skills, and developing expectations for their world.

As soon as infants are acting with purpose, they explore ways to make things happen, such as shaking a rattle, playing with a cause-and-effect toy, pushing the button on a busy box, turning a light on and off, or pointing at new people and things. The young child's curiosity turns to initiative, and these experiences build additional expectations, discovery of unexpected results, and additional explorations. This positive feedback loop of finding unexpected results motivates children to constantly look for new things and explore how the world changes. Piaget (1969) described curiosity as the urge to explain the unexpected.

Toddlers

Toddlers crawl and walk all around the room to explore things that they see and want to play with. Toddlers are constantly moving their bodies to investigate the world, and when they are sitting still, their minds are working hard to assimilate and accommodate all the new ideas they are learning. A toddler will take a chair to reach the desk where the phone is—a "toy" she loves to play with. Between 15 and 20 months, a child will demonstrate surprise when interacting with a pop-up toy. Between 18 and 30 months, she will demonstrate her understanding by bringing the toy to a trusted adult to show that parent or caregiver what she can do!

Toddlers ask questions about what they are seeing and doing, and older toddlers will frequently ask, "Why?" These questions become more sophisticated as children get closer to 3 years of age. Toddlers are also very curious about what the caregivers in their lives are doing and try to learn what caregivers are interested in. Whereas infants often explore items with their mouths, toddlers touch and move things. They want to manipulate what they find and play with it to understand it. For example, an older toddler might pretend she is the mail delivery person and put all her papers into the laundry basket "mail truck" to understand what it feels like to be in the other person's shoes and do that job she sees in the community.

Preschoolers

Preschoolers demonstrate their curiosity by asking questions, taking things apart, building structures to try new ideas, and exploring new ways to use familiar things. Preschoolers show eagerness to learn about a variety of topics and ideas, try to figure out how things work, and ask "what" or "how" questions (Center for Child and Family Studies, 2010). Children's curiosity will follow their interests and engagement in activities. Some preschool-age children develop very a specific curiosity, wanting to know everything they can discover about a specific topic, such as trains, dinosaurs, cars, or drawing.

With their language skills and vocabulary growing every day, preschoolers ask "why" questions frequently and work to learn the answers and study how things work. They frequently will jump right in and try different activities and explore multiple solutions to a problem. Preschool-age children start to develop classification systems and sort objects based on their attributes. These children are curious about things they are seeing and hearing about in their environment and their community, so they may be inquisitive about the weather, things in the garden or the park, or what they saw on the way to school or over the weekend.

KEY GOALS FOR CURIOUS THINKING EXPERIENCES

The following set of key words helps explore ways to support young children by describing their actions when they are engaged in curious thinking. These action words can be helpful when creating lesson and unit plan goals for children. It is helpful to think about these terms as guiding words for what children are working on at a metacognitive level. In other words, when watching children engage in the activities in this chapter or other activities designed to promote curious thinking, look for children doing these things.

**Key Words and Phrases for
Curious Thinking for Goal Setting**

- Taking initiative
- Exploring
- Inquiring
- Answering questions
- Seeking new information
- Investigating
- Asking how/why questions

Some of these words are more appropriate for preschoolers, whereas other words will describe what infants or toddlers are expected to be doing during these activities and investigations. For example, all children will explore, engage in inquiry, and seek and ask questions. Infants and toddlers will do the open-ended exploring, whereas preschoolers will engage in more formal investigations and answer "how" and "why" questions. Initiative for infants will involve using their bodies to reach and crawl and manipulate objects to understand how they work. They will seek out objects or processes in their environment that make them curious. For toddlers, initiative will involve trying a different tool or a different method. For example, a toddler may try to fill the bucket in the sand table with a large fork but then switch to a spoon to see if it is more effective. Preschoolers will demonstrate initiative in different ways, such as changing the design of a fence after the first version is unsuccessful by using what they have learned from earlier trials.

Look for these key words in the early learning experiences in this chapter and keep them in mind when working with and assessing the development of curious thinking in the young children you are working with.

Strategies for Facilitating Curious Thinking

We will be discussing many strategies in this book for promoting each thinking skill. Here are some key strategies for facilitating curious thinking in young children. Stimulating the senses is one way to help develop young children's curiosity; provide rich and varied experiences that stimulate all their senses: sight, hearing, taste, smell, and touch. Through these varied experiences, children have the opportunity to seek patterns, test expectations, form new ideas, and spiral through periods of equilibrium and disequilibrium.

A challenge for the adult is to match new experiences with the individual child's sensory tolerance. Young infants especially experience sensory overload and shut down, sleeping through unexpected noise and activity. An older toddler in sensory overload, after a morning walking around, might have a temper tantrum. Finding a balance between new and novel and order and routine is one of the great challenges in working with young children. This balance can be influenced by a child's past experiences, sensory integration tolerance, health, and other factors.

The environments where children spend time are also critical. Although teachers want a predictable, safe, and stable environment where routines are reliable, teachers also need to provide an environment for enrichment and flexibility. Research shows that young children attend to that which is novel and new (Shutts, Banaji, & Spelke, 2010). Early childhood settings where young children may spend 25 to 50 hours a week, where the same equipment and toys are available every day, could quickly become monotonous, uninteresting environments. Providing a rich curriculum with new experiences and new materials for children to explore can eliminate boredom and prevent negative behaviors that stem from a lack of stimulation. Storybooks also enrich children's lives and give them new ideas to "play" with.

Sustained time to engage in play is also critical. If the schedule requires frequent transitions, children do not have time to think through the problems that arise in play, or to develop the themes for their play, or to implement a creative idea. Extended periods of free or loosely structured play, in which adults follow the children's lead, support children to explore their environment, be curious, and try new things. For example, when introducing new materials or toys that will be used in a structured lesson, it is important to allow children some free playtime to explore the materials on their own before asking them to use the toys in a specific way. In the preschool lesson in this chapter, children use blocks to build a wall. Before using the blocks to build the wall, children should have time on previous days to play with and build with the blocks in whatever way is fun for them.

By talking to children about what you do, you are modeling curiosity and showing them how to make sense of the world by exploring and seeking information. Admitting what you do not know and demonstrating your interest in finding out teaches children to enjoy the process of learning and discovery. For example, you can admit, "I don't know why the sky is blue; that's a great question. Let's look it up." Acknowledge an unexpected question or answer by saying something like, "Wow, I hadn't thought of that! We can find that out. Thanks for sharing that idea." Ask children open-ended questions and encourage them to formulate questions to learn more about a topic.

Adults can model creativity by playing with words during a storybook reading or substituting words in a very familiar story. Toddlers and preschoolers will often notice and correct the teacher. Teachers and parents should ask open-ended questions that prompt the child to explain their thinking or explore a new combination of ideas. For example, when children are building with blocks during free play, a teacher can ask, "What are you building? What is that going to be? Why did you build it? Why did you use that piece?" When reading a story, teachers can ask, "What do think will happen? Why do you think the character did that? What would you do?" To keep a feedback loop going between a child and an adult during a building activity and to help the child delve deeper into an idea, encourage many possible answers (brainstorming) by asking, "What else could we do?"

The phrase "children are naturally scientists" is one people hear often. Children's curiosity and their need to make the world a more predictable place drive them to explore, draw conclusions, and develop and test theories from their experiences. But children need practice and support to develop their skills as natural scientists. Children need guidance and structure to turn their natural curiosity and activity into something more scientific. They need to practice science—to engage in rich scientific inquiry (Worth, 2010). The following activities offer some guidance on how to encourage scientific inquiry among young children.

CURIOUS THINKING EXPERIENCE FOR INFANTS

Curious thinking in infants is demonstrated when an infant shows interest in someone or something—for example, by picking up an object, putting an object in her mouth, rolling over to reach for an object, or focusing attention on someone. In planning curious thinking activities, educators should ask the following question: How can I encourage babies' curiosity and exploration? How can I encourage babies to actively explore new things?

As with each activity in this book, we have provided a completed activity template for the Hide-and-Seek infant activity as well as blank templates for you to use to modify these ideas to meet the needs of your babies and to design new activities.

The Hide-and-Seek Experience

This curious thinking experience centers around a Hide-and-Seek board book: *Where's Spot?* by Eric Hill (2003). Other similar Hide-and-Seek/lift-the-flap books can be used in place of or in addition to this book. *Where's Spot?* is the story of a dog, Sally, who cannot find a puppy, Spot. In this lift-the-flap board book, Sally the dog looks in various places until she finally finds Spot hiding in a basket.

Materials

- *Where's Spot?* by Eric Hill (2003; lift-the-flap board book)

Read the Book Together

Read this book aloud several times with one or more babies. Invite the babies to sit on your lap or in close proximity while you read and explore the book together.

Wonder and Ask Questions

As you read, pause after each question to invite the baby to respond: to wonder with you where Spot is and to lift the flap to discover if Spot is hiding on that page.

Explain and Discuss the Problem

Clearly stating and presenting the problem creates an opportunity for the infant to become curious about the problem of finding the missing dog, Spot.

Provide a description of the infant's initial actions to solve the problem. For example, if the baby has lifted the flap to look for Spot, you can say, "You looked in the closet, but Spot isn't in there. Where could Spot be?" It is important that you describe, but not judge, the effectiveness of the attempt to find Spot. Describing the attempt encourages the infant to repeat it. To support younger infants, you can model and describe his or her actions lifting the flap and discovering if Spot is there or not.

Engaging the baby in understanding the problem and then tapping into this curiosity to begin the search for Spot is at the heart of this experience.

Follow the Infant's Lead

It is important for the educator to follow the infant's lead. Notice what the baby does or says, always being responsive to and supportive of the infant's level of understanding and skill. This activity can be repeated often and with babies of all ages and abilities, so be sure that the challenge and language of the experience stays fresh by continuing to scaffold each infant's opportunities to develop skills and interact in a variety of ways with the materials. To deepen the activity, experiment with ways to make it slightly more difficult or a way to make it just a little different. Figure 3.1 is a rubric that will help you evaluate how well the infant engaged in the persistent learning experience. Examples are provided of the information you would record based on the infant's performance on the activity.

Rubric			
Rate the child's level of participation and understanding on the continuum. **Add evidence/ descriptions for each child.**	**Uses senses to explore the immediate environment; shows eagerness and interest in people, objects, experiences**	**Shows eagerness and interest in people, objects, experiences; explores and investigates ways to make something happen**	**Explores and investigates ways to make something happen; asks questions to get information; shows interest in learning new things and trying new experiences**
Child 1	Sarah reached out to touch the pages of the book as the teacher read. She took the book in her hands and turned it over and opened and closed it.		
Child 2		Brandon carried the book to his teacher and crawled into her lap. He turned each page, asking "Spot?" each time and then smiled when he finally found Spot on the last page.	
Child 3			Guerda was able to open the flaps with her fingers. On each page, she opened and closed the flap several times, saying, "Where's Spot?"

Figure 3.1. Infant curious thinking experience rubric.

Universal Design for Learning Supports for Infants

Because infants are just at the beginning of their development, many of the developmentally appropriate strategies used in a high-quality classroom are very similar to the UDL supports suggested. For example, offering an infant a choice of different textured balls to explore is both developmentally appropriate and a UDL support. In other words, UDL supports facilitate learning for all children but may have been chosen for use in the classroom based on the needs of a specific child. The suggestions for infants in the text boxes in these thinking

 UDL Supports for Infants

- Use hand-over-hand guidance to help infants point, touch, and lift the flap. [David]
- Add picture symbols to the book to support infants who will learn communication using picture symbols. [All]
- Provide a plush dog that looks like Spot to touch and hold for added sensory input during the activity. [Julia]
- Use supportive seating options such as a corner sitter or a wedge for children with low muscle tone. [David]
- Limit distractions in the room or play soft music without words to help focus the infants. [All]
- Use a few basic signs to engage infants in the experience and offer them opportunities to communicate (e.g., MORE, DONE, YES, NO). [Julia]

chapters are aimed at all children but address some needs of infants who have physical or multiple challenges that prevent them from independently manipulating the objects around them or from independently coming to engage in an activity. In the text box, it will be noted if these accommodations are geared toward all children or a specific profile child.

CURIOUS THINKING EXPERIENCE FOR TODDLERS

This activity is based on the children's book *One Duck Stuck,* written by Phyllis Root (1998). In this repetitive book, the duck gets stuck in the mud, and several different animal friends try to help him get unstuck. In addition to the repetitive phrases, the number of animals helping increases from 1 to 10. At the end of the book, their teamwork helps the duck to free himself. This book provides the opportunity to work on patterns, animal names and movements, numbers, and sequencing. Toddlers enjoy repeating the common phrase and imitating the animal movements to help free the duck from the mud. This activity could be done with other similar books, but we chose this book because it is a high-quality children's book that is readily available and popular in toddler classrooms.

Toddlers can readily identify the problem the duck faces and suggest a variety of people or animals to help solve this problem. Toddlers offer various ideas for how the duck can get out of the mud. In this activity, teachers and caregivers are encouraged to talk about the consistency of mud, what mud is made of, and how mud forms.

This activity emphasizes children's curious thinking skills—exploring with different senses, predicting, and offering various solutions. Children are encouraged to explore, predict, and investigate mud and make their own mud to learn more about the duck's predicament.

Introducing the Experience

To start the activity, read the first part of the story *One Duck Stuck*. Do a picture walk of the cover and first page: Look at the cover of the book with the children and ask them what they see. Based on their answers, ask what they expect the book to be about and why they think that is the case. In a typical picture walk, teachers and children look only at the pictures and use them as a tool to identify the topic of the book and to make predictions. Teachers can also use this time to introduce new vocabulary through the pictures and discussion.

Start reading and then stop after the page with three moose and the line "Help! Help! Who can help?" Ask the children, "What is mud? Have you ever played in it? What does it feel like?" Try to elicit some ideas about mud being dirty or clean and that it is made of water and dirt. Ask the children what they think is going to happen to the duck in the story. Explain that the duck has a problem because he is stuck in the mud. Ask the children who can help the duck. Children may suggest different animals or a mommy or daddy duck. Write down their suggestions on a piece of chart paper or a board for later. Ask the children, "What can the animals do to help the duck? Why is he stuck?"

Record the children's answers. Tell the children they will finish the book tomorrow (in another experience), but today they will investigate what mud looks and feels like and see if they can learn more about mud to help the duck.

Hands-On Engineering Experience

Organize the children into groups of two to four and prepare stations or centers for children to rotate through to do a variety of activities with mud. The stations can be completed in one or more activity periods, depending on your schedule. Thinking about the ages and developmental levels of your toddlers, assess whether they might do better with two stations now and the third station as a small group activity at a later time in the day.

Set up three stations for children to explore water, dirt, and mud:

1. At station 1, place three tubs (one with each consistency) on a table so children can put their hands in and see, touch, smell, and listen to the substance as they move it around. Talk to them about what they are feeling and seeing.

2. At station 2, set up quart-size zip-top bags with the three substances. Also, set up zip-top bags with mud of different consistencies for children to explore and describe the differences.

3. At station 3, set up for painting with brushes using water, mud, and dirt. For the dirt, use contact paper (sticky side up) on the paper to help the dirt stick. If children start to mix the dirt and water to make their own mud to paint with, ask the children how much water and how much dirt they used, or ask them to show you how they made the mud.

Ask children to cycle through the stations, exploring each substance in different ways. Encourage them to use their senses, and ask them to describe what they are investigating. Toddlers will use vocabulary to compare and contrast and start to describe similarities and differences and connect what they are doing during this activity with a previous experience with mud. Start with simple questions, such as "Are the two bags the same or different?" and then "Why? Can you show me or tell me how they are different or the same?" Focus on either similarities or differences in a loop of questions and then move to the other concept. Offer vocabulary to help deepen their descriptions.

Use a camera to document the children's work and their experiences. Photographs and videos are helpful for a later activity in this series on mud explorations. After all the children have gone through the stations, talk to the whole group about how the mud felt and what it looked like, sounded like, and smelled like. Write down the descriptive words the children use. Look at how the words are similar to or different from what they said after reading the first part of the book and before completing the hands-on engineering investigation.

Universal Design for Learning Supports for Toddlers

The UDL principles emphasize that supports provided in the classroom help all children to learn and engage in the curriculum. Educators may decide to use a specific support

---

 Self-Reflection Checklist

- Did I encourage children's enthusiasm to learn about mud and its properties?
- Did I ask children to make predictions, and did I document their predictions about the duck's problem?
- Did I model how to make "I wonder if . . ." statements, and did I document children's "I wonder if . . ." statements?
- Did I scaffold children to use their words to describe the mud and the process and give them new vocabulary?
- Did I encourage the children to try their own ideas for how to make mud?
- Did I offer multiple materials to find out what makes mud squishier or harder?
- Did I let the children try to manipulate the tools on their own?

Toddler Experience Planning Template

Problem-solving focus skill	Curious thinking
Motivating engineering problem	In the book *One Duck Stuck* by Phyllis Root (1998), the duck goes into a marsh and gets stuck in the mud. Various animal friends try to get the duck out of the mud, but it takes all of them working together to free the duck.
Focus of this particular learning experience	This activity focuses on exploring what mud feels and looks like and comparing and contrasting it to water and dirt.
Learning objectives for this particular experience	• Children will use at least three senses to explore and describe mud. • Children will use descriptive words to describe mud, water, and dirt.
Materials needed	• 3–6 tubs • Paper • Water • Contact paper • Dirt • Camera • Mud • Book (regular or big book) • Plastic zip-top bags • Chart paper and markers • Magnifying glasses • Rubber gloves • Paintbrushes • Trays/bags

Elements of the learning experience		UDL supports
Introduce children to the problem	Read the beginning of the book and discuss how the duck could get stuck in the mud. Ask the children what it looks and feels like and what their past mud experiences have been.	• Provide the book on an iPad or tablet computer. • Preteach key animals/vocabulary. • Use pictures/picture symbols for the animals.
Help children understand the problem-solving goal and constraints	Ask the children, "What could the animals do to help the duck? Why is he stuck?" Record the children's answers.	• Provide prepared sentence strips with possible answers and matching picture symbols. • Review with some children individually.
Support children in demonstrating their thinking	Set up three stations for children to explore water, dirt, and mud. Encourage them to use at least three senses (not taste).	• Offer stations at different tables to provide separation between children. • Supply gloves (for children not comfortable getting dirty). • Provide individual trays/bags for children. • Provide the book on an iPad or tablet computer. • Use a picture symbol board with key vocabulary. • Use grips for paintbrushes or large-handle paintbrushes. • Provide individual trays/areas to rotate through.
Provide opportunities for feedback and for trying again	Ask them to describe what they are investigating. Facilitate comparing and contrasting of the mud, dirt, and water. Offer vocabulary to help deepen their descriptions.	• Provide picture symbols. • Offer dichotomous picture choices for children to express opinions. • Use pictures for comparison/contrast.
Help children share and learn from one another	Use a camera to document the children's work and their experiences. Photographs and videos are helpful for a later lesson in this series on mud. After all the children have completed the stations, talk to the whole group about what they did and learned. Write down the descriptive words the children use.	• Offer small groups or large groups for debriefing. • Add pictures to chart responses from the activity.

Figure 3.2. Toddler curious thinking experience overview and rubric.

(continued)

Figure 3.2. *(continued)*

Rubric			
Rate the child's level of participation and understanding on the continuum. **Add evidence/ descriptions for each child.**	**Uses senses to explore the immediate environment** *Is the child touching and looking at the mud, dirt, and water?*	**Uses senses to explore the immediate environment; investigates ways to make things happen in the environment** *Did the child mix dirt and water to make mud and discuss?*	**Investigates ways to make things happen in the environment** *Did the child mix mud, trying different consistencies and/or mixtures?*
Child 1			Damien put dirt in the bag and then added water slowly to mix the mud. Then he tried a different bag and added more water to make it runnier.
Child 2		Cora touched all the textures and commented on the water being cold and the dirt feeling warm.	
Child 3	Will put his hands in each tub but wanted very quickly to wash his hands and be finished. He looked at it and pointed to pictures.		

because they know an individual child in the class has a need, but they can open that support up to all children so they can benefit as well. For example, this activity uses picture symbols to support vocabulary development and speech because Tam and Jesse both are English language learners and need the additional support to connect words to concepts, but all young children can benefit from picture symbols to support literacy development.

Figure 3.2 provides several UDL supports for this activity in the lesson template that are geared toward the profile children but can also be used with others in the classroom. For example, Jessie benefits from her own individual tray and workspace, but other children may prefer that as well. As the educator, you can decide whether you want to provide individual material sets or have children work in small or larger groups. Gloves and grips for the paintbrushes are also important supports for children with sensory and/or fine motor challenges. Tam needs these supports to develop his fine motor skills and works with the occupational therapist 1 day a week using grips

 Essentials to Remember

- Encourage children to explore with their senses.
- Ask children to describe what they are doing and learning.
- Ask them to identify what is the same or different and ask why.
- Offer multiple opportunities/ways to explore the mud/dirt/water.

and holding brushes and pencils. All children in the class can decide to draw, talk with the teacher, or use pictures to demonstrate their learning about mud. Within this mud theme, many of the supports are used in several of the activities to teach all the thinking skills because of the similarity of activities and the strengths and needs of the children. For example, picture symbols and pictures of animals are used throughout the unit. The UDL Planning Sheet provides a summary of all the UDL supports used for this toddler unit.

CURIOUS THINKING EXPERIENCE FOR PRESCHOOLERS

This learning experience is based on the children's book *Muncha! Muncha! Muncha!* by Candace Fleming (2002). In this whimsically illustrated book, a gardener's many efforts to protect his vegetables are no match for three determined bunnies and their abilities to jump, dig, swim, and climb. Mr. McGreely tries to keep the bunnies out with a wire fence, a wooden wall, a water-filled trench, and a stone enclosure. But each time he engineers a new structure, the bunnies manage to find a way in to munch his carrots and sprouts. Preschool children are delighted by the bunnies' antics and empathetic with Mr. McGreely's efforts to save his food. They readily identify the problem that he faces and have a range of opinions on whether his attempts to solve the problem will succeed. The variety of predictions that preschool children make about the fate of Mr. McGreely's vegetables makes this book a rich context for exploring curious thinking.

This experience emphasizes children's curious thinking skills—their fluency in asking questions, making predictions, and exploring and investigating to find answers. Children are encouraged to wonder, predict, and investigate as they practice some "garden engineering" alongside Mr. McGreely. In particular, they ask questions and explore answers about what makes sturdy garden walls.

Although the activity could be done with other similar books, we chose this book because it is a high-quality children's book that is readily available and popular in preschool classrooms.

Preparing for the Learning Experience

To prepare for this activity, decide what materials you will offer children to build model garden walls. Options include wooden unit blocks, DUPLO bricks, Bristle Blocks, cardboard boxes, magnetic tiles, and wooden planks. You can limit the available materials to one type, or you might want to offer an assortment of building materials and allow the children to explore the sturdiness of walls built out of different materials. The next preparation step is to create at least one model vegetable garden (Figure 3.3). The model helps make the goal of sturdy garden walls more concrete for children. To make a model vegetable garden for several children to share, you can cut out paper vegetable shapes and tape them to a large poster board or piece of cardboard. If you would like children to have their own individual model gardens, you can make several prints or copies of a garden illustration on paper and laminate them. Another option is to create a three-dimensional model garden by placing toy vegetables (perhaps from a dramatic play area) into a shallow box or bin. Finally, for this activity, you will also need to find a small stuffed animal or bean bag to use as a model bunny rabbit.

Asking Questions to Introduce the Experience

To begin the activity itself, tell the children that they will soon have a chance to practice being engineers. If you have not talked about engineering before, you can describe

Figure 3.3.   A model vegetable garden made out of poster board

engineers simply as people who design and build things that solve people's problems. Engineers learn how to do their work by practicing creating things that solve problems. Show children the book *Muncha! Muncha! Muncha!* (Fleming, 2002) and explain that in this book, Mr. McGreely has a big problem, and you would like to help the children find his problem and investigate one way to solve it.

Before opening the book, show children the cover illustration and ask anticipation questions such as "What do you think this book might be about?" "How many of you have planted a garden?" and "What are some of the things you have to do when you plant a garden?" Respond to children's ideas with more probes of their thinking. For example, if children predict that the book is about a farmer or a gardener, you can ask, "Why do you think this man might be a gardener?" By asking many questions about the book and about children's thinking, you can model curiosity and set the stage for this activity's focus on curious thinking.

Finding the Problem

After previewing the book cover, read aloud the first part of the story and stop just after the first time the line "Muncha, muncha, muncha!" appears. Ask, "How do you think

Mr. McGreely felt when the bunnies ate his vegetables?" Help children identify the problem faced by Mr. McGreely and then ask, "What are some ways that Mr. McGreely could solve his problem?" It is a good idea to document children's ideas at this point by drawing a visual of each idea or listing each one on a chart. This documentation can serve as a list of children's predictions about what Mr. McGreely will do. As you read the book throughout the coming days, they can look back at their predictions and check them against the events of the story. The children will be eager to find out if Mr. McGreely tries to protect his garden using any of the ideas that they proposed.

Making More Predictions

When you are ready to return to the story, continue reading only through the part where Mr. McGreely builds a wall. Here, stop to take another survey of children's thinking: "Will the wall solve the problem by keeping the bunnies from eating the vegetables?" This time, you might make the survey a data collection exercise by drawing a T-chart and titling one column "Yes" and the other column "No" (Figure 3.4). Have each child give his or her prediction one at a time, and record the prediction with an *X* in the appropriate column. Help the children count the number of "X's" in each column and record the total number of "yes" and "no" predictions. Ask a few children to explain why they predict that the wall will or will not solve the problem and then announce that before reading any more of the book, the children will have a chance to build their

Figure 3.4. T-chart used to document children's predictions about whether Mr. McGreely's wall will protect his vegetable garden from bunnies.

own pretend garden walls and see if they can make them sturdy enough to protect a pretend garden.

Other preschool learning experiences in this book will make use of the rest of *Muncha! Muncha! Muncha!* (Fleming, 2002), but before reading further, children will investigate how walls work to protect gardens. What makes a sturdy garden wall? Help the children understand that *sturdy* walls are walls that do not fall over easily when disturbed in some way.

Each child will use blocks to build a wall around a pretend "garden" (e.g., a paper with a garden drawing). Then they will test it by seeing if it remains standing when a pretend bunny "hops" toward it.

It is now time to help children think about what kind of wall they want to investigate. Show them what materials will be available for their investigation. Ask them to think about how they will build a wall out of these building materials. How do they think they can arrange the blocks (or bricks, etc.) to make a sturdy wall? To elicit children's ideas, predictions, and questions about garden walls, you can model thinking curiously about garden walls. You can make statements that begin with the phrase "I wonder if . . ." and ask children to do the same. For example, "I wonder if a garden wall that uses round blocks will protect the garden," "I wonder if a very tall garden wall will be sturdy when a bunny hops toward it," "I wonder if I can make a sturdy garden wall out of triangle-shaped blocks," "I wonder if fat or skinny garden walls are sturdy," and so forth. These wonderings are the work of a curious thinker.

Using Curiosity to Investigate

For the rest of the learning experience, you might choose to work with children individually or in small groups. Have a child or a small group join you in an open floor space such as a block area. Present the model vegetable garden and announce that you have a challenge for the children. How can they build a sturdy wall to protect this vegetable garden? Show them the stuffed animal or bean bag (or allow them to choose one) that will serve as the pretend bunny rabbit. To test whether a wall is sturdy, children will toss the bunny gently at the wall and see if the wall remains standing. The goal is for children to use their curious thinking to build different kinds of walls and explore which ones are best at standing up to the hopping bunny.

As children build, ask them questions about the way they are putting blocks together into a wall and about their wonderings about how their wall will work. How did the children come up with their wall designs? What inspired them to make their walls the way they did? What building pieces are they curious about? Ask each child to predict what will happen to his or her wall when the bunny "hops" toward it, and be sure to take a photograph of each wall before the child tests it with the bunny. You can echo back to the children the questions and wonderings they have shared with you.

Take a photograph after the bunny-hop test as well, whether or not the wall falls over. After each test, help children make sense of what happened by asking them to try to describe and then explain the outcome. Focus on describing what happened first, before moving on to explanations. Support children's observations of what happened by asking questions such as "So what happened?" "What did you notice?" and "Do you want to try it a couple more times?" After the children have described what happened, you can shift toward supporting their reasoning about *why* that happened. You might ask, "What do you think made this wall stay standing?" "What do you think made this wall fall over?" "Why do you think this wall was so good at protecting the garden?" and "So what do you know about your wall now?"

Encourage children to observe each other's work and ask each other questions about what they notice. Invite other children to watch when a wall is about to be tested.

You might find that when testing the sturdiness of their walls, children toss the stuffed animal or bean bag "bunny" only very gently, or only in such a way that it does not make contact with their walls. This strategy makes sense when children do not want to see their walls fall over! But remind the children that they are trying to find out what makes a wall sturdy enough to protect a garden from a hopping bunny, and the only way to find that out is to let the bunny really hop. Reassure the children that if the bunny knocks down their wall, they will learn something new about walls, and they will be able to build a new wall right away. You can encourage them to test the sturdiness of the wall by saying something like, "That was a very soft throw. I'm sure you want to make sure the bunny doesn't get hurt. But it's a strong bunny and we'd like to observe what happens when it hops into the wall. Can you throw it a little bit harder?" You could also choose to designate yourself as the bunny tosser.

Over the course of the day or week, offer all the children a chance to build and explore the sturdiness of different kinds of garden walls. Continue to take photographs of their work, and when you can, write down the predictions they make, their descriptions of what happens when they test their walls, and their explanations for those results.

Finally, bring all the children together to return to the question, "What makes a sturdy garden wall?" Share photographs of the children's walls before and after testing. Discuss what children notice about the different walls, and help them create a list of characteristics of sturdy walls. Continue to foster their curious thinking by modeling "I wonder" statements. You can sort the wall photographs into two piles: one with walls that fell over and one with walls that did not. You could then say, "I wonder if there's anything that is the same among all the walls that fell over," or "I wonder if there's a difference between walls that protected the garden and walls that did not." Ask children to help you investigate your wonderings and to share and explore their own wonderings about all the walls they built and tested.

Figure 3.5 provides a brief overview of the activity and a rubric to evaluate the children's development as persistent thinkers through this learning experience.

Universal Design for Learning Supports for Preschoolers

In the overview, a variety of UDL supports are suggested for each part of the activity, along with additional materials that should be on hand to support all children. Expressive language and communication are challenges for both Brandon and José, our profile preschool-age children. To support both children and facilitate their learning of picture symbols, use of an iPad or tablet computer communication device and pictures will be very important. Both boys are physically able to construct the wall and problem-solve with peers or independently ways to create a wall to keep the bunnies out, but both boys may also struggle with expressing why they made certain design choices and expressing

"Window into a Classroom" Anecdote

Teacher:	(Concludes her read-aloud with the line about McGreely's confidence that the bunnies won't get over the wall.) So here's what I want you to think of: I want you to do some thinking work.
Emmett:	I think only people can get in!
Teacher:	Well, I don't know. We'll take a vote, and we'll do a survey about your thinking. So don't yell out yet. Take a minute just to think. (She points to the data table she has drawn on the easel and reads its title.) Do you think the wall will protect the garden from the bunnies? Do you think that the wall is going to work? So just keep thinking.
Emmett:	I think yes!
Teacher:	So, Emmett, part of thinking work is that you hold on to it until it's your turn. So if you say "Yes," I'll put you here (points to the left column of the data table). And if you say, "No," I'll put you here (points to the right column of the data table).
Teacher:	(She asks each child in turn to share his or her response and records an "X" in the corresponding column of the data table. She asks one child to count the X's in the "No" column, and another child to count the X's in the "Yes" column. She helps the whole group count aloud to double-check each quantity, and then records the numeral underneath each set of X's. There are 11 "Yes" votes and 5 "No" votes.)
Teacher:	So which one do more of us think? Do more of us think "yes" the wall is going to work, or do more of us think "no"?
Children:	Yes, yes, yes!
Teacher:	So more people think "yes," the wall is going to work. The number 11 is more than the number 5. So more of us think the wall is going to work. Yes, Caleb?
Caleb:	But they can hop, they can go in the back, though, 'cuz there's no wall in the back, and they can come around the sides.
Teacher:	Okay, well, Caleb is starting to have a theory. Here's the challenge for you all. . . .

 ## Self-Reflection Checklist

- Did I encourage children's enthusiasm to learn about Mr. McGreely's garden problem and about what makes a wall sturdy?
- Did I ask children to make predictions, and did I document their predictions?
- Did I model how to make "I wonder if . . ." statements, and did I document children's "I wonder if . . ." statements?
- Did I ask children to explore and investigate multiple ways to make sturdy walls?
- Did I offer multiple resources to find out what makes a sturdy wall?

Preschool Experience Planning Template

Problem-solving focus skill	Curious thinking
Motivating engineering problem	In the book *Munch! Munch! Munch!* by Candace Fleming (2002), three bunnies keep sneaking into Mr. McGreely's garden and eating his vegetables. Children can recognize that the bunny break-ins are a problem for Mr. McGreely and explore better garden protection.
Focus of this particular learning experience	Mr. McGreely tries to protect his garden by building a wall around it, but the bunnies are able to get into the garden anyway. The question "What makes a good wall?" is the focus of this learning experience.
Learning objectives for this particular experience	• Children will explore and investigate ways to make strong structures. • Children will ask questions about strong structures and about gardens.
Materials needed	• Unit blocks or other building elements for walls • *Munch! Munch! Munch!* by Candace Fleming • Small stuffed animals or bean bags • Paper or poster with illustration of vegetable garden • Poster paper and markers for recording children's ideas • Camera

Elements of the learning experience		UDL supports
Introduce children to the problem	Begin to read the story *Munch! Munch! Munch!* Stop reading after the bunnies appear, and ask the children, "What do you think the bunnies are going to do?" Read the next page of the story and ask, "How do you think Mr. McGreely felt when the bunnies ate the vegetables?" Explain that Mr. McGreely has a *problem* with the bunnies.	• Use picture symbols for key vocabulary. • Use an audio or interactive version of the book on a tablet computer. • Preteach key vocabulary. • Offer Spanish/English vocabulary cards.
Help children understand the problem-solving goal and constraints	Ask, "What are some ways that Mr. McGreely could solve his problem?" Record children's ideas. Continue reading only through the part where Mr. McGreely builds a wall. Take a vote: "Will the wall solve the problem by keeping the bunnies from eating the vegetables?" Tell students that they are going to investigate how walls work to protect gardens. Each student will use blocks to build a wall around a paper or cardboard garden model. Students should begin thinking about what kind of wall they want to investigate. How will they build a strong wall?	• Allow children to complete this part again in a smaller group for time to think through ideas. • Provide blocks that are easy to assemble. • Provide a sticky or nonslip surface for easier building.
Support children in demonstrating their thinking	Support individual children or groups of children in building garden walls. Model questioning and wondering about how the walls will work and why they are making particular building choices.	• Provide communication boards or interactive communication tools to support expressive communication. • Group children so that they are supported by a peer or an adult.
Provide opportunities for feedback and for trying again	Show children how to use a small stuffed animal or bean bag "bunny" to test whether their walls stay standing when bumped by a "bunny-hop." Have children predict what will happen to their walls, and take photographs before and after the bunny-hop tests.	• Allow multiple trials to test and predict. • Position children so that their throws are successful.

Figure 3.5.   Preschool curious thinking experience overview and rubric.

(continued)

Figure 3.5. *(continued)*

Help children share and learn from one another	At "engineering circle" time, help children share photographs of their walls before and after testing. Discuss what children notice about the walls that protected the gardens and the walls that did not.	• Use a board to hold pictures so children can look at them and talk at the same time. • Use a turn-taking stick or other tool to determine the speaker. • Allow children to discuss in smaller groups or with the teacher.

Rubric			
Rate the child's level of participation and understanding on the continuum. **Add evidence/ descriptions for each child.**	**Explores and investigates ways to make something happen**	**Shows eagerness to learn about a variety of topics and ideas; uses a variety of resources to find answers to questions**	**Observes and asks questions about observable phenomena; plans and implements investigations using simple equipment (from MA Pre-K STE) (Massachusetts Department of Elementary and Secondary Education, 2014)**
Child 1			Hayden announced her plan to build and test a wall out of seven cardboard blocks. She wondered out loud if it would work better than her last wall, which had nine blocks and fell down.
Child 2		The day after reading *Muncha! Muncha! Muncha!*, Damon talked about exploring the walls of the raised garden beds in his backyard at home.	
Child 3	Without much verbalizing, Sylvia built, knocked down, and rebuilt several walls out of unit blocks.		

 Essentials to Remember

- The goal of the activity is not to re-create the *Muncha! Muncha! Muncha!* (Fleming, 2002) story but to support children's curious thinking as they engage in early engineering problem solving.

- The purpose of building walls is not to replicate the structure illustrated in the picture book but to explore the question "What makes a sturdy wall?"

- The key practices to elicit from children in this experience are making predictions (about what Mr. McGreely will do, about how his wall will work, and about how the children's walls will work) and asking questions, often in the form of "I wonder if . . ." statements.

- Your role as the facilitator is to model prediction making and question asking and to document the predictions, questions, and discoveries made by the children.

their brainstorming on how to build the best wall. Offer children multiple ways to communicate, and videotape the construction to gain a better insight into their process rather than relying more on their words. Work with them to use their words and develop their vocabulary around engineering and building, because these terms and concepts will be revisited throughout the activities in the following chapters. To help José limit his frustration, offer him a choice of building materials so he can focus on the bunnies' problem and not any issues with building. Because Brandon has autism spectrum disorder and can become overstimulated by lots of noise in the classroom, offer him a quieter corner of the room to work with one or two peers or an opportunity to complete the building part of the activity in rotating small groups to limit the noise and commotion.

Other suggestions, such as using a nonslip surface and special Bristle Blocks that are easier to connect, are listed in the UDL supports to help children with fine motor issues. The grouping and peer support strategies are useful for Brandon and José but may also benefit other children in the classroom. Several different alternative materials are listed throughout the UDL supports overview section to be used as needed in addition to the regular materials needed for this activity.

RESOURCES

Developmental Trajectory and Key Standards and Guidelines

Dichtelmiller, M.L. (2001). *Omnibus guidelines: Preschool through third grade.* Ann Arbor, MI: Rebus Planning Assoc.

Heroman, C., Burts, D.C., Berke, K., & Bickart, T.S. (2010). *Teaching strategies GOLD: Objectives for development and learning: Birth through kindergarten.* Washington, DC: Teaching Strategies, Inc.

High/Scope Press & High/Scope Educational Research Foundation. (2003). *Preschool Child Observation Record.* Ypsilanti, MI: Authors.

Office of Head Start. (2010). *Head Start child development and early learning frameworks: Promoting positive outcomes in early childhood programs serving children 3–5 years old (2010).* Washington, DC: U.S. Department of Health and Human Services. Retrieved from https://eclkc.ohs.acf.hhs.gov/hslc/tta-system/teaching/eecd/Assessment/Child%20Outcomes/HS_Revised_Child_Outcomes_Framework(rev-Sept2011).pdf

Ohio Department of Education. (2012). *Ohio early learning and development standards.* Retrieved from http://education.ohio.gov/getattachment/Topics/Early-Learning/Early-Learning-Content-Standards/The-Standards/ELDS-ATL-FINAL-21-October-2012-pdf.pdf.aspx

PBS Kids. (2014). *Child development tracker: Approaches to learning.* Retrieved from http://www.pbs.org/parents/childdevelopmenttracker/five/approachestolearning.html

Publications

Conezio, K., & French, L. (2002, September). Capitalizing on children's fascination with the everyday world to foster language and literacy development. *Beyond the Journal.* Retrieved from http://www.naeyc.org/files/yc/file/200209/ScienceInThePreschoolClassroom.pdf

Nuner, J. (2007). Foster creativity that will last a lifetime. *Texas Child Care Quarterly, 31*(2), 16–21. Retrieved from http://www.childcarequarterly.com/pdf/fall07_creativity.pdf

Ogu, U., & Schmidt, S.R. (2009, March). Investigating rocks and sand: Addressing multiple learning styles through an inquiry-based approach. *Beyond the Journal.* Retrieved from http://www.naeyc.org/files/yc/file/200903/BTJSchmidt_Ogu_Expanded.pdf

Perry, B. (n.d.). Why young children are curious. *Early Childhood Today.* Retrieved from http://www.scholastic.com/teachers/article/why-young-children-are-curious

Perry, B. (2001). *Curiosity: The fuel of development.* Retrieved from http://teacher.scholastic.com/professional/bruceperry/curiosity.htm

Seizt, H.J. (2006, March). The plan: Building on children's interests. *Beyond the Journal.* Retrieved from http://www.naeyc.org/files/yc/file/200603/SeitzBTJ.pdf

Texas Child Care. (2014). Science and discovery. *Texas Child Care Quarterly, 34*(4). Retrieved from http://www.childcarequarterly.com/pdf/spring14_basics.pdf

ZERO TO THREE. (2012). *Tips on nurturing your child's curiosity.* Retrieved from http://www.zerotothree.org/child-development/social-emotional-development/tips-on-nurturing-your-childs-curiosity.html

Additional Suggestions for Encouraging Curious Thinking

- Wonder out loud: "How can a bird fly?" or "Why is Juan so sad?" When adults share the things they wonder about, it models the behavior they want to see from children.

- Appreciate when a child is trying to figure something out, whether it is a friend's behavior or how something works. Comment in a positive way: "You are trying to figure out why the block tower fell; that is how we learn new things."

- Start activities with questions: "What would happen if . . . ?"

- Provide opportunities for children to make choices.

- Initiative is often linked with resiliency, as a child who is able take initiative can get his or her own needs met.

- Incorporate dramatic play by having children act out the parts of the gardener and the animals who are trying to sneak in to the garden.

- Explore this activity with both collaborative and individual building.

- Try this extension activity with a nonfiction text: Read *Garden* by Robert Maass, which has very clear photographs of gardens (Maass, 1998). Have children generate questions and predictions about what kinds of protection the gardens in the book will need from animals.

- Consider your environment; is there something new for children every day? It may just be a new song or story.

- Provide things for children to explore. Nature is rich with opportunities: seashells, pinecones, or various rocks.

- Go on a walk and ask the children to tell you if they see something that is new or different from the last time.

- Remember to present key concepts in as many ways as you can think of them: visually, through sound, with movement, and so forth. The more senses you use, the more likely you are to engage every child.

4 Persistent Thinkers

Persistence is both a self-regulatory and an academic skill needed for success across all developmental domains. Persistence includes both attention and task completion (Li-Grining, Votruba-Drzal, Maldonado-Carreño, & Haas, 2010; McClelland, Acock, & Morrison, 2006; Schaefer & McDermott, 1999). Rothbart and Bates (2006) state that interest and persistence are two important and separate parts of learning behavior. For the most effective learning, children must first engage in the activity and then maintain that engagement over a period of time. Engagement and persistence develop from the first year of life. Persistence and interest are observable throughout early childhood and across contexts (Martin, Ryan, & Brooks-Gunn, 2013). Children react to stimuli in their environment and then adjust their reaction to different stimuli based on their needs and interests (Rothbart & Bates, 2006). For example, children will react to blinking lights but then continue to watch them to understand their patterns and why the lights blink for an extended period of time.

A child's ability to regulate his or her emotions supports cognitive functioning "because a child who is more skilled at regulating her emotions is better able to direct her attention to, and sustain attention on, cognitive tasks" (Blair & Ursache, 2010, quoted in Martin et al., 2013, p. 659). Parents and early caregivers play a critical role in the development of persistence (Frodi, Bridges, & Grolnick, 1985; Kelley, Brownell, & Campbell, 2000; Yarrow, Morgan, Jennings, Harmon, & Gaiter, 1982). Children who received positive feedback and encouragement for their persistence at age 2 were more likely to demonstrate persistence at age 3 in clinical studies (Kelley et al., 2000). Parents and caregivers need to be sensitive to children's cues and support their efforts at a task. Risk taking and persistence promote self-regulation and help children better manage in emotionally challenging circumstances. Parent and caregiver modeling of positive self-regulation reinforces children's own self-regulation (Eisenberg, Smith, & Spinrad, 2010).

As children become toddlers and preschoolers, they start to work specifically on task persistence, an important component of academic self-regulation. Task persistence requires sustaining attention toward a specific task and resisting distractions or the impulse to flee (Martin et al., 2013). Drake, Belsky, and Fearon define task persistence as a "child's capacity to engage consistently in a challenging task without becoming distracted or irritable" (2013, p. 5). Robson and Rowe, in their study on creativity in preschools, examined persistence defined as a triad of skills: 1) persisting, when the child shows "resilience, and maintains involvement in an activity in the face of difficulty, challenge

or uncertainty"; 2) risk taking, when the child "displays a willingness to take risks, and learn from mistakes"; and completing challenges, when the child "shows a sense of self-efficacy, self-belief and pleasure in achievement: shows conscious awareness of his/her own thinking" (2012, p. 352). For example, toddlers like to put shapes in the shape sorter toy. This can be a challenging task at that age due to both their developing fine motor control and their ability to understand how to make the shapes fit into the correct hole. Toddlers who try multiple times to put the shapes in the holes, try different orientations for the shapes, and continue to problem-solve which shapes go into which holes over several minutes show persistence.

Persistence is also highly correlated with engagement and motivation and is a component of executive functioning. Motivation predicts a child's level of engagement in activities and can affect the child's level of performance in these activities. As children become more engaged for longer periods of time in tasks, engagement tends to provide opportunities to practice existing skills and to acquire new ones (Wigfield, Eccles, Schiefele, Roeser, & Davis-Kean, 2006). Motivation is necessary for development of academic skills because knowledge can only be successfully learned when children are able to persist in challenging activities, sustaining their engagement until learning occurs (Mokrova, O'Brien, Calkins, Leerkes, & Marcovitch, 2013).

WHY IS PERSISTENT THINKING IMPORTANT?

Persistent thinkers actively take risks and repeat their experiments over and over to verify results and look for new outcomes. They remain with an activity for a sustained period of time to try to solve the problem or understand the problem better. For young children, persistence is correlated to development and intelligence (Belsky, Friedman, & Hsieh, 2001; Kelley et al., 2000; Kelley & Jennings, 2003) and is a key predictor of cognitive development (La Paro & Pianta, 2000; Rimm-Kaufman, Pianta, & Cox, 2000). Six-month-old infants' levels of persistence predicted their levels of cognitive development at 14 months (Banerjee & Tamis-LeMonda, 2007). In addition, studies have shown that children with high levels of persistence at kindergarten entry have higher levels of achievement both in kindergarten and longitudinally (Banerjee & Tamis-LeMonda, 2007; Razza, Martin, & Brooks-Gunn, 2010, 2012). Hauser-Cram, Bronson, and Upshur (1993) found the degree to which children with disabilities were able to exercise choice in their activities is significantly related to increased social interaction, higher rates of engaging peers, higher levels of task persistence, and less distraction from tasks. With choice-making, children can exercise control over their environment and begin to understand the consequences of certain choices. Mokrova et al. (2013) found that parents and caregivers need to encourage young children's engagement in challenging activities and help them sustain that engagement.

Persistence is important because it supports and promotes learning and self-regulation. Critically, persistence is a skill that can be nurtured and grown through responsive and sensitive parenting and caregiving. In addition, parents and caregivers play a crucial role in limiting children's stress and anxiety during learning and play so that children are encouraged to take risks and make mistakes (Neitzel & Stright, 2003; Yarrow et al., 1982). Stress and anxiety affect development and limit persistence and self-regulation, two aspects of executive functioning that are important for learning and development (Thompson & Haskins, 2014).

NAEYC's accreditation standards for assessing early childhood programs specifically call for the development of problem-solving abilities:

- *1.B.04:* Teaching staff encourage and recognize children's work and accomplishments.

- *1.F.02a:* Teaching staff will help children manage their behavior by guiding and supporting the children to persist when frustrated.

- *2.B.04:* Children have varied opportunities to develop a sense of competence and positive attitudes toward learning, such as persistence, engagement, curiosity, and mastery (NAEYC, 2014, pp. 3, 8, 12).

Within the Head Start Approaches to Learning Domain 7, which addresses school readiness, one set of indicators specifically promotes engagement and persistence. Children will

- Grow in abilities to persist in and complete a variety of tasks, activities, projects, and experiences.

- Demonstrate increasing ability to set goals and develop and follow through on plans.

- Show growing capacity to maintain concentration over time on a task, question, set of directions or interactions, despite distractions and interruptions. (U.S. Department of Health and Human Services, Administration on Children, Youth and Families, Head Start Bureau, 2003).

As part of Domain 7, children also work on initiative and curiosity indicators and reasoning and problem-solving indicators. These are all linked to school readiness.

DEVELOPMENTAL CONTINUUM OF PERSISTENT THINKING

Infants

Infants try to understand their impact on the world and learn and test out the concept of cause and effect. When a young infant smiles and her mother smiles back and continues the interaction back and forth, the infant is learning that she has an impact on her mother and persists to gain a response again. Infants are learning to explore and figure out whom they can affect. According to Banerjee and Tamis-LeMonda,

> When infants are presented with a new task, they typically transition from inattention to passive exploration (mouthing, touching and holding objects) to goal-directed, persistent behavior in which they actively explore the features of objects, for example by turning, banging, shaking or pushing buttons in purposeful ways to achieve effects. (2007, p. 480)

At 6 months, infants start to purposely manipulate toys, and at 9 months, infants can be selective in their actions, choosing the best action for each task. By 15 months, children want to do things on their own without adult support. Infants are often learning through nonengagement and passive engagement. Passive engagement means that infants spend a lot of time watching and listening to the people and the world around them but are not actively manipulating it. When infants are placed in reclining car seats and carried, they are often experiencing the world through nonengagement, because they cannot move or see beyond their seats. As they develop motor control, they can be more actively engaged with manipulatives and other toys and explore and in turn maintain their engagement with activities and objects.

Toddlers

When toddlers start to use the shape sorter and look for the hole that fits the square when holding the square and not just try the square in all the holes, they are displaying a persistent task approach (Messer, 1995). A frequent activity enjoyed by toddlers is stacking blocks as high as they can and seeing them fall. When a 2-year-old experiments with which blocks form the most solid base and considers how best to balance the blocks as the tower gets taller, she is learning what steps are involved in reaching her goal through careful planning and persistence.

An 18-month-old will want to take her shirt off by herself. If she is struggling, scaffold one or two steps and then let her finish taking it off herself. A toddler will do a puzzle and try the pieces in a few different ways but will keep trying until he has finished the puzzle. At this age, toddlers are starting to take pride in their accomplishments and benefit from encouragement and specific feedback both for trying and for accomplishing a task.

Preschoolers

Preschoolers are very actively engaged in problem solving and should be persisting to find an answer and trying different solutions. One would expect a 5-year-old to use constructive engagement more often than a toddler would. For example, in the sandbox, a 4-year-old child tries to fill a truck with sand, but he notices that it is a slow process, so he looks around and finds a shovel to use to make the process go faster. In another part of a preschool classroom, a 5-year-old is working with playdough. She is making a pizza but notices that the rolling pin has marks on it and wants a smooth pizza, so she decides to use her hands and smooth out each edge with the flat edge of a knife and her hand. Finally, a 3-year-old finishes drawing at the table and shows the teacher his picture. The teacher asks him what his picture is and he explains. He then puts his paper down again and writes the first letter of his name. He proudly shows the teacher and says that he wrote his name. In this last case, the child is attempting a difficult task for him, and he tried and produced a good approximation for his age. Each of these are examples of persistence in preschoolers.

KEY GOALS FOR PERSISTENT THINKING EXPERIENCES

The following set of key words helps explore ways to support young children by describing their actions when they are engaged in persistent thinking. These action words can be helpful when creating lesson and unit plan goals for children. It is helpful to think about these terms as guiding words for what children are working on at a metacognitive level. In other words, when watching children engage in the activities in this chapter or other activities designed to promote persistent thinking, look for children doing these things.

Some of these words are more appropriate for preschoolers, whereas other words will describe what is expected of infants or toddlers doing during these activities and investigations. For example, all children will explore and engage in various tasks and activities. For very young children, these tasks are play and learning combined. But in their play, children

Key Words and Phrases for Persistent Thinking for Goal Setting

- Taking initiative
- Repeating
- Maintaining attention
- Engaging
- Solving problems
- Noticing patterns

also use the scientific method repeatedly to test their ideas and repeat their experiments over and over to make sure the same thing happens every time. For example, an infant may press the button on her musical toy over and over to see that music does play each time. Peekaboo is a repetitious game where the goal is the same every time, but the reward or what is found can be different. Infants want to find that person or toy that they seek as a comfort or as a novelty. As children grow into toddlers, they maintain their attention on a task for a longer period of time. Children engage with people and with objects from birth, but the nature and duration of engagement changes as children's learning and play develop over time.

Patterns are everywhere, and children look for them. Patterns can exist in different ways, such as a set of shapes in a particular order that children are supposed to recognize and extend, but first children must learn the attributes of different objects or activities. For example, from infancy, children start to classify people and objects by their attributes, first at basic levels and then using more intricate characteristics. A persistent child will study the pattern or system of classification and figure out how to extend it. Young children may think all animals are dogs at first but then learn the differences among dogs and horses and fish based on the animals' adherence to or lack of certain attributes. A persistent child might also look for additional examples of a particular animal or block type to better understand the classification system.

Finally, children are constantly solving problems, and persistence is critical to finding the solutions. Understanding cause and effect is the precursor to both language and communication and problem solving. Infants cry and learn that this action brings a caregiver to solve their problem. Toddlers learn that by saying certain words, such as *mama* or *milk*, they are able to receive what they want more efficiently. By trying closer approximations of the solution through trial and error, young children learn to solve their problems in several domains of their lives.

Strategies for Facilitating Persistent Thinking

Parents and caregivers can use several strategies to facilitate the development of persistence and foster motivation and engagement in children. First, adults can provide children with metacognitive strategies—that is, strategies to help children think about their thinking and what they are learning. For example, when playing or interacting with infants and toddlers, it is important to narrate their actions and your actions not only to support their language development but to help them think through and process what is happening.

In preschool, teachers use think-alouds or self-talk to model how to mix primary colors to make green or purple or to count one more or one less with manipulatives. For example, to model the mixing of primary colors, after putting pots of red, blue, and yellow finger paints and paper on the table for the children, a teacher might say, "What colors do we have? What do think would happen if we mixed red and blue on our papers? What do you think would happen if we mixed red and yellow? Let's try red and blue. Look! When I mix the two colors together with my fingers, I get purple! Now why don't you try red and yellow on your papers? See what color you get." Teachers are providing and modeling the metacognitive strategies necessary to complete the task and reducing the cognitive demands of the task for their children by breaking down the task. Teachers present information in small steps, reviewing the steps and discussing progress in relation to the overall task goal (Rogoff et al., 1993; Stright, Neitzel, Sears, & Hoke-Sinex, 2001). For example, when children learn to put on a coat, teachers do not ask them to put their arms in and zip it up all at once for the first time. They break the task down so children start with one arm and then the other. They offer one instruction at a time or teach the method of putting on a coat from the floor so children flip the coat overhead. By breaking the task down, children learn and master a few steps at a time so they can become more confident and persist with this task and harder tasks. For infants and toddlers, this metacognitive process is just as important. Children who have information about strategies and about the general nature of academic tasks are best equipped to cognitively manage their learning when they get older (Schraw, 1994). In the older grades, parents who provide metacognitive information during problem-solving interactions have children who can look for and recognize errors and self-correct and find the right strategies to use for different tasks (Stright et al., 2001).

At the same time, children should be encouraged to try different ideas and ways of playing with a toy rather than just being told or shown how it works. Two studies found that children need both the metacognitive support and the emotional support to use their metacognitive strategies and to try different solutions when solving problems (Neitzel & Stright, 2003; Stright et al., 2001). Scaffolding is also very important and supports children's individual learning needs through support and feedback to guide children in their learning. When scaffolding children's learning, adults provide hints, offering children choices to find the solution and guiding them to use additional resources. For example, if a child can draw a straight vertical line, adults can show her how to draw a straight horizontal line. To help her draw that line, the adult can draw dashes on the page and let her trace them until she can independently draw the line from left to right. After those two skills are mastered, she can put them together to draw a square. Parents and caregivers can use scaffolding to support the learning process and increase engagement to help children persist longer at the task; this helps children make progress in small increments toward each goal, and they feel emotionally supported in their learning. Studies show that parents who support their children's autonomy in learning and problem solving increase their children's achievement and have children who view themselves as having agency in their learning process (Grolnick & Ryan, 1989; Hess, Holloway, Dickson, & Price, 1984; Pianta, Smith, & Reeve, 1991). Children who feel free to use different materials and be creative in their learning and problem solving are more imaginative. Adults have great influence in facilitating how children think and how supported and motivated they are to persist and take risks in their learning (Robson & Rowe, 2012).

Persistent thinking is fostered not just by encouraging children to keep trying and supporting their risks and mistakes but also by providing them with the metacognitive strategies to be successful. Head Start Approaches to Learning recommends the following strategies to promote engagement and persistence in young children:

- Play games in which children must listen carefully and follow more than one direction, such as "Simon says, 'Stand on one foot and touch your nose.'"

- Assign children important, necessary tasks that involve following multiple-step directions: "Take your coat off, hang it in the cubby, and pick out a book to enjoy."

- When children quit or give up too easily, gently encourage them by saying, "Try one more time" or "Think of something else you could try."

- Gradually lengthen the time children are expected to remain engaged in activities or experiences; for instance, read longer stories to extend children's attention span.

- Engage children in prior planning of their own and remind them of their plans as needed: "What was it you planned to do today? Are you finished?"

- Provide ways for children to revisit and reflect on their experiences and learning.

- Make frequent comments about children's efforts: "Look how hard you've been trying to put that puzzle together. You're almost finished" or "You didn't give up until you got just the right color. You must be very proud."

- Help children identify successful strategies for problem solving: "It really helps when you look for the very first letter of your name to find your cubby" or "Let's repeat the directions together so everyone will know what to do next."

- Offer praise that is specific and meaningful to what children have actually done: "You really had to push hard to turn the pedals" or "You all spoke in such a kind, gentle way when José hurt his foot." Avoid vague words such as "Nice" and exaggerated praise such as "You're the best painter in the whole world." (U.S. Department of Health and Human Services, Administration on Children, Youth and Families, Head Start Bureau, 2003)

From infants to preschoolers, narrating and extending children's actions to facilitate their problem solving and modeling thinking strategies increases their persistence, engagement, and self-concept by increasing confidence and developing the important executive functioning skills that will be important in school and life.

PERSISTENT THINKING EXPERIENCE FOR INFANTS

Persistence is the desire to expend continued effort toward a goal. Imagine an infant reaching for a toy just out of reach again and again and then inching his body forward just enough to finally grab hold of the toy. This is persistence. Infants who have many opportunities to reach, crawl, and verbalize to get what they desire are building the foundation for persistent thinking. Children who develop persistent thinking skills are learners who are less daunted by challenges, which helps them cultivate the ability to focus on complex problems.

Supporting the Development of Persistent Thinking: The Peekaboo Experience

This persistent thinking experience involves a game that builds on the book *Baby Says Peekaboo!* by DK Publishing (2006). This board book has large flaps that can be opened to reveal a hidden picture. Manipulating these flaps to look under them requires persistence. The theme of the book is to find the infant that may be hiding under the large, colorful images on the flap, such as a big beach ball. The last page of the book is a mirror where infants see themselves. The activity can also be done with other similar books.

Materials

- *Baby Says Peekaboo!* by DK Publishing (2006; lift-the-flap board book)

- Soft scarf or other fabric for Peekaboo games

Read the Book Together

This book lends itself to one-to-one interactions between the teacher and the infant so the infant can explore and master how the book flaps work. Read the book with the infant next to you or on your lap.

Wonder and Ask Questions

As you read, you can provide commentary or self-talk as the infant works to open the flaps: "I think the baby is going to be there this time, do you? I hope we can find that sneaky baby! Where on earth could that baby have gone? That silly baby must be somewhere!"

Explain and Discuss the Problem

As you are reading the book, you can say, "We don't know where that baby is, do we?" By reminding the infant of the problem—in this case, the missing baby—you are restating the goal that the infant is working toward, encouraging his or her persistent focus on solving the problem at hand.

Rubric			
Rate the child's level of participation and understanding on the continuum. Add evidence/ descriptions for each child.	Shows interest in and excitement with familiar objects; shows interest in favorite activities over and over again	Repeats actions many times to obtain similar results; finds pleasure in causing things to happen	Attends for extended periods of time when engaged, despite distractions; tries several times until successful; seeks help when encountering a problem
Child 1	Sawyer picked up the Baby Says Peekaboo! (DK Publishing, 2006) book and handed it to his teacher to read.		
Child 2		Billy wanted to open each flap in the book himself and then loudly said "Peekaboo" each time he uncovered the hiding infant.	
Child 3			Greta tried to put the scarf on her head to play Peekaboo with the teacher. But each time she put the scarf on her head, it fell off. After three tries, she put the scarf farther over the top of head and then it didn't fall off. When the teacher asked where she was hiding, she pulled off the scarf and shouted, "Peekaboo!"

Figure 4.1. Infant persistent thinking experience rubric.

Start Your Own Peekaboo Game

Using a soft scarf or other fabric, pull the scarf up over your face. Then pull the scarf down, give a big smile, and say "Peekaboo!" Soon, the infant might start to make sounds or movements to prompt you to pull the scarf down again, smile, and say, "Peekaboo." Infants who can reach out can be encouraged to pull the scarf down, causing your (and their) happy reaction. You can further encourage infants by saying, "I am hiding. Can you find me?" or even, jokingly, "Don't look under the scarf!" and then, as they reach out to pull the scarf, you can exclaim, "You found me again! You keep finding me!" Many infants also enjoy being the ones to hide under the scarf, and either you or the infant can be the one to pull down the scarf.

When playing Peekaboo, asking the baby, "Where did I go?" and saying, "I am going to go away again! Good-bye!" clarifies the problem again and again. Statements such as "I did not think you were going to find me that time!" can foster repeated attempts to obtain this same happy result.

Follow the Infant's Lead

Read the infants' cues and follow their lead. For example, if an infant jumps when you say "Peekaboo," tone down your exuberance to a level that allows the infant to enjoy it. On the other hand, if the infant does not seem terribly interested after a "Peekaboo" or two, try something different from your smile, such as making a funny noise, pretending to sneeze, or having a hat or sunglasses on as a surprise. Your efforts will often encourage the infant to try again. There are many ways to vary this game. As your relationship with the infant grows, you will be able to continually modify the game to the developmental capacity and interests of the infant. Figure 4.1 is a rubric that will help you evaluate how well the infant engaged in the persistent learning experience. Examples are provided of the information you would record based on the infant's performance on the activity.

Universal Design for Learning Supports for Infants

As a reminder, the suggestions for infants in the text box are aimed at all children but address some needs of infants who have physical or multiple challenges that prevent them from independently manipulating the objects around them or from independently

---

 UDL Supports for Infants

- Use hand-over-hand guidance to help infants point, touch, and lift the flaps or grab the scarves. [David]

- Add picture symbols to the book to support infants who will learn communication using picture symbols or a single switch with a message. [All]

- Provide scarves with different levels of opaqueness and different textures that make various sounds (e.g., crunchy fabric, soft fabric that whooshes together). [Julia]

- Use supportive seating options such as a corner sitter or a wedge for children with low muscle tone or a gait trainer to move to the object. [David]

- Limit distractions in the room or play soft music without words to help focus the infants. [All]

- Use a few basic signs to engage infants in the lesson and offer them opportunities to communicate (e.g., MORE, DONE, BYE, HELLO). [Julia]

coming to engage in an activity. Some UDL supports are geared toward all children or a specific profile child. Use any of the UDL supports with any child who might benefit.

PERSISTENT THINKING EXPERIENCE FOR TODDLERS

This activity is based on the children's book *Ten Dirty Pigs, Ten Clean Pigs* by Carol Roth (1999). This is a different children's book than the one used for the other activities, but it maintains the same theme. It is helpful to do this activity after at least two of the other mud activities (Chapters 5 or 7) or as the last thinking experience after completing all other toddler experiences in this book, because the children are now focusing on cleaning up the mud. This activity could be done with other similar books, but we chose this book because it is a high-quality children's book that is readily available and popular in toddler classrooms.

In this repetitive book, the pigs start out very dirty, get clean one by one, and then get dirty again. In addition to the repetitive phrases, children can practice counting the 10 pigs and identifying the ways pigs get clean and dirty. At the end, the book can be flipped around, and you can count the pigs getting dirty after they just got clean. This book provides the opportunity to count, learn colors and vocabulary, and talk about getting dirty and getting clean. Toddlers love the colorful pigs and the playful nature of the story.

In this story, the pigs are dirty and they need to get clean. Toddlers can identify with this problem because they are expected to take baths to clean up and to wash their hands. The pigs also take fun toys in the bath with them at times. This story focuses on the persistent nature of cleaning and the need to scrub repeatedly and use water and soap to get clean.

This activity emphasizes children's persistent thinking skills—initiating the cleaning process, repeating actions to complete an activity or test a theory, noticing patterns, and maintaining attention with a given task. After reading the story, the children will use the water table to wash toys that they used in mud in previous activities.

Introducing the Experience

To start the lesson, do a "picture walk" of the cover and first page, looking at each picture without reading the words, instead asking the children what they see in the picture and what they think the book might be about. Ask the children what the picture reminds them of that they did in their classroom and try to elicit conversation about the different mud activities. Then ask the children, "What problem do the pigs have? What are they doing to solve it? What do you think will happen?" Ask the children, "How do you think the pigs got dirty?" After the children talk about getting clean, ask, "How do you think the pigs will get clean? What can they do to get clean?" Give all the children a chance to respond to the question and record their answers.

Read the book *Ten Dirty Pigs, Ten Clean Pigs* (Roth, 1999) through to the end so that all 10 pigs get clean. Review the children's responses to the questions see if the pigs used any of their suggestions to get clean. Tell the children that today they are going to clean the toys/friends that went in the mud in the water table. Organize the children into groups of two to four children and prepare the water table and individual water tubs for them to use. Decide which children can work together and which children may need more space or their own materials. Review with the children what materials and tools they might need to clean their toys like the pigs cleaned themselves.

The Water Table Wash

At the water table or individual water tubs, provide children with two to four toys to clean. Set up the water table/tubs with water, tools used at the beach, water table toys, sponges, brushes (e.g., toothbrushes, paintbrushes), towels, and a space for clean toys. Buckets, cups, scoops, and other small containers are all helpful. At the water table, encourage children to work together or maybe form an assembly line. Soap can be used as well, but it is helpful to have a separate tub for the soapy water. Encourage the children to brainstorm how they want to clean the toys and talk through the process with them as they are cleaning and washing. Talk to the children throughout their play in this activity, narrating and extending their actions to provide language for their learning.

Ask children to show an adult when a toy is clean and ask them to tell why they think it is clean and how they cleaned it. When it is time to stop and/or all toys are clean, ask the children to count (with support) how many toys they cleaned. Facilitate children to use new vocabulary, and use picture symbols to support that vocabulary during the activity.

Summarizing the Experience

Use a camera to document the children's work and their experiences. Photographs and videos are helpful for a later lesson in this series on mud explorations (Chapter 6). After all the children finish washing their toys, talk to the whole group about what they did to wash the toys and what tools they used. Highlight creative ways that children washed the toys, such as creating an assembly line or putting the toys under a water wheel and letting water from the wheel pour over them. Discuss how long it took to wash certain toys, and encourage persistence and sustained attention. Help children think about how they solved the pigs' problem of being dirty.

Universal Design for Learning Supports for Toddlers

This book offers various UDL supports for the profile children and other children in the class. This activity uses picture symbols to support vocabulary development and speech because Tam and Jesse are both English language learners and need the additional support to connect words to concepts, but all young children can benefit from picture symbols to support literacy development. The picture symbols are also used with words to support

 Self-Reflection Checklist

- Did I encourage children's enthusiasm to try different ideas for washing?
- Did I ask children to make predictions, and did I document their predictions about the pigs' problem?
- Did I model how to make "I wonder if . . ." statements, and did I document children's "I wonder if . . ." statements?
- Did I scaffold children to use their words to describe washing and the process and give them new vocabulary, such as *scrub* or *dry*?
- Did I encourage the children to try their own ideas for creating a cleaning assembly line?
- Did I offer multiple materials to find out what makes it easier or harder to clean different toys?
- Did I let the children try to manipulate the tools on their own?

Toddler Experience Planning Template

Problem-solving focus skill	Persistent thinking	
Motivating engineering problem	In the book *Ten Dirty Pigs, Ten Clean Pigs* by Carol Roth (1999), the pigs get clean and then get dirty again. This book is a fun exploration of clean and dirty, as well as counting to 10.	
Focus of this particular learning experience	This activity focuses on getting all 10 pigs clean and the process of scrubbing and cleaning to get the pigs/toys clean after mud play.	
Learning objectives for this particular experience	• Children will count the number of toys cleaned. • Children will be able to clean the multiple toys using the tools provided.	
Materials needed	• Toys • 10 pigs from mud table • Water • Water tubs/water table • Towels • Sponges • Brushes • Soap • Smocks • Rubber gloves	

	Elements of the learning experience	UDL supports
Introduce children to the problem	Read the book *Ten Dirty Pigs, Ten Clean Pigs*. Discuss the process of getting all the pigs clean and how the children get clean.	• Use a big book. • Provide additional copies of the book for the reading center. • Preteach key vocabulary with picture symbols.
Help children understand the problem-solving goal and constraints	Brainstorm with the children how they could get the pigs clean and their toys clean at the water table. What tools do they have to use at the water table and/or in the classroom?	• Have possible tools at the reading circle as concrete representations. • Offer picture symbols for common ideas for cleaning toys.
Support children in demonstrating their thinking	Ask children to demonstrate and articulate when a toy is clean or dirty. Ask children to demonstrate and discuss how they get their toys clean. Facilitate children to clean and count the toys they have cleaned.	• Offer rubber gloves. • Use picture symbols for communication. • Provide grips for use with tools. • Use picture directions for cleaning. • Use liquid soap pumps and bar soap. • Provide individual tubs for children to use who do not want to work at the water table.
Provide opportunities for feedback and for trying again	Ask children to show or use words to demonstrate clean toys. If a child is struggling, suggest that he or she look for a different tool or use a different method to get the toys clean. Model cleaning or counting with children as needed.	• Use peer buddies or a teacher assistant to help children articulate ideas. • Have picture symbols available at water table/tubs. • Provide counting manipulatives and number symbols.
Help children share and learn from one another	This activity can be done together in groups or individually. Together they can count the clean toys and help clean up.	• Use peer buddies. • Provide grips and alternative tools for children with fine motor control challenges.

Figure 4.2. Toddler persistent thinking experience overview and rubric.

	Rubric		
Rate the child's level of participation and understanding on the continuum. **Add evidence/ descriptions for each child.**	**Repeats actions many times to achieve similar results** *Did the child wash the toy repeatedly to get it clean?*	**Repeats actions many times to achieve similar results; tries several times until successful** *Was the child able to consistently clean the toys with the tools provided? Did the child clean multiple toys using the same technique?*	**Tries several times until successful; creates and carries out a plan to solve a problem; plans and pursues a variety of appropriately challenging tasks; plans and pursues own goal until it is reached** *Was the child able to plan how to clean the toys and execute the plan with minimal supports?*
Child 1		Sarah put four toys in the water at the same time and swished with soapy water and then poured water on each to rinse.	
Child 2	José enjoyed playing in the soapy water and making the toy sudsy and then pouring water over it and doing it again.		
Child 3			Elan worked with Kayla to each take a part of the cleaning process "like Mommy and Daddy help." They worked together for their eight toys.

brainstorming responses to questions from the book. During the brainstorming phase, the teacher can provide actual tools to assist children in talking about the tools needed to clean the toys. This unit talked about toys and toy pigs that can be used getting dirty and clean. Assess the needs of your students and the materials available to determine if toys can be used interchangeably or children are still at a concrete stage where they need to be washing toy pigs to go with the story. This may vary across different children.

Figure 4.2 provides several UDL supports for this activity in the lesson template that are geared toward the profile children but can also be used with others in the classroom. For example, Jessie benefits from her own individual tray and workspace, but other children may prefer that as well. On the other hand, based on levels of engagement, this might

 Essentials to Remember

- Encourage children to use multiple tools and strategies.
- Ask children to describe what they did and what they have learned.
- Focus on praising persistence at the task and encouraging creativity.
- Offer multiple opportunities to explore the water and the cleaning process.

be a good activity to work on Jessie's areas of need and support her to work with a peer buddy. On the other hand, Tam should be placed with another child for this task, possibly at the water table for support and practice with fine motor skills. Tam can imitate other children and offer ideas as part of the group. Children with sensory issues around water will need to be monitored to keep them on task. Children who do not like water should be provided with waterproof smocks and gloves and encouraged to try the activity with support. The UDL Planning Sheet provides a summary of all the UDL supports used for this toddler unit.

PERSISTENT THINKING EXPERIENCE FOR PRESCHOOLERS

This preschool persistent thinking experience continues to make use of the children's book *Muncha! Muncha! Muncha!* by Candace Fleming (2002). Persistence is seen on the parts of both the protagonist and antagonists in this book. The bunnies are determined to make their way into Mr. McGreely's garden to feast on his vegetables, and Mr. McGreely is determined to find a way to keep them out. He revises his garden protection system four different times! Children can find inspiration for their own persistent thinking in both Mr. McGreely and the bunnies.

This learning experience is designed as an opportunity for children to practice persistent thinking skills, which are the skills that help children plan and pursue their own goals, often by practicing an activity many times until they are successful. Children can be persistent thinkers as they make their garden protection ideas a reality. With the building materials you make available to them, children can try and try again to build a garden protector that works the way they want it to. The goal for children in this activity is not to create perfect garden protection systems but to notice a way to improve something they create and to persist in making it better. Of course, teachers will want to encourage children's creative ideas about garden protectors, but the main focus is the cycle of building, testing, and trying again to make it better.

Because this activity is centered on the problem of bunnies sneaking into a vegetable garden, at least one model vegetable garden will be needed for children to build their garden protectors around. Teachers can create one for all the children to share out of large green or brown paper with vegetables placed on it, or they can make individual garden illustrations or posters for each child.

This activity is intended to take place after children draw (or talk about) plans for garden protection systems in the flexible thinking activity (see Chapter 5), but if they have not completed that activity, they can still participate in this persistent thinking activity as a stand-alone experience. However, teachers will need to start by reading at least the beginning of *Muncha! Muncha! Muncha!* so that children can identify the problem they are asked to solve. See the curious thinking (Chapter 3) and flexible thinking (Chapter 5) preschool activities for ideas about how to conduct the read-aloud sessions.

To orient the children toward the goal of persistent thinking, begin the discussion by recalling the determination and persistence demonstrated by the characters in *Muncha! Muncha! Muncha!* Ask the children if they remember how many times Mr. McGreely built a new system to keep the bunnies out of his garden (four times) or how many different ways the bunnies sneaked into the garden (four ways). Both Mr. McGreely and the bunnies kept trying and trying again. And that is the challenge for the children today. Ask them to build something that can keep the pretend bunny out of the pretend vegetable garden you have in the classroom. Show children the building materials that will be available to them. Talk with children about what it means to make a *model* of a real structure. A model is not the real thing but something that helps one see or understand how the real thing works. Often models are a different size or made of a different material than the real thing.

At this point, it is a good idea to help children remember the ideas they have already generated about how they could protect the garden. If they have created design plans with drawings or dictations, or if you have recorded their plans on chart paper, share those with the children at this time. If they have simply talked about their ideas, tell the children what you remember about their proposed solutions.

The next step is to agree on a test (or two or three) that the children can carry out on the models to determine whether the models really solve Mr. McGreely's problem. For example, you can say, "I'm wondering how we will know if the garden protectors you build are good garden protec-tors. We will need a way to test them. How do you think we could test your model garden protectors?" Show the children the model garden again and the stuffed animal, bean bag, or figurine that can be used as a model bunny, and help the children decide on a test for their constructions. We suggest guiding the children toward the "fit test," the "bunny height test," or "the bunny jump test," but you can use any test that gives the children visual feedback about whether their construction has a characteristic that you have all agreed is important. To conduct the "fit test," children check for whether the garden protector is big enough to fit around the model garden. For the "bunny height test," children compare their garden to a model bunny (a stuffed animal, figurine, or drawing of a bunny) and make sure the garden protector is taller than the bunny. For the "bunny jump test," the children toss a stuffed animal or bean bag gently at their construction to see whether it survives the impact.

When you are confident that all children understand the task of building a model garden protector, are clear about which materials they are permitted to use in their constructions, and will be able to carry out the test that you have agreed on, you can move on from the large-group discussion and work with children one-to-one or in small groups as they build their garden protectors. You might decide to simply make a large model garden available in the block area, and children can work on their protection systems when they make the choice to be in the block area. Be prepared, however, for an atypical influx of children to the block area! In one preschool classroom with about 10 children age 2.9 to 4 years old, a teacher used her morning meeting time to read *Muncha! Muncha! Muncha!*, discuss Mr. McGreely's solutions to his garden problem, and elicit children's ideas for other garden protection solutions. The next activity in the daily schedule was choice time, when different children typically played and worked in different areas of the classroom depending on their interests for the day. On this day, the teacher concluded the morning meeting by showing a large poster-board model garden and saying, "I will put this garden in the block area, and if you'd like to work on your garden protector, you may choose the block area for choice time today." She expected the two or three boys who typically chose block area to be the first to build garden protectors. Much to her surprise, when she closed the morning meeting and invited the children to make their choices, they *all* wanted to go to the block area. The teacher decided to delay choice time and respond to the children's collective interest. She moved a shelf to make the block area larger so that all 10 children could fit around the garden. Spontaneously, working as a team, the children all began pulling blocks from the shelves and placing them around the model garden (Figure 4.3). They naturally distributed themselves and worked in small groups of two or three to construct different corners and walls of their garden protector. Some children used unit blocks, others got out the basket of Bristle Blocks, and others added Mega Bloks to the structure. The teacher pointed out their wonderful teamwork and encouraged their persistence when parts of the structure fell over (which happened frequently with so many hands trying to help and pretending to be the bunny).

Another option is to set out several smaller model gardens at an art table or another area of the room where a few children can work in parallel on their constructions. Yet another option is to have an adult facilitate one small group of children at a time as a project group working on their garden protectors. This strategy can enable children to get more hands-on help manipulating materials to bring their design to fruition; the adult for the small group might be able to cut cardboard to a desired shape, tear off pieces of tape, and so forth. Observe as the children begin to work with physical materials to build their own garden protection systems. Often children's garden protectors will appear to be re-creations of the structures Mr. McGreely constructs in the storybook, but if you observe closely or talk with the children, you will find important ways that the children are going beyond the story or beyond what they have built before in the classroom. Share with them what you notice about their creations and ask them to tell you how they will work to protect the vegetables. When the children seem satisfied with what they have built, help them carry out a test of their systems and evaluate how their constructions could have passed the test even better. Encourage children to engineer like Mr. McGreely did and

Figure 4.3. Ten preschool children working together on a garden protection system around one large model garden in their classroom's block area.

"Window into a Classroom" Anecdote

One 4-year-old child named Evan responded to this garden protection design challenge by starting to build a structure that closely resembled the big stone castle at the end of *Muncha! Muncha! Muncha!* (Fleming, 2002). One of the teachers wondered if she should prompt Evan to branch out more from the story. However, she stood back and watched closely, and by waiting and watching, she was able to uncover and point out quite a bit of creativity and persistence in his work. He was innovative with the scale of his structure and with his choice of construction materials, and he was persistent in revising his structure until others were convinced it worked well. It turned out that Evan wanted his structure to be capable of protecting a life-size garden. As a result, to frame the walls of his enclosure, he decided to use his classroom's large, hollow wooden blocks instead of the smaller unit blocks being used by most of his classmates to construct their miniature garden protectors. These blocks allowed him to create an enclosure taller than himself. To test his structure, he invited two classmates from the dramatic play area to pretend to be bunnies. The two girls happily obliged, although they wanted to pretend to be squirrels instead of bunnies. They jumped like squirrels toward his structure and made their way inside by shifting some blocks around. The teacher noticed the friends successfully sneaking into the garden, articulated what had happened, and nudged Evan to improve his garden protector: "We have some squirrels that tried to get into your garden. How are we going to keep them out? What do we need to do? How are we going to keep them out? They were coming in this side. The squirrels were getting in right here. What are we going to do so the squirrels don't get in?"

Evan responded to his teacher's challenge with persistent thinking. He designed more elements to add to his protection system, and he invited his friends to join him in constructing those elements. One of the girls made a large paper lock for him to hang on the front of the enclosure, and the other helped him color white paper blue and lay it around the circumference of the garden. This paper represented water. The children were reordering and rearranging Mr. McGreely's designs to make their own new garden protection system at the scale of a preschool human being rather than at miniature scale. By standing back and observing these three children as they worked and played, the teacher was able to see how they persistently added elements and functionalities on top of what was presented in the story (see Figure 4.4). Figure 4.5 provides a brief overview of the activity and a rubric to evaluate the children's development as persistent thinkers through this learning experience.

 ## Self-Reflection Checklist

- Did I motivate children's persistent thinking by discussing the example of Mr. McGreely trying and trying again to protect his garden?
- Did I encourage children to refer to the plans they previously made or talk about their garden protectors?
- Did I include children in deciding which test or tests we would use to check whether their garden protectors worked? Did I model how to test a garden protector?
- Did I think aloud as I noticed what happened when I tested a garden protector?
- Did I offer multiple kinds of materials for children's construction of garden protectors?

Figure 4.4. A "garden protector" resulting from persistent engineering by a preschool child and his friends. They started with a simple block wall, but after some dramatic play testing, they added a lock, and a moat, and more walls.

to keep trying new solutions. When a child's construction passes the test on the first try, challenge him or her to try out another design idea. One teacher said to her children who had already been successful at protecting model gardens, "So this is like 'Take 2: Action.' We're going to try again, and we're going to see if we can build walls just as secure using *different* materials."

Universal Design for Learning Supports for Preschoolers

In the overview, a variety of UDL supports are suggested for all children for different aspects of the persistent thinking activity. Again, this activity is a very hands-on learning opportunity but also requires children to explain their reasoning and negotiate between a model or drawing and a 3-D creation of a model. For some children with spatial or cognitive challenges, this activity may be a struggle. Children such as Brandon would benefit from working in mixed-ability groups, where they can work together on the task and build on each other's strengths and weaknesses. Both Brandon and José will need additional support in expressing their thoughts and could benefit from practice with the vocabulary and time to formulate their responses for engineering circle ahead of time with an adult. To avoid frustration, José could use different types of building materials in his first and second creations. Children who need motor support can use larger, easier-to-grip blocks and a nonslip mat.

Preschool Experience Planning Template

Problem-solving focus skill	Persistent thinking
Motivating engineering problem	In the book *Munch! Munch! Munch!* by Candace Fleming (2002), three bunnies keep sneaking into Mr. McGreely's garden and eating his vegetables. Children can recognize that the bunny break-ins are a problem for Mr. McGreely and explore better garden protection.
Focus of this particular learning experience	Mr. McGreely builds many different structures around his garden, and the bunnies "test" each one and figure out a way through or around it. This learning experience is focused on repeated constructing and testing of children's own ideas for garden protectors.
Learning objectives for this particular experience	• Children will plan and pursue the task of constructing a garden protector. • Children will plan and pursue their own goals for constructing and testing their designs.
Materials needed	• *Munch! Munch! Munch!* by Candace Fleming • LEGO bricks, DUPLO bricks, Bristle Blocks, Magna-Tiles, unit blocks, other construction sets, or craft materials • Small stuffed animals or bean bags to serve as test "bunnies" • Paper or poster with an illustration of a vegetable garden or a large sheet of green or brown paper with toy vegetables placed on it • Poster paper and markers for recording children's ideas • Camera

	Elements of the learning experience	UDL supports
Introduce children to the problem	Help children remember all the garden protectors that Mr. McGreely builds in *Munch! Munch! Munch!* Emphasize that he kept trying and trying again. Remind children that they have made their own plans for garden protectors. Now they will have a chance to build and test models of their plans. If their first model does not work, they can try again just like Mr. McGreely did.	• Provide an opportunity to reread the book in centers or reading time. • Use an interactive version of the book. • Have a refresher on key engineering vocabulary.
Help children understand the problem-solving goal and constraints	Show children the building materials available for them to use to build their models. Talk with children about what it means to make a model of a real structure. Ask, "How can we test your model garden protectors?" Help the children decide on a test for their constructions. The following are some possibilities: • The "fit test": Is the garden protector big enough to fit around the garden? • The "bunny height test": Is the garden taller than a stuffed bunny? • The "bunny jump test": Does the garden protector survive a stuffed bunny being tossed gently at it?	• Provide a choice of different building materials (some easier or larger options and some smaller or harder options). • Use peer buddies in mixed ability groups. • Provide a stuffed bunny for children who are literal minded. • Use picture symbols for key vocabulary.
Support children in demonstrating their thinking	Show the children the vegetable garden image that you have printed or drawn on paper or cardboard. Their job is to build a garden protector that fits around this garden model and passes the test the class has agreed on.	• Provide an opportunity to talk through thinking and dictate ideas. • Draw as a group or use a computer or iPad or tablet computer to help.

Figure 4.5. Preschool persistent thinking experience overview and rubric.

(continued)

Figure 4.5. *(continued)*

Provide opportunities for feedback and for trying again	Let children know that after they test their first construction, you will ask them to try again—to rebuild in some way and try the test again just as Mr. McGreely did. Help individual children construct garden protectors, test them, and rebuild at least one time. Talk with children and take "before" and "after" photographs as they test their garden protectors.	• Complete in small groups or individually. • Use a nonslip mat for the building area. • Use a different material for the second try.
Help children share and learn from one another	At "engineering circle" time, help children share their garden protection models or photographs of their models. Talk about what it felt like to build something, test it, and try to build it again.	• Have individual or group discussions. • Document learning orally or by journaling. • Offer the opportunity to practice before group time and to formulate thoughts with an adult.

Rubric			
Rate the child's level of participation and understanding on the continuum. Add evidence/ descriptions for each child.	Tries several times until successful	Plans and pursues own goal until it is reached	Designs and builds a solution to a problem; tests solution and makes changes based on test results
Child 1			Lola used Magna-Tiles to construct a tower and called it a "garden scarecrow." A bean bag toss made the Magna-Tiles collapse. She moved to the block area and built another scarecrow from unit blocks.
Child 2		To add a "river" around his garden protector, Matt colored one piece of paper at a time with blue crayons and took it over to his structure. He continued coloring and placing paper until a 6-foot river had been created.	
Child 3	Kali used Bristle Blocks to make a "castle" around the garden. She asked for a bean bag to test the castle. Her initial bean bag tosses landed in front of the structure. She kept tossing the bean bag until it landed on the structure itself.		

Essentials to Remember

- The goal of this activity is not for children to create perfect garden protection systems but for them to notice a way to improve something they have created and to persist in making it better.

- The focus of this activity is on the cycle of building, testing, and trying again to make something better. Many children will need adult encouragement to move from building and testing toward making changes. Adults can accompany children as they test their garden protectors, think aloud about what happens during testing, and offer an explicit new task such as "Oh, I see the roof moved over a little bit! I have a new challenge for you. Can you build a roof that doesn't move at all when the bean bag hits it?"

RESOURCES

Developmental Trajectory and Key Standards and Guidelines

Dichtelmiller, M.L. (2001). *Omnibus guidelines: Preschool through third grade.* Ann Arbor, MI: Rebus Planning Association.

Head Start Child Development and Early Learning Frameworks. (2010). *Approaches to learning: Engagement and persistence.* Retrieved from http://eclkc.ohs.acf.hhs.gov/hslc/hs/sr/approach/cdelf/a2_learning.html

Heroman, C., Burts, D.C., Berke, K., & Bickart, T.S. (2010). *Teaching strategies GOLD: Objectives for development and learning: Birth through kindergarten.* Washington, DC: Teaching Strategies, Inc.

High/Scope Press & High/Scope Educational Research Foundation. (2003). *Preschool Child Observation Record.* Ypsilanti, MI: Authors.

National Governors Association Center for Best Practices & Council of Chief State School Officers. (2010). *Common Core State Standards for mathematics.* Washington, DC: Authors. Retrieved from http://www.core standards.org/Math/Practice/CCSS.MATH.PRACTICE.MP1

Ohio Department of Education. (2012). *Ohio early learning and development standards.* Retrieved from http://education.ohio.gov/getattachment/Topics/Early-Learning/Early-Learning-Content-Standards/The-Standards/ELDS-ATL-FINAL-21-October-2012-pdf.pdf.aspx

PBS Kids. (2014). *Child development tracker: Approaches to learning.* Retrieved from http://www.pbs.org/parents/childdevelopmenttracker/five/approachestolearning.html

Publications

Epstein, A.S. (2003, September). How planning and reflection develop young children's thinking skills. *Beyond the Journal.* Retrieved from http://www.naeyc.org/files/yc/file/200309/Planning&Reflection.pdf

Helm, J.H., & Katz, L. (2001). *Young investigators: The project approach in the early years.* Washington, DC: NAEYC.

Jablon, J., & Wilkinson, M. (2006). Using engagement strategies to facilitate children's learning and success. *Beyond the Journal.* Retrieved from https://www.naeyc.org/files/yc/file/200603/JablonBTJ.pdf

Rice-Lim, P. (2012). *Character building: Preschool lesson plan on perseverance.* Retrieved from http://www.brighthubeducation.com/preschool-lesson-plans/105110-perseverance-lesson-with-the-little-engine-that-could

Office of Head Start. (2010). *Head Start child development and early learning frameworks: Promoting positive outcomes in early childhood programs serving children 3–5 years old (2010).* Washington, DC: U.S. Department of Health and Human Services. Retrieved from https://eclkc.ohs.acf.hhs.gov/hslc/tta-system/teaching/eecd/Assessment/Child%20Outcomes/HS_Revised_Child_Outcomes_Framework(rev-Sept2011).pdf

Additional Suggestions for Encouraging Persistent Thinking

- Find the challenging but not frustrating level of activities for each child. This requires a deep knowledge of each individual child's skill level.

- Scaffold if the child starts to become frustrated.

- Encourage the child to ask a friend for help.

- Be sure your daily schedule has some longer blocks of time that allow children deep engagement in activities.

- Provide open-ended activities that are rich and varied.

- Reread stories frequently, as children learn from the repetition; ask different questions each time to help children focus on new vocabulary, story structure, ideas, and concepts.

- Recognize children's effort.

- Encourage children to return to unfinished work, be it a block building or a story.

- Remember your promises to children (write them down if necessary).

- Remember each child's temperament and need for novelty or consistency.

5

Flexible Thinkers

The invention and use of tools are hallmarks of human beings' problem-solving capabilities. Although other animal species have been shown to make simple tools to accomplish tasks such as retrieving food, it is believed that only humans can *engineer* tools—that is, humans are likely the only species that can apply insight to solve an unfamiliar problem in a new way without seeing an example of a solution (Cutting, Apperly, & Beck, 2011).

The type of thinking that is perhaps most important to this uniquely human capability is flexible thinking. Flexible thinking is foundational to the complex problem-solving practices required in the STEM domains. In our work with young children's problem solving, we define flexible thinking as thinking that adjusts to changing information and goals, that anticipates and plans for future scenarios, and that considers new or different perspectives to "think outside the box." Our shorthand for flexible thinking is open-mindedness.

Much of the understanding of flexible thinking comes from what cognitive scientists refer to as *cognitive flexibility*. This idea has its roots in Piaget's notion of reversible thought (Piaget & Inhelder, 1966), which is the ability to imagine how things were prior to having a particular thought and to imagine how things will be as a result of that thought. Different researchers define cognitive flexibility in slightly different ways. However, most agree that it entails the ability to control the focus of attention and working memory, to switch from one task to another, to be open to new knowledge, and to envision an object or state of events that does not currently exist (Adi-Japha, Berberich-Artzi, & Libnawe, 2010; McCormack & Atance, 2011). Cognitive flexibility in infants and toddlers is often measured by how well they can use their bodies and simple tools in different ways to complete different actions (Barrett, Davis, & Needham, 2007). Cognitive scientists also look at evidence that infants and toddlers are carrying out some sort of planning—for example, does an infant pause longer than normal before picking up one of two tools to activate a toy? In verbal children, one way to measure cognitive flexibility is to ask them to draw a familiar object and then to draw an example of that object that "does not exist" (Adi-Japha et al., 2010; Karmiloff-Smith, 1990): something the child invents, something strange the child has never seen before, or something make-believe or pretend. You can try this flexible thinking task by having a child draw a flower and then asking, "Now can you draw a flower that does not exist, a strange flower that you have never seen before?" Simply put, the more cognitive flexibility a child has, the more likely he or she is to propose a new kind of flower that combines different categories of things, such as a giraffe-flower. Children with less cognitive flexibility are more likely to respond to the request by changing one characteristic of their first drawing. For example, they might redraw their first flower, but with a much larger stem or without any petals.

Cognitive scientists and psychologists view mental flexibility as a key component of *executive function*, which is the set of mental processes that intentionally guide people to complete tasks and manage their behavior (Cartwright, 2012). Executive function develops from infancy as children begin to engage in deliberate mental actions. A growing field of research is showing that executive function is essential to both academic and personal success and that it underlies children's intellectual, social, and emotional development. That means that when teachers help children develop their flexible thinking skills, not only are they laying the foundation for STEM problem solving, but they are also supporting children's overall ability to regulate emotions and actions.

Ideas about flexible thinking in psychology and education are also related to the notion of creative thinking. Here we are not talking about what some researchers call big *C* Creativity, which refers to the invention of a device or work of art that is new to all of society. Rather, we mean little *c* creativity, which is a quality that all humans exhibit to varying degrees and that is defined as thinking that is new for the individual—but not necessarily all of society—and that produces ideas of value. Robert Sternberg, a well-known psychologist and expert on intelligence, success, and creativity, says that for children or adults to excel at creative thinking, they need to learn how to redefine problems, take sensible risks, deal with ambiguity, and allow for time and mistakes when analyzing and trying out ideas (Sternberg, 2003, cited in Robson & Rowe, 2012). When people learn these components of creative thinking, they are able to approach problems by applying prior knowledge in interesting and unexpected ways to try out ideas. In the process of solving the problem with creative thinking, they construct and gain new knowledge.

WHY IS FLEXIBLE THINKING IMPORTANT?

Flexible thinking is the primary "mental ingredient" of problem solving. Flexible thinking supports people whenever they need to make a mental action other than simply reacting immediately to something perceived in the environment. Anytime they need to pause and decide what to do next, they are drawing on flexible thinking abilities. The more developed their flexible thinking, the better they will be at considering a problem from multiple perspectives, adjusting their approach to new information, and successfully planning the next steps toward a solution.

Although flexible thinking is important for everyone, it is especially useful to the work of scientists and engineers. They solve problems all the time, in the form of scientific questions about the natural world or technological challenges faced by humans. To develop new explanations for how the world works or new technologies to solve the world's problems, they have to think creatively about how existing knowledge can be applied and combined in new ways (National Research Council, 2012). As they try out a model of a phenomenon or a prototype of a design solution, they find new information for how well it works. They have to adjust their ideas according to this new information. As they tweak their models and prototypes, they are flexibly anticipating the range of results they might obtain and planning for what they will do in each case. This is serious problem-solving work, and it requires great creativity and mental flexibility.

But problem solving and its component flexible thinking are not just important for scientists and engineers. All people need to be flexible problem solvers to navigate everyday tasks as well as major life challenges. On a typical day, many people problem-solve as they find alternate routes to work, choose the most affordable ingredients for dinner, and figure out how to get all the housework done before bedtime. They also problem-solve when managing family members' illnesses or cleaning up after bad weather events. Early childhood educators recognize the importance of problem solving to children's development. NAEYC's standards for assessing early childhood programs specifically call for the development of problem-solving abilities:

- *2.D.06(b)*: Children have varied opportunities and materials that encourage them to have discussions to solve problems that are related to the physical world.

- *2.G.01(b)*: Infants and toddlers/twos are provided varied opportunities and materials to discover that they can make things happen and solve problems (NAEYC, 2014, pp. 14, 18).

DEVELOPMENTAL CONTINUUM OF FLEXIBLE THINKING

Infants

When considering the world's great problem solvers, one might not initially think of infants. But actually, infants showcase quite a bit of flexibility when it comes to tackling the challenges they find in the physical world. For example, think of how infants use their hands to learn about objects and materials. Even very young infants adapt what they are doing with their hands to the properties of the substance that they are touching: They alter the strength of their grip or pressure of their touch when they are contacting things that vary in material structure, such as a toy that is soft cloth on one side but hard plastic on the other. This "adaptive action" by infants is one sign of flexible thinking (Fontanelle, Kahrs, Neal, Newton, & Lockman, 2007, p. 153). One can also see infants' flexible thinking when they are learning about tools and when they are constructing categories of characteristics.

Infants are very good at replicating the use of simple tools after seeing adults and older children modeling tool use. In other words, infants can copy what adults do with an object after watching the adult over a period of time. For example, a 6-month-old infant can hold a bottle or sippy cup with two hands and move the spout to his lips. And a 15-month-old infant can use a spoon by grasping the handle, placing the bowl of the spoon in her food, and lifting it to her mouth. This kind of tool use does not require flexible thinking. But when faced with another problem that can be solved with a spoon, some infants are able to adapt their use of the spoon to solve that problem. For example, imagine a toy light box with colorful lights that flash when a wand is passed into a small slot (Barrett et al., 2007). When the slot is big enough for the round end of a spoon, nearly all 12-month-old infants succeed at picking up the spoon and using it to turn on the lights. If you make the problem harder by decreasing the size of the slot so it is too small for the round end of the spoon, some older infants can pick up the spoon by the round end and insert its skinny handle into the slot to flash the lights. This is certainly flexible tool use! Infants tend to pause before they pick up the spoon by its round end, and this shows that they are using their mental resources to plan how to solve a problem.

Infants also show flexible thinking by using unfamiliar tools in new ways to solve problems. Thinking of that same light box toy, imagine an infant presented with an oddly shaped stick with one circular end and one skinny, straight end. Even if the adult only models how to use the circular end of the tool to flash the lights, the infant will figure out how to use the skinny, straight end when the slot is too small for the circular end (Barrett et al., 2007). Flexible thinking is easier with this unfamiliar tool than with a spoon, which infants are so accustomed to seeing held by the handle.

Cognitive scientists also look for infants' mental flexibility by measuring whether infants change their focus of attention to different characteristics in different contexts (Sloutsky & Robinson, 2013). They conduct experiments that show that infants can learn to focus on the color of a picture when it is presented on one background but focus on the shape of that same picture when it is on a different background. This result means that infants can consider both the background and the picture's characteristics at the same time, and they can flexibly shift among attending to different characteristics. They can learn multiple categories at once, and they can categorize the same set of characteristics—such as shape and color—in different ways based on the context (Ellis & Oakes, 2006).

Toddlers

Infants can apply flexible thinking to tool use, but by the time they are toddlers, they develop the ability to apply flexible thinking to tool *choice*. When faced with a problem, toddlers can change not just how they are using a certain tool but also which tool they are using (Chen & Siegler, 2000). They often just need a nudge from adults to make adjustments to their problem-solving strategies. Younger toddlers respond to adults' modeling of tool selection and use, and older toddlers are more receptive to adults' verbal hints about how to solve a problem (Daehler, 2000).

Toddlers also show more capabilities than infants do in their *planning* for problem solving. Infants often pause before picking up a tool, but older toddlers attempt to show or tell adult what they are going to do before they do it. Planning requires flexible thinking because when young children plan, they have to adjust not only to the current situation but also to what they anticipate will happen in the future.

Toddlers also show flexible thinking when they make distinctions between real-life and pretend stories. This is something that older, verbal toddlers can do; they can respond to adults' suggestions to use their imaginations and create alternate, pretend worlds. In one research study (Richards & Sanderson, 1999), 2-year-olds and 4-year-olds were shown nonreal scenarios, such as sheep riding bicycles and elephants roller skating, and then were asked questions about the pretend scenes. When the 2-year-olds were encouraged to imagine a fantasy planet where these scenes might take place, they answered the questions correctly, even though the answers contradicted what is actually true in real life. For example, in one trial, all the children were told that sheep ride bicycles, but only some children were asked to imagine the sheep riding bicycles on a fictional planet. When researchers then asked, "Tell me, what do sheep do?" the 2-year-olds who imagined the sheep on the other planet were much more likely to make the reality-contradicting statement that sheep ride bicycles. In fact, they performed just as well as 4-year-olds—that is, the toddlers could adapt their thinking to theoretical situations when given hints to be imaginative.

Preschoolers

As young children develop language, they grow substantially in their capacity to "think outside the box" and anticipate and plan for future scenarios. With their new language abilities, preschoolers can represent ideas in their minds, and these mental representations help them bring different categories together and consider new and different perspectives. Preschool children, from 3 to 5 years old, show the beginnings of thinking that is flexible enough to figure out creative solutions to problems.

Infants have enough flexible thinking to adapt how they use tools, and toddlers can flexibly choose which tools to use. By preschool age, the goal for children is to begin to apply flexible thinking to create new tools. In some situations, children in this age group can independently invent a tool to solve a problem. For instance, imagine a tiny bucket stuck at the bottom of a tall tube, and a pipe cleaner offered as a material one could use to make something to help retrieve the bucket. In one research study, about 1 out of 10 preschoolers successfully created a hook tool to retrieve the bucket. However, the other 9 out of 10 needed substantial hints from adults before they began to manipulate the pipe cleaner to make a tool (Cutting et al., 2011). This shows that when preschoolers are working independently, the task of actually engineering a new tool is typically just out of their developmental reach. However, with adult support, they can do it. Researchers think that preschoolers may have trouble independently creating new tools not because they lack mental flexibility, but because to create a new tool, a preschooler needs to know about mechanical properties and apply that knowledge to a relatively long sequence of cognitive tasks (Cutting et al., 2011).

Although not all preschoolers are ready to invent novel tools to solve problems without adult help, they *can* propose ideas and things that do not exist. Earlier, the "draw a flower that does not exist" task was mentioned. Preschoolers are quite successful on this task. They apply different flexible strategies, and some realize that you can combine different categories together, such as houses and flowers, to make a new representation: a house-flower. Others realize that you can invent a new category by changing a characteristic of the new one, such as flowers without stems. Preschoolers' ability to propose nonexistent objects reveals that they are nearing readiness to invent nonexistent tools to solve problems.

Preschoolers are also quite good at the flexible thinking task that cognitive scientists call switching. An important piece of executive function, switching develops significantly from 3 to 5 years old, and it allows children to shift among multiple strategies to figure out the best way to accomplish a task (Cutting et al., 2011). Preschoolers who demonstrate the ability to switch do not continue to try a strategy that is not working. Instead, they experiment with another strategy. For example, imagine the typical problem of a small toy stuck underneath a couch. A child who is good at switching might try once or twice to reach the toy with her arm, realize it is unreachable that way, and find a broom handle or some other tool to help swipe out the toy. Without the ability to switch, a child might try again and again to reach the toy with her hand and finally give up in frustration.

In some ways, preschoolers are actually more flexible in their thinking than adults are. Of course, 3- and 4-year-olds can often surprise adults with very unexpected (and often very humorous) statements. There is also research evidence, much of it generated by cognitive scientist Alison Gopnik and her colleagues, that young children are open to a wider range of possibilities for how problems might be solved (Gopnik et al., 2004). Because they have less experience with the world than adults have, they have less abstract knowledge about the cause-and-effect relationships that make things work. As a result, they are more open-minded about what solutions are worth attempting. Researchers describe this as children having "more diffuse expectations" than adults do (Lucas, Bridgers, Griffiths, & Gopnik, 2014, p. 294). Children's broader set of expectations leads them to explore and innovate.

KEY GOALS FOR FLEXIBLE THINKING EXPERIENCES

The following set of key words helps explore ways to support young children by describing their actions when they are engaged in flexible thinking. These action words can be helpful when creating lesson and unit plan goals for children. It is helpful to think about these terms as guiding words for what children are working on at a metacognitive level. In other words, when watching children engage in the activities in this chapter or other activities designed to promote flexible thinking, look for children doing these things.

STRATEGIES FOR FACILITATING FLEXIBLE THINKING

This chapter has been exploring all the ways that infants, toddlers, and preschoolers already exhibit flexible thinking, but how can teachers help them refine those skills and apply them in even more problem-solving situations?

Preschoolers are almost ready to engineer solutions to problems on their own but need a nudge from adults before they begin to explore how to combine physical materials in new ways to build tools. One strategy for providing this nudge is to engage in conversation with children about the properties of different materials and the ways in which those materials can be changed or brought together to perform a new function. Also look at existing everyday tools, such as kitchen utensils and sporting equipment, and talk about how the materials combine to make those tools and the role each material plays in helping the tool do its job.

Another strategy with preschoolers is to turn an ill-structured problem into a well-structured one (Beck, Apperly, Chappell, Guthrie, & Cutting, 2011, cited in Cutting et al., 2011). For example, instead of asking children to invent a new tool to retrieve a bucket from

 Key Words and Phrases for Flexible Thinking for Goal Setting

- Inventing
- Experimenting
- Exploring the environment and objects
- Solving problems
- Reasoning abstractly
- Using tools/materials to problem-solve
- Finding multiple solutions
- Creating
- Brainstorming

a tube, show them pictures of three different devices and have them choose which one would best retrieve the bucket if they built it out of the materials available in the classroom. When preschool children are shown a problem and given solution options to choose from, they are very good at recognizing the solution that will work (Cutting et al., 2011, p. 509).

Teachers can also help preschoolers build their flexible thinking skills by inviting them to try activities such as the "draw a flower that does not exist" task or to imagine scenarios that might happen on a "fantasy planet." These opportunities to think outside the box encourage children's creative and hypothetical thinking.

With toddlers as well as preschoolers, teachers can model thinking routines that show children how to flexibly consider what they observe from different perspectives (Salmon, 2010). In the "think/puzzle/explore" routine in Salmon's (2010) work, an adult notices a child trying to solve a problem and having some difficulty, and she attempts to give voice to the variables at play. She says something such as "Let's think about how this can work. You are puzzled about [variables that factor into the physical situation]. Do you want to explore more about [an idea that child seems to be attempting to implement]?" In the "circle of viewpoints" routine, an adult helps a group of children explore diverse perspectives by structuring a conversation in which each child shares his or her ideas for solving the problem and then the children compare across the different suggested ideas.

To help toddlers develop flexible thinking, teachers can set up interesting physical problems, provide an assortment of objects that might serve as tools to solve the problems, and offer modeling and hints about using the objects. Toddlers can learn to use different tools to accomplish tasks when adults demonstrate how to use helpful tools or provide verbal suggestions about which tool to use. In one research study of toddlers' strategies for solving a toy retrieval task, researchers found that although most toddlers would not spontaneously pick up a tool (such as a rake or ladle) to retrieve an attractive toy that was just out of reach, they would begin to pick up tools after an adult either showed or told them that a particular tool would retrieve the toy (Chen & Siegler, 2000). More impressively, the next time they faced a situation in which a fun toy was out of reach, many of the toddlers would immediately pick up a tool and try to use it to get the toy. Their flexible thinking (ability to change to new strategies based on new information) improved with adult help and experience with successful tool use to solve problems.

Infants' flexible thinking can be supported in a similar way to toddlers'. Adults can set up physical situations and offer interesting physical objects that give infants a chance to use familiar tools in novel ways. Adults can model how to use the tools in new problem-solving ways and guide infants in experiencing how the tools solve the problems. For example, an adult can play a drum with his hands and then introduce a spoon as an alternative drumstick. An adult can show an infant how to brush her hair and then use the hairbrush to open the lid of a box the infant has been struggling with and uncover a favorite toy.

FLEXIBLE THINKING EXPERIENCE FOR INFANTS

Flexible thinking involves experimentation, reasoning, and inventiveness. The foundation for flexible thinking involves reacting to a problem and seeking to achieve a specific goal.

Supporting the Development of Flexible Thinking: Hidden Animal Search

This experience centers around a board book featuring the search for a boy's missing cat. In Eric Carle's *Have You Seen My Cat?* (2009), a boy has lost his cat and travels around the world asking people if they have seen it. Each person he encounters points him to a different kind of "cat" (lion, puma, tiger, etc.). The book is designed as a "slide-and-peek" board book with flaps that are pulled out of the side of each page. The boy keeps asking until finally he finds his cat, who it turns out has had kittens. This experience combines a book with a game to provide opportunities for infants to build their flexible thinking skills for reacting to the problem of the missing cat. This activity can also be done with other similar books.

Materials

- *Have You Seen My Cat?* by Eric Carle (2009; "slide-and-peek" board book)
- Small stuffed or toy cat(s) (or other animals)
- Items to hide the stuffed cat(s) (soft scarves, fabric, blanket, small box, etc.)

Read the Book Together

Eric Carle's *Have You Seen My Cat?* (2009) is a story that can be read individually or with a group of infants. With the infants next to you or on your lap, read the book together, pulling out the flaps on each page to reveal the animal underneath (the infant can help or attempt to pull the flaps if you are reading one on one or with a small group). A book with a similar theme is *Where Is Spot?* (Hill, 2003), which depicts a search for a missing puppy. Read the book at various times so the infants become familiar with it.

Start Your Own "Have You Seen My Cat?" Game

Create an experience for infants that encourages them to look in different places to try to find a missing toy or stuffed cat (or other object). The goal is to find the missing cat or other object. Place the cat out of sight (e.g., under a scarf or box) or in places that an older infant can walk or crawl to. You can leave a little part of the cat visible as a hint. Putting on a worried expression, tell the infants you have lost your cat. Ask for their help and tell them you want to look everywhere until you find it.

Narrate Your Actions

With nonmobile infants, tell them where you are looking: "I am going to check on the shelf over here." You can also "find" some objects that turn out clearly not to be the cat (such as a ball or a book) and say, "Oh no, this is not my cat. This is a shoe! I need to keep looking for my cat! Can you help me? Where should I look next?"

Extend and Modify the Experience

With older infants, you can increase the challenge by hiding different animals and by having them search with you. "Let's go check near the blocks. Does anyone see my cat? Come here kitty, kitty! I think it might be over here." You can hold up a different object, asking, "Is this my cat? No! This is not my cat. This is a cow! Let's keep looking for my cat!"

Try extending this activity by hiding an object in a new or different place the second time around. You can also vary the game in silly ways, such as hiding the cat under a hat on your head. The infants will try to tell you the cat is there, but pretend you do not know what they mean for a short time and then "find" the cat on your head. With younger infants, you can also simply say, "Where is the kitty?" and move the kitty around (maybe "walk" the kitty around with a meow) out of their vision and then back in so the infants "find" the cat. When you can see that the infants are reacting to the cat, you can exclaim, "You found the cat, didn't you?" or find other ways to positively reinforce the infants' reaction to the problem by looking for, recognizing, and "finding" the cat.

Wonder and Ask Questions

These books and the experience are only limited by your creativity, so wonder and ask away with creative, new, or even silly questions! "I hope I don't find a scary monster under this blanket instead of my cat!" "Do you think my cat was hungry and went to find some food?" "I think I hear my cat meowing over there. Do you hear it?" "I hope we don't give up! We still have more places to look; let's go!"

Follow the Infant's Lead

Read the infants' cues and follow their lead. Pick a time when most infants are alert and not overly hungry or too tired to read a book or play a game in a group. If any infants do not participate, talk to them about it later: "Did you see us looking high and low for my cat? We finally found it in a chair; my cat was hiding! Do you want to see where the kitty was hiding?" You can modify the game to the developmental capacity and interests of the infants in your care. If a parent is there and not in a rush, invite him or her into the game: "William's dad is going to help us find that sneaky cat. I hope we can find the cat quickly, because his dad needs to get to work soon." Figure 5.1 is a rubric that will help you evaluate how well the infant engaged in the flexible learning experience. Examples are provided of the information you would record based on the infant's performance on the activity.

Universal Design for Learning Supports for Infants

As a reminder, the suggestions for infants in the text box are aimed at all children but address some needs of infants who have physical or multiple challenges that prevent them from independently manipulating the objects around them or from independently coming to engage in an activity. Some UDL supports are geared toward all children or a specific profile child. Use any of the UDL supports with any child who might benefit.

 UDL Supports for Infants

- Use hand-over-hand guidance to help infants point, touch, and lift the flaps or grab the scarves. [David]
- Add picture symbols to the book to support infants who will learn communication using picture symbols or a single switch with a message. [All]
- Provide objects of different textures that make various sounds (e.g., crunchy fabric, soft fabric that whooshes together, boxes). [All]
- Hide the stuffed cat in a soft-object obstacle course where the infants can crawl around independently looking for the cat. [Julia]
- Use cats of various sizes to promote different challenge levels to infants. [David]
- Use a few basic signs to engage infants in the lesson and offer them opportunities to communicate (e.g., MORE, DONE, YES, NO). [Julia]

Rubric			
Rate the child's level of participation and understanding on the continuum. **Add evidence/ descriptions for each child.**	**Reacts to a problem**	**Reacts to a problem; seeks to achieve a specific goal; observes and imitates how other people solve problems**	**Observes and imitates how other people solve problems; asks for a solution and uses it**
Child 1	Sam looked intently each time the teacher pulled the tab on the page to reveal the cat.		
Child 2		Brandon watched as the teacher put a scarf over the cat and then crawled over and pulled the scarf off to reveal the cat, saying, "Cat!"	
Child 3			Glory placed three stuffed cats on different locations on the rug, covered each with a scarf, and then asked, "Have you seen my cat?"

Figure 5.1.   Infant flexible thinking experience rubric.

FLEXIBLE THINKING EXPERIENCE FOR TODDLERS

Experience

This activity is again based on the children's book *One Duck Stuck* by Phyllis Root (1998). This activity extends the learning from the collaborative thinking activity (Chapter 7) in which toddlers dug objects out of wet mud. In this activity, the children again engage in a hands-on engineering experience in which they have to figure out how to find and release objects from the hardened, dried mud. This activity is very similar to archeological digging, but because it involves toddlers, it focuses on the process of finding and identifying objects rather than digging and preserving delicate artifacts. The book serves as a springboard for this activity, but this activity is specifically focused on the engineering problem and not on the information from the book.

This activity emphasizes children's flexible thinking skills—brainstorming ideas, experimenting, investigating the environment, using tools and materials to problem-solve, and trying multiple solutions. These are the skills commonly associated with problem solving and engineering, but flexible thinking is just one part of problem solving. This chapter focuses on flexible thinking, but children will use thinking skills from several chapters to complete the activity. After discussing what they have learned in previous activities about wet mud and what they think the characteristics of dried mud are, the children will excavate to find toys/animals in the dried mud using tools, clues, and problem solving.

Introducing the Experience

For this activity, it is necessary to prepare the tubs of objects in dried mud several days in advance. Depending on the time of year, it takes 2 to 3 days for mud to dry in the sun. We found that using aluminum roasting pans filled with five to eight objects and mud works well. When we did this activity in a toddler classroom, we used old toy cars, plastic animals and dolls, and toy tea set pieces with mud from a backyard. This activity was very messy, with dirt getting everywhere and on everyone.

Provide laminated pictures of all the objects in the tubs and keep track of which items are in which tubs as a UDL support for children. In thinking about your classroom, think about whether it would work better to have children at one big table or working at smaller tubs at tables or outside. Because this activity is about collaboration, try to have children work in groups of at least two or with at least two children negotiating the same workspace so that they can engage with and observe each other.

To start the activity, finish reading the book *One Duck Stuck*. Ask the children questions as you read: "What do you think will happen next? Will [animal] get him unstuck? How could he get him unstuck? How many animals will it take? Why are more animals better?" Depending on the ages of the toddlers, focus on counting the animals or making the animal sounds, the repetitive phrase, animal movements, or the animal pictures and their names. The goal of this activity is to help children remember the names of the animals and discuss how each animal can help the duck with his problem. Providing auditory, visual, and kinesthetic input assists children in making connections with what they are learning and connecting the information to previous information they have learned. For example, when children are looking pictures of the duck, the fish, or the moose, children are more likely to remember the names of the animals and their characteristics if they also move around like the animal and make the sound. Similarly, listening to the word *duck*, repeating the word *duck*, and physically matching a picture of a duck to a stuffed duck by putting the stuffed duck on the picture of a duck will reinforce what the children are learning. In addition, the reflective thinking activity (Chapter 6) focuses on sequencing the animals and story retelling. The unit helps build the children's knowledge about animals and mud and the thinking skills necessary for engaging in problem solving. Remind children about the objects they found in the wet mud. This time, children are going to look for objects in dried mud. Show them one object that is partially visible and partially hidden by dried mud. Ask the children to make a guess as to what the object is. Ask them for clues and why they think it is what they are guessing. In the large group, model using the tools to free the object from the dried mud. Talk about excavating and digging out objects. Remind the children to be careful not to damage an object but to use the tools gently to slowly remove the dried mud.

Dirt Excavations

In this activity, the children will try to identify objects in dried mud as they start to dig them out. Ask the children to make a guess as to what each is. Ask them for clues and why they think it is what they are guessing. At the mud table or individual mud tubs, arrange children so that they have the opportunity to find two to four toy animals.

Set up the mud tubs with mud; tools used at the beach or in a sand table for digging, such as shovels, spoons, brushes, and plastic hammers/mallets; and a space for the found toys. Buckets, cups, scoops, and other small containers are also helpful. At the mud table, prompt children to work together to locate and dig out objects. Encourage the children to brainstorm how they want to locate and dig out toys and talk through the process with them as they are locating and digging. Some children may engage in trial and error or random digging, whereas others may have a strategy, such as starting from one side of the tub and moving systematically to the other. Talk to the children throughout their play in this activity, narrating and extending their actions to provide language for their learning.

Keep pictures of the objects in the tub next to the tub to support the children. As children start to dig out an object, look at the pictures with them and ask them to predict what they are digging out and ask why they think it is that object. Discuss with the children what was found and what tools can be used to find objects and get objects unstuck. Encourage children to use shovels or scoops to move dirt. Facilitate by offering suggestions of strategies that are working for others (e.g., "Cindy is really making progress moving mud with the shovel.") Encourage children to try different tools and see what works best. When it is time to stop and/or all toys have been found, ask the children to count how many toys they found with support. Teach children to use new vocabulary from the story by introducing it, discussing its meaning, and providing a picture or context to help children connect the word to a real-life thing or experience. Use picture symbols to support that vocabulary during the activity for all children so that the words adults and children say and write are connected to concepts that children understand. For example, have toy objects or real objects for new

 Self-Reflection Checklist

- Did I encourage children's enthusiasm to try different tools and strategies?
- Did I ask children to make predictions, and did I document their predictions about the duck's problem?
- Did I model how to make "I wonder if . . ." statements, and did I document children's "I wonder if . . ." statements?
- Did I scaffold children to use their words to describe the digging and the search process and give them new vocabulary, such as *hammer* and *excavate*?
- Did I encourage the children to try their own ideas for finding the toys?
- Did I offer multiple materials to find out what makes it easier or harder to find toys?
- Did I let the children try to manipulate the tools on their own?

 Essentials to Remember

- Encourage children to try different tools and strategies.
- Ask children to describe what they did and what they have learned.
- Ask them to identify their tools and objects and use their new vocabulary.
- Offer multiple opportunities to find objects and to dig, praising creativity and flexibility.

vocabulary so that children can learn the word and the characteristics. When they find an object, have them draw and label the object on a piece of paper. Adults can help them write the words and let them draw their representation of the object.

Summarizing the Experience

Similar to previous activities in this book, use a camera to document the children's work and their experiences. Photographs and videos are helpful for a later lesson in this series on mud explorations (Chapter 6). After the children finish finding their toys, talk to the whole group about what they did to find the toys and what tools they used. Highlight creative ways that children found the toys and what tools worked best. Discuss what problem they had today (i.e., needing to find their hidden toys in dried, hard mud) and how they solved it. Start to familiarize children with the language involved in the engineering design process by discussing problems and solutions and what they tried that worked and what they tried that did not work. Remind them that engineers have to try many different ideas to find the best solution to a problem.

Universal Design for Learning Supports for Toddlers

All activities in this book have used picture symbols to support vocabulary development and speech. When choosing toys to hide in the mud, assess the needs of your students and the materials available to determine if toys can be used interchangeably or if children are still at a concrete stage at which they need to find toy animals to go with the story. This may vary across different children. This activity is very hands-on, and the focus is completely on the engineering process and the problem-solving work. All children should be actively involved in the digging and discovery process. Provide tools to children to help them be successful in digging out the toys, and guide certain children who may have fine motor challenges or who become easily frustrated with certain tasks to use specific tools. For example, Jessie may benefit from working on a section where she is successful early to maintain her motivation to continue with the task.

Figure 5.2 provides several UDL supports for this activity in the lesson template that are geared toward specific profile children mentioned but can also be used with others in the classroom. Jessie benefits from her own individual tray and workspace, but other children may prefer that as well. Children who do not like getting dirty should be provided with waterproof smocks and gloves and encouraged to try the activity with support. Grips will be important in this activity because the hardened dirt will take more physical effort to break up, and children will need to have a good grip on the tools they are using. Some children may need hand-over-hand assistance or fading prompts to help them dig for objects. Use adult assistance in the classroom to maximize the assistance to students who need physical support to remain actively involved in the activity.

The picture cards of hidden objects are another example of supports that are helpful for English language learners but also support all children. When using the pictures, children can look at the pictures as clues to predict what they are finding and connect the words to concepts. Picture symbols can also be used with children with physical challenges or linguistic challenges to ask them to choose what tools they want to use. To help scaffold children who may need to use pictures symbols in developing their reading skills, a choice of picture symbols is preferred over giving a choice between two actual tools, but both methods provide choices. The UDL Planning Sheet provides a summary of all the UDL supports used for this toddler unit.

Toddler Experience Planning Template

Problem-solving focus skill	Flexible thinking	
Motivating engineering problem	In the book *One Duck Stuck* by Phyllis Root (1998), the duck goes into a marsh and gets stuck in the mud. Various animal friends try to get the duck out of the mud, but it takes all of them working together to free the duck.	
Focus of this particular learning experience	This activity uses tools to find objects stuck in dried mud and/or sand.	
Learning objectives for this particular experience	• Children will hypothesize what objects are from seeing part of the object hidden by mud or sand. • Children will use tools and strategies to find and free objects from mud or sand.	
Materials needed	• Dried mud • Tubs • Various-size paintbrushes • Scoops • Plastic hammer/mallet • Metal spoons and forks • Sifters • Paper and markers • Rubber gloves *Note:* Prepare tubs/trays of objects in dried mud at least 3 days in advance.	

Elements of the learning experience		UDL supports
Introduce children to the problem	Remind children of the story. Review the previous activity on finding objects in wet mud. Ask children to guess what a partially hidden object is and suggest tools to get it free.	• Model digging and excavating an object out for children who are struggling with concepts. • Offer a choice of two tools that would help to reduce frustration. • Provide additional clues.
Help children understand the problem-solving goal and constraints	Ask the children to tell you if a tool would work. Have examples of tools to use and tools that would not work. Show children pictures of objects they might find.	• Give children pictures of toys to find (make sure they are in that tub). • Offer a choice of two tools that would help to reduce frustration. • Provide additional clues.
Support children in demonstrating their thinking	Give each child or group of children a tub with hidden objects in dried mud that they need to excavate. Discuss with the children what they are doing and scaffold their learning. Model as needed so children can imitate adults. Children can draw pictures of what they find and adults can label it with words.	• Have individual tubs for children as needed. • Give children pictures of toys to find (make sure they are in that tub). • Offer a choice of two tools that would help to reduce frustration. • Provide additional clues or physical assistance.
Provide opportunities for feedback and for trying again	Ask children why they choose a certain tool or to describe what it does. Ask children to describe and discuss what they are finding.	• Provide additional clues or physical assistance. • Model digging or excavating until the object is partially showing for the child to complete. • Suggest a tool to use.
Help children share and learn from one another	Take pictures of the process and have children share what they found with their classmates, both their objects and their labeled pictures of the objects.	• Show pictures to help children retell what they did and to practice key vocabulary.

Figure 5.2.   Toddler flexible thinking experience overview and rubric.

Rubric			
Rate the child's level of participation and understanding on the continuum. **Add evidence/ descriptions for each child.**	**Reacts to a problem; seeks to achieve a specific goal** *Did the child find at least one toy using the tools?*	**Reacts to a problem; seeks to achieve a specific goal; observes and imitates how other people solve problems; asks for a solution and uses it** *Was the child able to find the toys with the tools provided?* *Did the child imitate how a peer or teacher used a tool to find the toy?* *Did the child observe others and then try himself or herself?*	**Observes and imitates how other people solve problems; asks for a solution and uses it; solves problems without having to try every possibility; thinks problems through, considering several possibilities and analyzing results** *Did the child use multiple tools or techniques?* *Was the child able to figure out how to find a toy using clues or previous knowledge?*
Child 1			Sandra started to use a spoon to dig but noticed that Jay was making progress with a plastic knife and started burrowing the knife in the dirt to break up the mud. Then Sandra scooped the extra dirt away from the toy.
Child 2		Latoya watched the teacher move dirt out of the main container and started to use a scoop to scoop out the dirt near an object.	
Child 3	Felix used the fork to fling dirt out of the container. He moved dirt in front of him until he found a toy but only used one tool and technique.		

FLEXIBLE THINKING EXPERIENCE FOR PRESCHOOLERS

Like the curious thinking learning experience, this flexible thinking activity is also based on the children's book *Muncha! Muncha! Muncha!* by Candace Fleming (2002). The main character of this book, Mr. McGreely, problem-solves like an engineer. He uses flexible thinking to brainstorm four different methods for keeping bunnies away from his vegetable garden. But each time he constructs a new garden protection system, the bunnies manage to find a way in to munch his carrots and sprouts, and he has to put on his flexible thinking hat again. The range of ideas that Mr. McGreely generates to save his vegetables, and the fact that even at the end of the story he is not completely successful, make this book a motivating launching point for children's problem solving.

This learning activity emphasizes preschool children's flexible thinking skills—their openness to anticipating and planning for future scenarios and to considering new and different perspectives. Children are encouraged to brainstorm and represent multiple ways to solve a problem as they practice some "garden engineering" alongside Mr. McGreely. In

"Window into a Classroom" Anecdote

One teacher had her children reenact several of Mr. McGreely's solutions in the classroom before they began planning their own. During their first reading of the entire story, she paused at two points and sent them in small groups to model gardens that she had previously set up in the classroom. One model garden had fence pieces (from a construction set) next to it, and the others had wooden blocks. The children built their own replicas of the fence and the wall from the first part of *Muncha! Muncha! Muncha!* (Fleming, 2002). Then, after reading the next part of the story in which Mr. McGreely creates a moat, she added blue pieces of construction paper to all the stations, and the children re-created the moats around their model gardens. As they children re-created Mr. McGreely's solutions, they deepened their comprehension of the story and got inspired to brainstorm their own creations to protect their gardens.

particular, they will create plans for garden protection systems. Figure 5.3 provides an overview of teacher preparation and facilitation steps for this learning experience.

This activity was designed to follow the garden wall exploration from the curious thinking chapter (Chapter 3). However, if you have not already carried out the walls exploration, you can still jump into this activity. You just might want to spend a bit more time at the beginning of the activity discussing the problem that Mr. McGreely faces in *Muncha! Muncha! Muncha!* You can use the anticipation questions suggested in Chapter 3. You will also want to prepare at least one model vegetable garden. A large green or brown poster board with vegetables (cutouts or from the dramatic play center) works well; you can also draw and copy a bird's-eye view of a garden on letter-size paper.

Remind children about the story *Muncha! Muncha! Muncha!* Help them remember that in the first part of the story, Mr. McGreely discovers that he has a big problem: Bunnies are breaking into his garden and eating his vegetables! Mr. McGreely builds a fence and a garden wall, but neither of those things keeps the bunnies out of his garden. Mr. McGreely could use some help from engineers. The children are going to have the chance to practice being engineers by pretending to solve Mr. McGreely's problem with the materials in their preschool classroom.

If you have recently carried out the curious thinking exploration of sturdy walls (Chapter 3), you may want to give the children time to retell what kinds of walls they built and what they discovered out about their walls. Then emphasize to the children that now you want them to think about *other* ways to protect gardens from bunnies. The first step is to find out more about the ways that Mr. McGreely tried to keep bunnies from eating his vegetables.

Explain that you will now read the rest of the story, and you wonder what other ways Mr. McGreely will try to solve his garden problem. Ask the children to look for his other solutions—that is, the other things he does to solve his problem. With the children, read the entire story of *Muncha! Muncha! Muncha!* After reading, record the children's ideas about what Mr. McGreely did to solve his garden problem. Then count how many ways he tried to solve the problem. Ask children why they think Mr. McGreely had to build so many different protection systems for his garden. Help the children recall all the different strategies that the bunnies used to break into the garden. Talk about how it might have felt to try so many different ways. Help the children see that when people face big problems, they often have to think of more than one way to solve the problem before they find a solution that works. It can be hard to keep thinking of different ideas to try, but it can also be fun, like figuring out

Preschool Experience Planning Template

Problem-solving focus skill	Flexible thinking
Motivating engineering problem	In the book *Munch! Munch! Munch!* by Candace Fleming (2002), three bunnies keep sneaking into Mr. McGreely's garden and eating his vegetables. Children can recognize that the bunny break-ins are a problem for Mr. McGreely and explore better garden protection.
Focus of this particular learning experience	Mr. McGreely tries many different solutions to solve his problem of the bunnies breaking into his garden. This learning experience is focused on observing Mr. McGreely's attempts and suggesting new possible solutions to the problem.
Learning objectives for this particular experience	• Children will observe how a character in a story solves problems. • Children will think through a character's problem and suggest at least two possible solutions without yet trying them. • Children will identify at least one good idea in a solution suggested by another child. • Children will know what it means to make a plan.
Materials needed	• *Munch! Munch! Munch!* by Candace Fleming • Paper or poster with an illustration of a vegetable garden or a large sheet of green or brown paper with toy vegetables placed on it • Poster paper and markers for recording children's ideas • Paper, pencils, and other writing and drawing materials for students to use when creating their plans • Camera

	Elements of the learning experience	UDL supports
Introduce children to the problem	Read (or reread) the beginning of the story *Munch! Munch! Munch!* Help children recall the first two ways Mr. McGreely tries to solve his problem: He builds a fence and a wall. As you read the rest of the story, ask the children to look for the other ways Mr. McGreely tries to solve his garden problem. These were his other solutions. After reading, record the children's ideas about the solutions he tried.	• Provide an opportunity to reread the book in centers or reading time. • Offer an interactive version of the book. • Provide a refresher on key engineering vocabulary. • Help some students to develop answers ahead of the activity with an adult.
Help children understand the problem-solving goal and constraints	Count how many ways Mr. McGreely tried to solve the problem. Ask, "Why do you think he had to try so many different ways to solve his problem?" Tell the children about the task: "Today we are going to think of as many ways as we can to solve the problem of bunnies getting into a vegetable garden. That way, if some of the ideas don't work, we'll have others to try. Your job is to show at least two different ways you could protect a vegetable garden. We are just going to plan today. We will build our plans on another day."	• Provide peer buddies in mixed ability groups. • Provide individual work time with an adult as an option.
Support children in demonstrating their thinking	Help individual children create at least two plans for protecting a garden. Help children draw, dictate, or write to express their garden protection plans. Save the children's plans for the next learning experience, and take photos of them so that you can use them later in an engineering journal or documentation panel.	• Use a tablet or computer to create plans. • Provide precut shapes to use in drawing plans. • Allow some children to touch and move building materials while making plans.

Figure 5.3. Preschool flexible thinking experience overview and rubric.

(continued)

Figure 5.3. *(continued)*

Provide opportunities for feedback and for trying again	Ask children questions about their plans and have them look at each other's plans and try to describe what they think their friends' solutions are. Encourage them to ask each other questions and to add details to answer each other's questions. You can ask prompting questions such as "I see that you have a tall structure as part of your plan. Can you tell me about what that does?"	• Use picture symbols for key vocabulary. • Use a communication board or interactive communication device.
Help children share and learn from one another	At "engineering circle" time, help children share their plans for solving the problem. After some or all children share, ask, "What are some good ideas your friends had to solve the problem? Why did you like those ideas?" Record these ideas on a chart. Finally, count the children's ideas for solving the garden problem and discuss how they can be better problem solvers by thinking of more than one way to solve a problem.	• Provide individual or group discussions. • Document learning orally or by journaling. • Offer the opportunity to practice before group time and to formulate thoughts with an adult.

Rubric			
Rate the child's level of participation and understanding on the continuum. **Add evidence/ descriptions for each child.**	**Observes and imitates how other people solve problems; asks for a solution and uses it**	**Solves problems without having to try every possibility; thinks problems through, considering several possibilities and analyzing results**	**Represents solution to problem before actually trying it; applies own ideas to new situations**
Child 1			After a large-group reading of *Munchal Munchal Munchal*, Johan asked why Mr. McGreely did not try to build a scarecrow to scare the bunnies away from the garden. At choice time, he drew a picture of a scarecrow and said he wanted to make it out of Bristle Blocks.
Child 2		Darla suggested building a roof over the garden to keep the bunnies from jumping in over a wall. She drew a picture of the roof but chose not to build it because "it wouldn't let the sun get to the vegetables."	
Child 3	Rick suggested that the class build a wall around the garden and make rivers next to the wall. His idea was similar to the solutions presented in the book.		

a hard puzzle. People might feel tired after thinking of different ways to solve the problem. But when they do find a way to solve the problem, they feel very happy, like Mr. McGreely felt when his big stone castle kept the bunnies away from the garden for one night.

After discussing and recording all the garden protection systems that Mr. McGreely tried out, ask the children to recall the end of the story: "Did Mr. McGreely's last solution really work?" Make sure all the children understand that although the big stone castle kept the bunnies out for one night, eventually they found a way to sneak back into the garden. Mr. McGreely still needs new ideas for solving his problem.

The children's task is to think of at least two other ways to protect a garden from bunnies. They will make *plans* for their ideas before they try building them. Talk about what it means to make a plan for something. When engineers plan solutions to problems, they make lists of the materials they will need, they draw pictures, they tell each other about their ideas, and they write down the steps they might follow to build their ideas. Tell the children about their task:

> Today we are going to think of as many ways as we can to solve the problem of bunnies getting into a vegetable garden. That way, if some of the ideas don't work, we'll have others to try. Your job is to show me at least two different ways you could protect a vegetable garden. We are just going to plan today. We will build our plans on another day.

One way to get the children's planning started is to ask the whole group of children to tell you what materials in the classroom they think they might be able to use for their garden protection systems. If you are willing to obtain materials from home or the store, you can also ask them what materials from outside the classroom they think they might like to use. Record their ideas for materials and let them know which of these materials will be off-limits and which they will actually be able to use.

The next step is to help children brainstorm garden protection systems. Show children the model garden and stuffed bunny and say, "Here's my pretend garden and my pretend bunny. Can you be engineers and make a plan for something you can build to protect this garden from this bunny?" If you have model gardens for each child, make these available now. If all children will work with the same large model garden, tell them where this model garden will be placed in the classroom.

Depending on the strengths and needs of your children, you might decide to do all the planning as a large or small group. Children can share their ideas in the group setting, and you can write down their ideas as they talk. Hopefully you will be delighted by the

---

 Self-Reflection Checklist

- Did I help children make sense of Mr. McGreely's plans before I asked them to begin engaging in their own planning?

- Did I encourage children to generate more than one idea for how to protect the garden?

- Did I ask children to explain why they thought each garden protector idea would work?

- Did I model how to brainstorm possible solutions by thinking aloud about previous experiences that might provide inspiration (e.g., gardens I have seen, strategies I have used to scare away animals)?

- Did I offer multiple modes for children's expression and documentation of plans (e.g., dictating to an adult in a one-to-one setting, drawing, whole-class conversation with teacher note-taking, voice recording on a computer or tablet)?

Essentials to Remember

- Keep in mind that the goal of this learning experience is to foster children's flexible thinking—that is, their open-mindedness or abilities to "think outside the box." It is much less important that children propose feasible garden protectors than that they generate some ideas that diverge from those presented in the book.

- There are many different ways to document a plan: written text, drawing, audio/video recording, and physical construction. Just be sure that children's plans are documented in such a way that they can be revisited later, both by the children who proposed them and by peers.

- Children may need extra encouragement to think of garden protection systems that are not stationary structures such as walls and fences. Try to help them think of completely different strategies for deterring the bunnies. If you focus on this part of the activity, you will make the greatest impact on children's flexible thinking.

variety of ideas generated by the children. We have seen 3- and 4-year-olds suggest everything from "a top for the garden" to "tubes and balls so the balls would knock the bunnies back" to "a wind turbine that will blow the bunnies away." We have also seen many ideas that take their cue from illustrations in the book, such as "a super super super giant lock" and "a boat so the garden can float in the water."

If you have the children do their planning in a group setting and you are recording their ideas, make sure your writing is visible to the children, and read back to them what you write. Invite them to add illustrations to your writing. Deliberately refer to this writing and drawing activity as *planning*, and emphasize how impressed you are that the children are trying to think of more than one plan.

If some children can draw independently, provide them with paper and drawing supplies to make pictures of their garden protection plan. You can add a caption describing each plan using words dictated by each child.

Universal Design for Learning Supports for Preschoolers

In the overview, a variety of UDL supports are suggested for all children for different aspects of the flexible thinking activity. This activity encourages children to create a model or drawing of what they want to build. For some children with spatial or cognitive challenges, this activity may be a struggle. Children such as Brandon would benefit from working in mixed-ability groups, where they can work together on the task and build on each other's strengths and weaknesses. Both Brandon and José will need additional support in expressing their thoughts and could benefit from practice with the vocabulary and time to formulate their responses for engineering circle ahead of time with an adult. To avoid frustration, encourage children to try not to worry about finding a correct answer; rather, tell them to design several different possible solutions. Focus on supporting children like Brandon and José to be able to verbalize their reasoning behind their designs with pictures, picture symbols, or words.

RESOURCES

Developmental Trajectory and Key Standards and Guidelines

Dichtelmiller, M.L. (2001). *Omnibus guidelines: Preschool through third grade.* Ann Arbor, MI: Rebus Planning Association.

Head Start Child Development and Early Learning Frameworks. (2010). *Approaches to learning: Initiative & curiosity*. Retrieved from http://eclkc.ohs.acf.hhs.gov/hslc/hs/sr/approach/cdelf/a2_learning.html

Heroman, C., Burts, D.C., Berke, K., & Bickart, T.S. (2010). *Teaching strategies GOLD: Objectives for development and learning: Birth through kindergarten*. Washington, DC: Teaching Strategies, Inc.

High/Scope Press & High/Scope Educational Research Foundation. (2003). *Preschool Child Observation Record*. Ypsilanti, MI: Authors.

Ohio Department of Education. (2012). *Ohio early learning and development standards*. Retrieved from http://education.ohio.gov/getattachment/Topics/Early-Learning/Early-Learning-Content-Standards/The-Standards/ELDS-ATL-FINAL-21-October-2012-pdf.pdf.aspx

PBS Kids. (2014). *Child development tracker: Approaches to learning*. Retrieved from http://www.pbs.org/parents/childdevelopmenttracker/five/approachestolearning.html

Publications

Gandani, L. (1992). Creativity comes dressed in everyday clothes. *Child Care Information Exchange, 85*, 26–29. Retrieved from https://ccie-catalog.s3.amazonaws.com/library/5008534.pdf

Morin, A. (n.d.). *6 ways kids use flexible thinking to learn*. National Center for Learning Disabilities. Retrieved from http://www.ncld.org/types-learning-disabilities/executive-function-disorders/ways-kids-use-flexible-thinking-to-learn

Mullins. S. (2011). *How to build flexible thinking skills*. Retrieved from http://bitsofwisdomforall.com/2011/09/16/how-to-build-flexible-thinking-skills

Ortieb, E. (2010). Pursuit of play within the curriculum. *Journal of Instructional Psychology, 37*(3), 241–246. Retrieved from http://www.creighton.edu/fileadmin/user/AdminFinance/ChildCareCenter/docs/The_Pursuit_of_Play_Within_the_Curriculum.pdf

Stephans, K. (2004). 20 ways to encourage children's resourcefulness and creativity. *Child Care Information Exchange*. Retrieved from http://www.ccie.com/library/5017500.pdf.

Additional Suggestions for Encouraging Flexible Thinking

- One way to be open to new ideas is to make the routines in your classroom very stable and predictable for children.

- There is a wide variety of newness that any person can tolerate, and although this varies from child to child, just as it does from adult to adult, routines and consistency allow everyone to open up to new ideas.

- Adults also need to model flexibility. Play around, whether by changing a storyline, inserting a new rhyming word into a poem, or providing a variety of ways to make a transition from the circle. Your own playfulness shows that it is okay to "think outside the box."

- Acknowledge children's creative ideas while providing safety limits.

6 Reflective Thinkers

Perhaps the easiest way to define reflective thinking is to describe what it is not: Reflection is the opposite of reaction. To think reflectively is to keep yourself from immediately reacting to an object or an event and instead to represent the object or event in your mind, remember it later, analyze it, and then plan and carry out your next step. For example, a 10-month-old infant can exhibit reflective thinking during this classic Hide-and-Seek trick (Piaget, 1954). Imagine that an adult hides a beautiful toy car under a green blanket 13 times. The infant learns to look for the car under the green blanket. But then on the 14th round, the adult hides the car—while the infant is watching—under the blue blanket. The typical infant will look for the car under the green blanket even though she saw the adult hide it under the blue blanket. This is because she has formed a habit of looking under the green blanket, and her reaction to the car disappearing from view is to immediately use the strategy that has been accomplishing her goal. But the infant with early reflective thinking can stop, realize that the car is not under the green blanket this time, and find the car under the blue blanket.

Another way that cognitive scientists define reflective thinking is having a thought about something that is already represented in your mind. An infant's thinking about a ball is one example (adapted from Marcovitch, Jacques, Boseovski, & Zelazo, 2008). The first level of the infant's reflection about the ball would be going from seeing and appreciating the ball to noting that it is called a "ball." The next level would be thinking *about* that now-labeled "ball"—perhaps by relating this ball to the one she played with yesterday. The next level (probably not possible for an infant) would involve thinking about that relationship between the two balls—perhaps considering which of the two balls is more fun to play with and why. Reflective thinking entails moving from one representation of a thought to another representation. Each level of thought provides more ways to respond to the situation—beyond responding to only its most obvious aspects (Marcovitch et al., 2008).

In his classic text on the role of reflection in professional work, Schön (1983) tells us that reflection involves naming the things to attend to within a situation or problem. In other words, reflection starts with intentional focus of attention. The next step in reflection is then evaluating those things to which you attended. So reflection can also be defined as "acknowledging and evaluating" (Watkins, Spencer, & Hammer, 2004, p. 46).

Of course, the nature of reflective thinking depends on what is reflected upon. Teachers often want children to reflect on the strategies they are using to try to solve problems so that they can determine which strategies work well (and therefore which ones they should keep using) and which strategies are unsuccessful (and therefore should be discarded). Reflection in this sense can be described as "remembering with analysis" (Epstein, 2003, p. 2). Teachers want children to recall plans for solving the problem and then answer the question "How did it go?" This cognitive task fits into the realm of metacognition, or thinking about thinking (Trudeau & Harle, 2006). Reflecting on a problem-solving strategy requires remembering how you thought about the problem and then thinking about how well those thoughts worked for you.

Research on reflective thinking in children shows that it is related to their executive function—that set of mental processes that intentionally guides the regulation of behavior. When children are guided to plan, carry out, and reflect on their own learning activities, they show more purposeful behavior and more success on intellectual measures (Sylva, 1992). Reflection allows them to have more control over their mental processes because it increases the chances that they will not act just based on habit; reflection gives their conscious thoughts more influence over their behavior.

The brain has to do quite a few things to carry out reflective thinking. First, reflective thinking requires *planning to remember* some object or event. To plan to remember something, a person has to create an organizational structure in his or her mind to help decide where to focus attention as the object is in sight or as the event is happening. After focusing attention on specific aspects, he or she has to create a mental representation of those aspects. Later, he or she has to consciously retrieve those representations from memory. Research shows that talking about an event *as it unfolds* can help with the storing-in-memory task, and talking about an event experienced in the past can help with the accessing-from-memory task (Larkina, Guler, Kleinknecht, & Bauer, 2008).

WHY IS REFLECTIVE THINKING IMPORTANT?

Reflective thinking is the backbone of scientists' and engineers' work. At every step of a scientific investigation or an engineering design process, scientists and engineers have to make decisions about what to do next. To make those decisions, they must acknowledge what actions they have already taken and what data they have already gathered. They evaluate those actions and data to determine whether or not they are a step closer to answering a question or designing a solution. The national *Framework for K–12 Science Education* tells us that one of the three key spheres of activity for scientists and engineers is *evaluating*, which is very closely related to reflecting (National Research Council, 2012). Scientists evaluate the theories and models that their peers propose to explain observations of the natural world, and engineers evaluate the designs that their peers propose to solve problems in the world. Reflective evaluating is a practice used by scientists and engineers when they develop and critique arguments:

> Scientists and engineers use evidence-based argumentation to make the case for their ideas, whether involving new theories or designs, novel ways of collecting data, or interpretations of evidence. They and their peers then attempt to identify weaknesses and limitations in the argument, with the ultimate goal of refining and improving the explanation or design. (National Research Council, 2012, p. 46)

Whereas scientists and engineers apply reflective thinking to evaluate each other's arguments about theories or designs, in everyday life people need reflective thinking to take stock of what has happened and determine what to do next. The National Association for the Education of Young Children expects all early education programs to offer children opportunities to develop the skills of reflective thinking. The following NAEYC standards are most closely related to reflective thinking skills:

- *2.G.01:* Infants and toddlers/twos are provided varied opportunities and materials to (a) use their senses to learn about objects in the environment and (b) discover that they can make things happen and solve simple problems.

- *2.G.05:* Children are provided varied opportunities and materials to (a) collect data and to (b) represent and document their findings (e.g., through drawing or graphing).

- *2.G.06(a):* Children are provided varied opportunities and materials that encourage them to think, question, and reason about inferred phenomena.

- *3.A.06(a):* Teachers create classroom displays that help children reflect on and extend their learning (NAEYC, 2014, pp. 18–19, 26).

DEVELOPMENTAL CONTINUUM OF REFLECTIVE THINKING

Infants

One way to think about reflective thinking is as the opposite of pure reaction. This idea is helpful when looking for the beginnings of reflective thinking in infants. When infants notice a stimulus but deliberately pause before acting in response to that stimulus, they are showing an early form of reflection. For example, imagine a 9-month-old who has learned to crawl and is now eagerly exploring every floor-level feature of the room. He starts to tug on a lamp cord, and his mother says, "No, no. No, thank you. We don't touch cords." The infant turns toward his mother's voice, looks at her, and stops moving his hand for 2 seconds. Then he tugs on the cord again to see what his mother does next. He may not understand the meaning of his mother's words, but he has paused his action to consider whether they are connected to what he is doing, and he has decided what to do next.

An even stronger sign of reflective thinking in infants is when they are confronted with a choice between two or more tools and they pause before choosing one to use. Cognitive scientists conduct studies with infants (who have developed grasping abilities) in which the scientists place a toy out of reach, and between the infant and the toy, they place two long objects that might serve as tools to reach the toy. They measure the length of time between the placement of the tools and the infant's first reach for a tool. For some infants, almost no time passes. They do not pause but immediately grasp one of the two objects. Other infants wait and gaze at both tools, allowing measurable time to pass before they grasp one and use it to swipe at the toy. Researchers speculate that these infants are using reflective thinking skills to decide which tool will work better for retrieving the toy.

Of course, infants also show the foundation for reflective thinking when they carry out the "remembering" part of reflection's "remembering with analysis." When they show recognition of familiar faces, objects, and events, they are using thinking skills in order to make connections across experiences.

Toddlers

Reflective thinking in action can be seen in toddlers when they begin to be successful at playing Hide-and-Seek games with objects. They can certainly carry out the "remembering" part of reflection. Eighteen-month- and 2-year-olds watch carefully as an adult places a toy in a hiding place, and they can use intentional strategies to remember where the toy is among different possible locations (DeLoache, Cassidy, & Brown, 1985). For example, some toddlers use their early oral language skills to talk about the toy or its hiding place. Nonverbal toddlers sustain their gaze at the location where the toy was hidden, or they point at it or walk toward it and stand next to it until they are asked to find it. These behaviors of verbalizing, looking, pointing, and approaching are all toddler strategies for keeping something in their minds.

Toddlers also begin to show clear capabilities of the "analysis" part of "remembering with analysis." They can ponder experiences with a focus on one or two objects or events that really stood out to them. Especially when the experiences arise from toddlers' own plans, they can consider what happens and compare it to what they wanted to have happen. Imagine an older toddler who has built a tall tower out of blocks until it becomes unbalanced and tumbled down. If a teacher asks her what happened in the block area, she can use gestures and simple language to recount what happened (Epstein, 2003). She might point to the ceiling and say, "Blocks," and then point to the ground and say, "All fall down." Her teacher can encourage this early reflective thinking by revoicing the child's descriptions with more elaborate language and by thinking out loud about why the tower might have fallen down.

Preschoolers

As they become verbal, preschoolers can go beyond gesturing and simple phrases and participate in extended conversations about what they have done and what they are going to do next. They can recollect experiences with "layered explanations and hypotheses" (Epstein, 2003, p. 3). For preschoolers, reflecting on action becomes a self-reinforcing experience. The more often they reflect on what they have done, the more language and concepts they develop, and the more able they are to generate and share complex reflections and to develop multipart sequences when they plan next steps (Epstein, 2003). Teachers can see preschoolers' reflective thinking simply by noticing the things they create and asking questions about how they have done that creating: "I see your tower. How did you make it so tall?" or "I see your red swoosh on your painting. How did you make it so big?" When teachers comment on children's activities, children often respond by elaborating on what is noticed. They then remember the experience more easily and are more likely to revisit it at a later time.

Preschoolers also show expanded abilities in the specific area of remembering objects, locations, people, and so forth. They can attend selectively to characteristics they are asked to remember and use intentional strategies to remember them, including naming the characteristics and physically manipulating the related objects when possible (Larkina et al., 2008).

KEY GOALS FOR REFLECTIVE THINKING EXPERIENCES

The following set of key words helps explore ways to support young children by describing their actions when they are engaged in reflective thinking. These action words can be helpful when creating lesson and unit plan goals for children. It is helpful to think about these terms as guiding words for what children are working on at a metacognitive level. In other words, when watching children engage in the activities in this chapter or other activities designed to promote reflective thinking, look for children doing these things.

Strategies for Facilitating Reflective Thinking

Purposeful listening, conversation, and documentation by an adult can help young children reflect on their activities through remembering and analysis (Epstein, 2003). Some simple strategies can be practiced to foster memory skills. "Self-talk" can even be modeled with infants when adults talk about the process of remembering by saying things such as "I wonder where I put that book. Did I put in on the bookshelf in your room or in the kitchen? Oh, I remember! We read it in the kitchen at lunchtime." With older toddlers and preschoolers, adults can help develop remembering capabilities by being elaborate when reminiscing together about past events, such as a family birthday party. Provide rich narratives about who was there, what happened, what food was eaten, and how everyone felt about it. Try to elicit information from children about the event and build on their responses. For example, say, "That's interesting that you remember Grandma was the one who lit the candles on the birthday cake. Did you notice how many times Grandpa had to blow before all the candles went out?" In addition to initiating focused conversations about past events, adults can also bring them up more often during natural family talk. Research shows that this is positively correlated with how well children perform on recall and recognition memory tasks (Ratner, 1980).

A focus on strategies for metacognition can facilitate the growth of analysis skills. Model thinking about thinking: "You know, I've been thinking . . ." Nudge children to consider the genesis of their ideas by asking, "How do you know that?" or "What makes you think that?" Encourage children to think in their heads before answering

 Key Words and Phrases for Reflective Thinking for Goal Setting

- Remembering
- Analyzing
- Connecting
- Making patterns
- Understanding cause and effect
- Recording and sharing
- Analyzing data
- Classifying
- Comparing and contrasting
- Evaluating
- Reasoning logically

questions. It also helps to acknowledge children for being thinkers and to point out to others when they make connections from one activity to another (Trudeau & Harle, 2006).

Finally, Ann Epstein (2003) offers six strategies that can be permanent tools for building young children's reflective thinking skills. Epstein encourages reflection as a consistent part of the daily routine. Soon after children have carried out some activities that they planned, ask them what happened and why. Another essential strategy is to ask open-ended questions that begin with "What happened when . . . ?," "How did you . . . ?," or "Why do you think . . . ?," rather than questions that ask children to repeat what is already known about what they did. These questions can still be asked of nonverbal infants and toddlers, and then any kind of response the infant or toddler offers can be interpreted and elaborated on. For example, adults can narrate a young child's facial expressions and gestures: "Oh, it made you happy when you painted on the long paper with your feet? Did the paint feel warm or cold to you?" In addition to asking questions and elaborating on children's responses after the activity, also comment on observations made during the children's playtime. They will often respond to comments with more details about what they are doing or with their ideas for their next steps. This leads to the next strategy for facilitating reflection: recording the children's reflections in writing. When adults write down what children say, this lets them know that their ideas are important enough to keep, and it creates something permanent that can be returned to later. Finally, when encouraging reflection among verbal toddlers and preschoolers, be prepared for conflicts among different children's accounts. Facilitate reflection among peers by accepting conflicting viewpoints and interpretations when they occur. For example, if two children offer a different account of what they were enacting in the dramatic play area, say, "Some friends were pretending to visit an animal doctor's office, and some friends were pretending to give a dog a bath."

REFLECTIVE THINKING EXPERIENCE FOR INFANTS

Reflective thinking first develops as infants remember and connect experiences, recognizing familiar people, places, and objects. These skills build the foundation for reflective thinking.

Make an Infant Faces Game

Laminate large photographs of each infant's face. With all the laminated photographs in hand, tell the infants that you need their help to find one infant's picture. With younger infants, look at the infants' photographs and name the infants and their facial features, such as nose, eyes, mouth, and ears. You can hold up two photographs and ask them to show you which one is the infant's face you were looking for. Add more photographs and look for a different infant. With older infants, put all the photographs on the floor and ask them to find their own pictures. The goal is to have infants look for and recognize the photographs of their classmates, thus building reflective thinking skills.

Materials

- Photographs of each infant in the class

- Laminator and laminating sheets (one per infant in the class)

- Optional: *Baby Faces Peekaboo* by Roberta Grobel Intrater (1997) or another book with large photographs of infant faces

Narrate Your Actions

With nonmobile infants, tell them you are trying to find one of the infants in the pictures you have. Hold up photographs one at a time and ask, "Is this Billy? No, this isn't Billy; this is Joshua. Is this Billy? Yes, there he is. Do you see his eyes and his smile? That is definitely Billy's picture." Older infants can go looking for the correct photograph themselves, and you can similarly narrate their searching and recognizing process.

Wonder and Ask Questions

Model wondering—for example, say, "I am not sure where I put that picture of Kyli. Can you help me find Kyli's picture? I see you found Maria's picture. Let's keep looking for Kyli's." Point out details about the pictures. For example, "I can't remember if Kyli has on a hat in her picture. Do you remember?" or "I think Billy was smiling in his picture, or he might have been laughing. Maybe he saw something silly when we were taking his picture!"

Extend and Modify the Experience

Take photographs of children holding their own pictures or simply enjoying the game. Copy the photograph with a note to parents or caregivers about the activity. This will extend the reflective learning skill that much more if parents are encouraged to talk about the photograph and also play the game with their infants. For the reading extension, consider *Baby Faces Peekaboo* by Roberta Grobel Intrater (1997) or another book with large photographs of infant faces.

Follow the Infant's Lead

Read the infants' cues and follow their lead. Pick a time when most infants are alert and not overly hungry or too tired to play a game in a group. You can have the infants all look for their own photograph as described or you can all look for one infant's picture. If any infants do not participate, talk to them about it later: "Did you see us looking for Kyli's picture? We did finally find it. Do you want to see it? Let's look for your picture in the stack, too!" If infants are tired, hold them in your lap and look at, touch, and talk about the photographs as you would with a book during quiet times.

Figure 6.1 is a rubric that will help you evaluate how well the infant engaged in the reflective learning experience. Examples are provided of the information you would record based on the infant's performance on the activity.

Universal Design for Learning Supports for Infants

As a reminder, the suggestions for infants in the text box are aimed at all children. This activity is more about recognition and cognition and less about action. In the text box, it will be noted if these accommodations are geared toward all children or a specific profile child. In this collaborative activity, one goal is to use UDL supports to increase interactions with adults and peers.

Rubric			
Rate the child's level of participation and understanding on the continuum. **Add evidence/ descriptions for each child.**	**Recognizes familiar people, places, and objects**	**Looks for hidden objects based on their previous location; looks for familiar people and recognizes names; makes connections between objects and events**	**Recalls familiar people from the past; recalls one or two items removed from view; remembers sequence of personal routines/ experiences with support**
Child 1	Sam looked at Madeline's photograph and then looked at Madeline, who was on the floor next to him.		
Child 2		When asked to find the picture of Lee, Brandon crawled across the rug, looking at each picture until he found Lee's picture, and he pointed to it.	
Child 3			Glory found a picture of Pam, a former teacher in the classroom, picked it up, and said Pam's name.

Figure 6.1.   Infant reflective thinking experience rubric.

 UDL Supports for Infants

- Use hand-over-hand guidance to help infants point. [David]

- Use mirrors to look at the infants' features and faces. [All]

- Offer only two pictures of known friends or caregivers to start and expand. [All]

- Use a few basic signs to engage infants in the lesson and offer them opportunities to communicate (e.g., MORE, DONE, YES, NO). [Julia]

- Incorporate a switch with YES to give the children another way to respond. [All]

- Use a corner sitter or wedge for supported sitting in the group or with an adult. [David]

- Minimize distractions and/or play instrumental music to help focus the children's attention. [All]

- Use the same pictures in this activity as are used in other activities to create continuity and greater recognition possibilities by infants. [All]

REFLECTIVE THINKING EXPERIENCE FOR TODDLERS

This activity is a continuation of the "mud explorations" theme based on the children's book *One Duck Stuck* written by Phyllis Root (1998). There are mud experiences in Chapters 3, 5, and 7. In this activity, children participate in a series of steps to recall the story, retell the story, and create a new ending.

This activity emphasizes children's reflective thinking skills—recalling information; recognizing and creating patterns; connecting information to previous learning; and comparing, contrasting, and classifying. Although some of these thinking skills may not seem as if they are part of reflection, for toddlers, skills such as classifying and comparing are prerequisite skills to the analysis of reflection and evaluation. Children learn through increasingly complex categorization techniques and by recognizing and extending patterns. After reviewing the story, the children will participate in activities to recall and extend patterns and connect what they have learned to real-world knowledge by creating a new ending to the book.

Introducing the Experience

Engage children in this learning experience by telling them that they will have a chance to share what they know about making mud. Bring out *One Duck Stuck* and do a picture walk to review what it was about. Then show some pictures from the children's mud making in the curious thinking activity (Chapter 3). Talk about what they did and how they did it. Encourage children to use their new vocabulary and provide them with picture symbols or real pictures to prompt their use of the words. The goal is to be able to retell and recall information and describe what they have learned. Children can participate in four different activities; each child can do just one or rotate through each one of the four. Start in a large group and then move to centers. The following activities will help the children do this.

Recalling and Retelling Centers

Children should be presented with a choice of the following four centers:

1. Retelling *One Duck Stuck* in sequence and/or with at least 5 out of 10 animals

2. Recreating through pictures and retelling the making of mud

3. Retelling and extending or changing the ending of *One Duck Stuck* with pictures and words

4. Creating a picture collage of the animals in the book and attempting to place them in order along a path on the paper

In the first center, children can make pictures describing how the duck got stuck and unstuck. In these pictures, they can work on sequencing at least five animals. In the second center, children can help make sequence cards about how to make mud. Children can use words and draw pictures, and adults can help them write to make the cards. In the third center, children can talk to an adult and/or create a picture or verbal story to create a different ending or change some aspect of the book. This is a more advanced

---

 Self-Reflection Checklist

- Did I encourage children's creativity in extending the story?
- Did I ask children to retell their versions of the story?
- Did I model how to retell and recall what we did with mud?
- Did I scaffold children to use their words to describe the book and the mud activities and give them new vocabulary?
- Did I offer multiple modes of assessment and multiple activities to practice reflective thinking?

reflective thinking skill and can be used as a UDL center for children who need a higher level of challenge beyond basic recall and sequencing. In the fourth center, children can create a picture collage of the animals in the book. It is helpful to use a longer piece of construction paper and make a path with a line or string and place the animals on it in order to again work on sequence and story recall.

Based the on size of your class and classroom, you can have children go to just two centers each session or you can even do some of these activities as a large group. This activity is very flexible, but we wanted to provide a variety of ideas for how to work on the prerequisite skills for reflective thinking for use in problem solving. Adults can work with children individually and in groups to check for their understanding and the accuracy of their answers. Teachers can scaffold the children's learning by offering them the activity choices that fit their developmental levels. Feel free to modify the centers in this activity to meet the needs of your students and classroom.

Summarizing the Experience

At the end of the time or after all children have engaged in several center choices, children can share and talk about their pictures in a small group. Children who created an alternative ending can tell their new story to the group. Reflective thinking can be very language and literacy based—an area of rapid growth for toddlers—but they are still building their vocabulary and are not reading and writing yet. Encourage the use of pictures and speech as much as possible, and scaffold and extend children's language to support all learners in the classroom. Figure 6.2 provides an overview and rubric to guide you through the activity.

Universal Design for Learning Supports for Toddlers

This book offers various UDL supports that benefit all children in the classroom, including the specific profile children mentioned. This particular activity is language and literacy focused and supports children's expressive language skills. On the other hand, toddlers are just learning expressive language, and English language learners may be learning to express themselves in multiple languages. Picture symbols with words can be used to support retelling and recalling responses to questions from the book *One Duck Stuck* (Root, 1998) by providing children with language they can remember by using the picture symbols as cues. For example, in this activity, a child may not remember all the animal names, but a picture can give the child a clue, such as the color or shape of an animal, to help him or her remember its name. For this activity, having *One Duck Stuck* on an electronic device such as an iPad or tablet computer, where children can listen to it orally with the pictures, is a standard UDL support. Because *One Duck Stuck* has many vocabulary words, such as

 Essentials to Remember

- Encourage children to use their words.
- Ask children to share their own ideas about the book and the activities.
- Ask children to sequence the story and talk about what they learned about the animals from the book.
- Offer multiple models of recall and reflective thinking.

Toddler Experience Planning Template

Problem-solving focus skill	Reflective thinking	
Motivating engineering problem	In the book *One Duck Stuck* by Phyllis Root (1998), the duck goes into a marsh and gets stuck in the mud. Various animal friends try to get the duck out of the mud, but it takes all of them working together to free the duck.	
Focus of this particular learning experience	In this activity, children will retell two stories: first the story of the duck in *One Duck Stuck* and then the story of how they made mud and played with it.	
Learning objectives for this particular experience	• Children will use words and pictures to describe how to make mud. • Children will use words and pictures to retell the story of the duck.	
Materials needed	• *One Duck Stuck* • Crayons and markers • Paper • Pictures of mud activity • Pictures of animals in *One Duck Stuck* for felt board or story board • Picture symbols	• Video camcorder (optional) • Grips for markers • Picture symbols for key vocabulary • Sequence board • Multiple felt/story boards for children to use in centers • Electronic version of book

Elements of the learning experience		UDL supports
Introduce children to the problem	Children can participate in four different activities. Children can do just one or rotate through each one. Start in a large group and then move to centers. Picture walk children through the story to retell it as a group. Use pictures of animals and place in order. Discuss how the children made mud. Move to centers to do different activities.	• Use picture symbols for key vocabulary. • Use a sequence board. • Provide multiple felt/story boards for children to use individually. • Provide multiple pictures of the mud activity (for sequencing and retelling).
Help children understand the problem-solving goal and constraints	Today's goal is to be able to retell and recall information and describe what they have learned. The following activities will help the children do this: 1. Retelling *One Duck Stuck* in sequence with at least 5 out of 10 animals 2. Recreating through pictures and retelling the making of mud 3. Retelling and extending or changing the ending of *One Duck Stuck* with pictures and words 4. Creating a picture collage of the animals in the book and attempting to place them in order along a path on the paper	• Provide multiple pictures of the mud activity (for sequencing and retelling). • Use grips for markers. • Use picture symbols for key vocabulary. • Provide a sequence board. • Offer multiple felt/story boards for children to use in centers. • Provide an electronic version of the book. • Use a videocamera to capture children retelling the story (optional). • Provide glue sticks or use paintbrushes to apply glue to paper.
Support children in demonstrating their thinking	Children will complete at least one of the center activities to demonstrate recall of the story, retelling skills, and sequencing using pictures, words, and symbols.	• Use all supports listed in centers.
Provide opportunities for feedback and for trying again	Adults will work with children individually and in groups to check for their understanding and offer them the best level of activity based on their strengths and needs.	• Provide peer or teacher support as needed. • Offer children more or fewer choices based on their level for this activity and thinking skill.
Help children share and learn from one another	At the end of the time, children can share and talk about their pictures in a small group.	• Children can share just with one adult or with the class. • Children can share orally or show a product (including a video).

Figure 6.2. Toddler reflective thinking experience overview and rubric.

(continued)

Figure 6.2. *(continued)*

Rubric			
Rate the child's level of participation and understanding on the continuum. **Add evidence/ descriptions for each child.**	**Recognizes familiar people, places, and objects; looks for hidden objects based on their previous location; looks for familiar people and objects by name; makes connections between objects and events** *Did the child recognize and identify the animals from the story?* *Did the child identify the key vocabulary words from mud making?*	**Recognizes familiar people, places, and objects; looks for hidden objects based on their previous location; looks for familiar people and objects by name; makes connections between objects and events; recalls familiar people and so forth from the past; recalls one or two items removed from view; remembers sequence of personal routines/experiences with support** *Could the child retell any part of the story? Could the child partially describe how to make mud? Could the child sequence at least three animals in the story?*	**Talks about experiences to evaluate and understand them; recalls three or four items removed from view; draws on daily experiences and applies this knowledge to similar situations or applies it in a new context** *Could the child sequence at least five events in the story? Could the child fully describe how to make mud? Can the child tell about a time he or she made mud?*
Child 1	Dana was able to name six animals from the story and said, "I put mud and water together. It was mushy."		
Child 2			Steve put five animals in order and could tell the teacher three more. He put the sequence cards for mud making with pictures in order.
Child 3		Leslie talked about the duck and his friends who helped and said that Mommy and Daddy did not help. She listed four animals in sequence. She put mud cards in sequence for three out of five steps.	

the animal names and sounds, it is helpful to reteach the words using picture cards to children who may need more time to learn the words and connect them to prior knowledge. In addition, the book or e-book can be used at reading centers for more opportunities. For some children, retelling the story can be facilitated through the use of pictures with picture sentence strips. Computer-based painting and picture programs can help children for whom drawing is difficult create their own pictures with less physical work. Also, putting the story into a program such Intellikeys allows the user to re-create a custom large keyboard layout so children can press a picture of an animal and it will play that animal sound. Intellikeys can also be used to create a game to let children sequence the story using a switch or simplified keyboard; this program will read through the story again with the support of a switch.

The picture cards of animals are another example of supports that are helpful for English language learners but also support all children. To help scaffold children who may need to use picture symbols in developing their reading skills, a choice of picture symbols is preferred over giving a choice between two actual toy animals, but both methods provide choices. In addition, children could use a felt board of animals in a "mud pit" to retell the story. The UDL Planning Sheet provides a summary of all the UDL supports used for this toddler unit.

REFLECTIVE THINKING EXPERIENCE FOR PRESCHOOLERS

This preschool learning experience is designed to help children think reflectively about their planning, building, and testing and to reach conclusions about how well their problem-solving strategies worked. It is intended to follow the preschool persistent thinking activity (Chapter 4), in which children take on the role of engineers to build and test garden protection systems for the main character of the book *Muncha! Muncha! Muncha!* (Fleming, 2002). If you have not completed that activity, you can still use the basic framework of this chapter's activity, as long as children have carried out the steps of planning, building, and testing to solve a problem. This reflective thinking activity works as a follow-up to any physical problem-solving experience in which you have kept records of children's plans and constructions.

This activity focuses on children's reflective thinking skills by supporting them in remembering how they planned to solve a problem, how they created their initial solution, and what happened when they tried it out. Then, with assistance, they compare their problem-solving experience to that of other children and consider what they can learn from this comparison. The key tool used to scaffold all this reflection is the *engineer's notebook*.

Beginning the Experience

Initiate children's reflection by reminding them that they have been using engineering to build and test models of garden protectors for Mr. McGreely's vegetables. Show the children some of the "before" and "after" photographs from their tests of their garden protection systems. Ask the children if they feel like they are finished with the garden protection project. Have they solved the problem? You will probably find that most children feel that they have finished the work when their garden protector passes the test. Particularly if you asked them to pose for a photograph in front of it, they will have felt a sense of completion. Acknowledge this sense that their work is done, but then reveal that there is still more work to do! Let the children know that engineers do not stop when they have solved the problem. Their very important final step is to record what they have done so that others will know how to solve the problem, too, and will learn from the mistakes the engineers made along the way to solving it. Explain that each time an engineer tries out a solution to a problem, he or she makes a record of what happened and what worked and did not work. Then the whole engineering team can use these records to decide on the next steps they should take to solve a problem. You might ask children what it means to make *a record* of something or *to record* something that happened. For example, have the children noticed you taking notes while they are playing? Do they see their parents taking photographs when they learn to do something new? Have they seen their doctor typing information into a computer during a checkup? You can help the children think about all the different methods of documentation, including writing words, taking photographs, drawing pictures, and capturing video. Many engineers keep their records in a special book called an *engineer's notebook.*

Share with the children at least a few pages from a notebook created by an engineer. You can access some design notebook pages at the web site ScienceBuddies.org (2014), or you could view some samples from Rutgers University's extensive online collection of Thomas Edison's notebooks (The Thomas Edison Papers, 2012). If you do not have time to let the children really study the engineer's notebook pages during your large-group discussion, tell the children where you will make it available for them to browse during another time in the day.

When you feel that the children understand the purpose of an engineer's notebook, tell them that they will have a chance to create their own engineering notebook about how they tried to solve Mr. McGreely's garden protection problem. Every child will have his or her own page or pages in the notebook. These pages can include the plans the child made before building, drawings of what the child actually built, and/or photographs of what it looked like before and after testing. You will ask the children to describe how they came up with their ideas and what happened when they constructed their models, and you will write down what they tell you. It is important to have children try to remember their thoughts from both before and after the actual building part of the design process. Strong reflective thinking skills depend on remembering both what you *planned* to do and how it went in practice. It is not adequate to reflect only on how well a solution worked.

Tell the children that you will combine all their pages into a class engineering notebook. Children will be able to read the class notebook and think about what they learned from their own and their friends' engineering solutions.

Finally, because creating notebook pages requires adult assistance, explain how you will go about helping the children with their notebook pages. This activity can be set up in a writing center or art station, and you can plan to focus your presence in that area during free choice time. Children can work on their notebook page when they choose to be in that area. Another option is to gather all the notebook elements that you have (children's plans from before building, children's drawings, photographs of children's constructions) and invite children in small groups to come and work with you or another adult in a space dedicated to engineering notebooking for the time being. A third strategy—which works well with older preschool children—is to conduct this activity in parallel with the persistent thinking activity (Chapter 4) and simply encourage children to sit down and draw and write immediately after they test out their garden protection systems.

Many children will need substantial support to get started on their notebook pages. It can be easier for them to start with a photograph and then add a drawing or sentence (dictated to an adult) next to it in response to a question posed by an adult. You can show them a photograph of their garden protector and say, "Tell me what's happening in this photograph" or "What do you notice about the construction in this photograph?"

Remember to prompt children to record both about their planning and about their building/testing. To help children reflect on their planning, ask questions such as the following:

- "How did you get inspired to build this?"

- "How do you think your brain thought of this idea?"

- "Was it easy or hard to think of something that could protect the garden? Why?"

After the children have thought about their initial thinking, then you can move on to questions about how well that thinking solved the problem. Your second set of questions can include the following:

- "What did you find out when you started to build your idea?"

- "How did your garden protector work?"

- "What worked well about your garden protector?"

- "What did you like most about your garden protector?"

- "What would you change about your garden protector?"

Offer feedback on the notebook pages by telling children what you notice about their photographs and the drawings or sentences that they added. You can also

---

 "Window into the Classroom" Anecdote

In one public school preschool classroom with 4- and 5-year-old children, the teacher decided to conduct this engineer's notebook activity on the same day as the task of building and testing garden protection systems. When she felt that a child had reached a stopping point in constructing and carrying out tests of his or her garden protector, she invited that child to find his or her journal and sit down to draw and write. In her classroom, children already used journals to document much of their class work, so she told them that they would simply create their engineering notebook pages within their journals. Later on, they could add photographs to the pages.

This way of structuring the engineer's notebook activity allowed the children to reflect with each other and plan next steps while the building experience was fresh in their minds and the building materials were still available. For example, one child, Ben, brought his journal over to his garden protection system and began to draw his structure. His partner, Thatcher, then also retrieved his journal, and the two boys decided to take their work over to the classroom's art table (see Figure 6.3). They inspected each other's drawings and talked with each other about their work. Ben gave Thatcher feedback and shared an idea for a next step:

Ben: You know what you could do? You could draw a long arrow showing how far he [the bunny] will jump.

Thatcher: I need the same color as the blocks!

Ben: (*While continuing to draw*) How about we try this with a marble run?

Figure 6.3. Two preschool children draw, write, and comment on each other's engineering notebook pages where they reflected on their designing, building, and testing of garden protection systems.

ask, "If a friend looks at your notebook page, will she know how you tried to solve Mr. McGreely's problem? What else could we put on your notebook page to help show or tell what you tried?"

Finally, compile all the notebook pages into one class engineering notebook. At "engineering circle" time, read the notebook to the children. Talk about things that are the same about most of the pages in the notebook and things that are different across different children's pages. Ask some of the following questions:

- "What does this notebook tell us about our engineering work?"

- "Did your friends give you any good ideas?"

- "What kinds of garden protectors worked well?"

- "Can you think of anything we could do differently the next time we work on protecting a garden?"

- "What do you think we should do differently the next time we use engineering to solve a problem in our classroom?"

Figure 6.4 provides an overview and rubric to guide you through the activity.

Preschool Experience Planning Template

Problem-solving focus skill	Reflective thinking
Motivating engineering problem	In the book *Munchal Munchal Munchal* by Candace Fleming (2002), three bunnies keep sneaking into Mr. McGreely's garden and eating his vegetables. Children can recognize that the bunny break-ins are a problem for Mr. McGreely and explore better garden protection.
Focus of this particular learning experience	Mr. McGreely learned something new from each of his attempts to keep the bunnies out of his garden. This learning experience focuses on documenting children's engineering work and facilitating their thinking about what worked well and what did not work so well.
Learning objectives for this particular experience	• Children will talk about and document their building and testing of garden protectors by creating an engineering notebook. • Children will use their engineering notebooks to evaluate their engineering experiences and compare with friends.
Materials needed	• Printouts of the "before" and "after" photographs of all the garden protectors built by children in the curious thinking and/or persistent thinking learning experiences

Elements of the learning experience		UDL supports
Introduce children to the problem	Remind children that they have been practicing being engineers by trying to solve Mr. McGreely's garden problem. When engineers try out solutions to problems, they keep records to remind themselves and other people what worked and what did not. Engineers often keep their records in a special book called a *notebook*.	• Provide a refresher on key engineering vocabulary. • Allow some students to develop answers ahead of the activity with an adult.
Help children understand the problem-solving goal and constraints	Using photographs of each child's garden protector models, help each child add descriptions to the photographs to tell what happened when they tested their models. Combine all the photographs and descriptions into a class engineering notebook.	• Offer adult support to children with challenges. • Provide a peer buddy to help organize and glue photographs.
Support children in demonstrating their thinking	Help individual children create their engineering notebook pages. Children can glue their garden protector photographs onto paper. They can draw pictures or dictate sentences to show more about what happened when they built and tested their models.	• Offer a choice of crayons, markers, or other drawing tool to document the process. • Use a tablet or computer to make the notebook (Pictello app).
Provide opportunities for feedback and for trying again	Offer feedback on the notebook pages by telling children what you notice about their photographs and the drawings or sentences that they added. Also tell them what confuses you, and ask them if they can add to their pages so that you are not confused.	• Provide immediate feedback from an adult. • Use a picture communication board to help formulate and write sentences. • Provide a help sign to give students a noninvasive way to ask for help.
Help children share and learn from one another	Compile all the notebook pages into one class engineering notebook. Read the notebook to the children. Talk about things that are the same about most of the pages in the notebook and things that are different across different children's pages.	• Create a copy on a tablet. • Put a laminated notebook in the reading corner to review. • Create an engineering picture word wall.

Figure 6.4. Preschool reflective thinking experience overview and rubric.

(continued)

Figure 6.4. *(continued)*

Rubric			
Rate the child's level of participation and understanding on the continuum. **Add evidence/ descriptions for each child.**	**Remembers and recounts sequence of personal experiences with support**	**Talks about experiences in order and evaluates experiences; applies knowledge of everyday experiences to new context**	**Documents experiences and thinking; constructs theories based in experience about what might be going on; supports thinking with evidence**
Child 1			Serena drew a picture that showed her garden protector scarecrow and a bean bag being tossed at it to test its sturdiness. She dictated a sentence to the teacher: "The scarecrow was strong."
Child 2		The teacher asked Thomas what happened to his garden wall. He said, "It was sturdy and the bunny lovey couldn't knock it down. Then I tossed it again, and the lovey got in through the top! It's like when I climb into my brother's crib at home."	
Child 3	When asked, "How did you build your garden castle?" Hakeem at first said he did not know. The teacher offered, "I noticed your castle had some very tall parts. How did those get built?" Hakeem then responded, "I picked out all the long blocks and then I stacked them together."		

Universal Design for Learning Supports for Preschoolers

In the overview, a variety of UDL supports are suggested for all children for different aspects of the reflective thinking activity. In this activity, children create a class engineering notebook. For some children with communication or cognitive challenges, this activity may be a struggle. Children such as Brandon would benefit from working in mixed-ability groups, where they can work together on the task and build on each other's strengths and weaknesses. Both Brandon and José will need additional support in expressing their thoughts and could benefit from practice with the vocabulary and time to formulate their responses for engineering circle ahead of time with an adult. Picture communication boards can be helpful for all students to help them think about their vocabulary and spell words. A board with all the key words from the unit can be put on tables with the words below the pictures. Children can use the pictures to remember the concepts and know how to write the words for their journals. In addition, the

Self-Reflection Checklist

- Did I take time to discuss with children what it means to "record" ideas, plans, and results?
- Did I talk about the word *reflection* with children?
- Did I model how to create an engineering notebook page?
- Did I offer children access to the plans they made for their garden protectors or photographs of what they created?
- Did I offer children multiple means of expressing their reflections about their garden protectors (e.g., discussion, drawing, writing, dictation, reenactment)?

 Essentials to Remember

- Help children remember the plans they initially made for their garden protectors.
- Help children compare and contrast what they actually created with the plans they made.
- Ask open-ended questions to prompt further reflection. These are questions that request information that is not already obvious. Try question starters such as "What happened when . . . ?," "How did you . . . ?," or "Why do you think . . . ?"
- Tell children what you notice about their engineering notebook pages.

engineering words can be added to a word wall with pictures or picture symbols to help children remember the words and connect the concepts to the written words, enhancing their language development.

RESOURCES

Developmental Trajectory and Key Standards and Guidelines

Dichtelmiller, M.L. (2001). *Omnibus guidelines: Preschool through third grade.* Ann Arbor, MI: Rebus Planning Assoc.

Heroman, C., Burts, D.C., Berke, K., & Bickart, T.S. (2010). *Teaching strategies GOLD: Objectives for development and learning: Birth through kindergarten.* Washington, DC: Teaching Strategies, Inc.

High/Scope Press & High/Scope Educational Research Foundation. (2003). *Preschool Child Observation Record.* Ypsilanti, MI: Authors.

Ohio Department of Education. (2012). *Ohio early learning and development standards.* Retrieved from http://education.ohio.gov/getattachment/Topics/Early-Learning/Early-Learning-Content-Standards/The-Standards/ELDS-ATL-FINAL-21-October-2012-pdf.pdf.aspx

PBS Kids. (2014). *Child development tracker: Approaches to learning.* Retrieved from http://www.pbs.org/parents/childdevelopmenttracker/five/approachestolearning.html

Publications

Epstein, A. (2003, September). How planning and reflection develop young children's thinking skills. *Beyond the Journal.* Retrieved from http://www.naeyc.org/files/yc/file/200309/Planning&Reflection.pdf

High Scope Videos. (2014). *Recall time.* Retrieved from http://www.highscope.org/Content.asp?ContentId=381

Hong, S.B., & Broderick, J.T. (2003). Instant video revisiting for reflection: Extending the learning of children and teachers. *Early Childhood Research & Practice, 5*(1). Retrieved from http://ecrp.uiuc.edu/v5n1/hong.html

Nimmo, J., & Hallet, B. (2008). Children in the garden: A place to encounter natural and social diversity. *Beyond the Journal.* Retrieved from https://www.naeyc.org/files/yc/file/200801/BTJNatureNimmo.pdf

Project Approach. (2014). *Project approach.* Retrieved from http://www.projectapproach.org/project-approach-m3

Tools of the Mind. (2014). *Preschool: Play plans.* Retrieved from http://www.toolsofthemind.org/curriculum/preschool

Additional Suggestions for Encouraging Reflective Thinking

- Encourage children to remember what they have done during meal/snack.

- Create photographic histories of the class.

- Talk about the children who may have left the group, especially when the present children mention them.

- Encourage parents to reflect with children on things they have done at the end of each season.

- Provide opportunities for children to share in pairs or small groups.

- Engage in journaling, a reflective activity that can build drawing and literacy skills.

- Let children take digital photographs and write or dictate the captions later in the day.

7 Collaborative Thinkers

Collaborative thinking is an essential component of the engineering design process. Collaboration is a familiar concept for most educators. They collaborate among themselves as teachers and with parents and families. Similarly, educators seek to foster collaboration among children working together to accomplish a goal. This chapter focuses on 1) the development and importance of collaborative thinking and 2) strategies educators can use to support the development of young children's collaborative thinking.

Although *collaboration* is a common term, what does it really mean? To collaborate means to work with someone or a group to produce or create something. Collaboration involves two or more people coordinating their actions in order to achieve a common goal. Therefore, collaboration involves social interactions such as expressing oneself and listening to and contributing ideas. Collaboration also involves cognitive tasks, such as integrating information and concepts, remembering prior events, and critiquing ideas. Thus, collaborative thinking requires both cognitive and social competencies and enables a child to effectively engage in collaborative action.

Collaborative thinking begins in infancy and develops rapidly over the first 5 years of life. Early collaborative behaviors can be seen in games and routines with infants—for example, when an infant and a caregiver pass a ball back and forth. Toddlers and preschoolers demonstrate collaborative thinking when they work together to figure out how to stabilize a tall block tower. They might plan and build as a team, with one child implementing the idea and the other observing the tower's stability and suggesting modifications.

Young children require active experiences with collaboration in order to develop their understanding of it. Very young children can begin to understand that partners share a common goal. In the early months and years, children develop the capacity for joint attention, in which they share a focus on an object with an adult or another child. Then, during the toddler and preschool years, children develop their cooperative play skills and begin to develop an awareness of their role as a collaborative partner (Brownell, Ramani, & Zerwas, 2006; Henderson, Wang, Matz, & Woodward, 2013). Research shows that active experiences with collaborative games and activities improve the collaborative thinking skills of infants and young children (Henderson et al., 2013).

Caregivers play an important role in scaffolding the development of collaborative thinking in young children. Being an effective member of a problem-solving team is a skill that can be taught and learned. The importance of collaborative thinking is recognized in early learning standards such as those found in the areas of social competence, approaches to learning, cognitive development, and language development.

WHY IS COLLABORATIVE THINKING IMPORTANT?

Collaborative thinking is the primary "social ingredient" of problem solving, and its importance cannot be overstated. Few real-world problems are solved by a single individual. Instead, groups and teams of individuals must work together effectively, asking questions, pooling information, contributing to and critiquing concepts and ideas, and jointly testing solutions. The skills needed to collaborate in intellectual inquiry processes are complex, high-level skills that rely on social and cognitive competencies. Collaborative thinking requires competencies in language and communication, social skills, and critical thinking, and collaborative action requires the integration of these competencies.

Collaborative thinking is important in science and engineering and also for all domains of development and early learning. Success in educational settings, as well as in the workplace, requires effective collaboration and teamwork. Thus, collaborative thinking is essential not just for engineering and problem solving but for healthy development and early learning more broadly.

Early learning standards provide a framework against which educators can align their efforts to promote collaborative thinking. For example, the Head Start Child Development and Early Learning Framework includes multiple components of collaborative thinking not just in the domain of Science Knowledge and Skills but also in the domains of Social and Emotional Development, Approaches to Learning, Language Development, and Logic and Reasoning (Office of Head Start, 2010). The Next Generation Science standard for kindergarten (K-PS2-1) states, "With guidance, [children] plan and conduct an investigation in collaboration with peers" (Next Generation Science Standards [NGSS] Lead States, 2013). Collaboration is thus clearly established as an essential area of early learning.

The teacher's role in promoting the development of collaborative thinking is emphasized throughout the NAEYC standards for early childhood program accreditation (NAEYC). As described earlier, collaborative thinking involves joint problem solving and therefore requires a complex combination of communication, reasoning, and social competencies. In high-quality early care and educational programs, teachers must consistently do the following:

- *1.C.01:* Facilitate an infant's social interaction when he or she is interested in looking at, touching, or vocalizing to others.

- *1.C.02:* Support children's development of friendships and provide opportunities for children to play with and learn from each other.

- *1.D.05.d:* Ensure that each child has an opportunity to contribute to the group.

- *1.D.05.e:* Encourage children to listen to one another.

- *1.F.02.b:* Guide and support children to play cooperatively with others.

- *3.D.11:* Create opportunities for children to engage in group projects and to learn from one another.

- *3.G.09:* Engage in collaborative inquiry with individual children and small groups of children (NAEYC, 2014, pp. 5–6, 8, 32, 36).

DEVELOPMENTAL CONTINUUM OF COLLABORATIVE THINKING

Infants

As infants develop the foundation for collaborative thinking, they begin by establishing positive relationships with caregivers as well as the other infants or children in their lives. They begin by showing an interest in others. Infants may reach out to touch a caregiver's face, for example. They also begin to react to the emotional expressions of others and participate as a member of a family and their classroom or child care setting.

The trusting relationships adults build with infants serve as the foundation from which infants can safely and securely explore the world, take risks, and seek solutions to everyday problems. One such everyday problem might be a toy just out of reach for a nonmobile infant. To obtain the toy, the infant might look at the toy, reach out in the direction of the toy, and then look up at the caregiver. A responsive caregiver understands what the infant is asking, talks with the infant, and helps him or her achieve the goal. These everyday interactions build trust and foster communication skills that are the foundation for collaborative thinking early in life.

Toddlers

The development of trusting relationships and attachment during infancy provides the safe foundation through which toddlers begin to explore the world beyond the immediate physical proximity of caregivers. Toddlers may venture away from a caregiver to explore a toy or another person, periodically checking back to see if the caregiver is still nearby. With the new-found independence that comes with crawling and walking, toddlers begin to encounter new challenges and they begin to understand collaboration in new ways. A toddler might pick up a shape sorting toy, and bring it back to the caregiver for help matching the shapes to the correct holes. Although this interaction might not yet be considered collaboration with a shared goal, the toddler is seeking help from another to achieve his or her goal. Seeking help from others and offering help to others are early prosocial skills that set the stage for more complex collaborative thinking.

Toddlers are developing their capacity to share a common goal with others and to coordinate their actions with others to achieve a goal. As they do so, they acquire the essential skills for cooperative thinking. Toddlers are often immersed in learning early prosocial skills such as sharing and turn-taking. Parents and teachers of toddlers are quite familiar with the joys and challenges of teaching these early prosocial skills. When a toddler is shouting, "Mine, mine, it's mine!" it may seem hard to imagine a collaborative toddler. At the same time, however, toddlers can surprise adults with their awareness of and concern for the feelings of others. Toddlers may share another's joy and excitement or respond with deep empathy at another's sorrow. A toddler may approach a crying child to offer a hug or concerned expression. Toddlers' empathic response develops over time, and they can become increasingly sensitive to others' perspectives. For example, a toddler might learn that when Lucas is sad, he likes his teddy bear, but when Maria is sad, she likes her blanket. This can be seen in action when a toddler brings Maria her blanket to try to comfort her. Through such actions, teachers can observe the development of social competencies such as understanding the perspectives and feelings of others. Learning how to share, take turns, comfort others, and interact with others in prosocial ways is an important foundation for collaborative thinking for toddlers and young preschoolers.

Preschoolers

During the preschool years, far more sophisticated social interactions and relationships develop. Children often develop their first friendships during the preschool years. They may seek repeated opportunities to engage collaboratively with peers. Much of this takes place in the context of pretend or dramatic play. To collaborate effectively, preschoolers must have an interest in engaging with others and be able to understand the perspectives of others, listen to and communicate ideas, and participate cooperatively and constructively in group situations. In early childhood settings, small-group activities and choice time provide rich opportunities for preschoolers to practice their emerging cooperative thinking skills.

Preschoolers often exhibit a drive to collaborate with others—for example, to build a city together out of blocks or to get dressed up and "play house." Researchers attribute this drive to an intrinsic motivation to work together with others in order to overcome challenges (Butler & Walton, 2013). Of course, some children demonstrate a preference for more solitary play and activities, with little apparent interest in collaborative play. Either way, children need support and guidance to develop the skills and knowledge to effectively collaborate with others. The next section turns to approaches and strategies for supporting the development of collaborative thinking among infants, toddlers, and preschoolers.

KEY GOALS FOR COLLABORATIVE THINKING EXPERIENCES

The following set of key words helps explore ways to support young children by describing their actions when they are engaged in collaborative thinking. These action words can be helpful when creating lesson and unit plan goals for children. It is helpful to think about these terms as guiding words for what children are working on at a metacognitive level. In other words, when watching children engage in the activities in this chapter or other activities designed to promote collaborative thinking, look for children doing these things.

 Key Words and Phrases for Collaborative Thinking for Goal Setting

- Trusting others (attachment)
- Observing
- Engaging with others
- Demonstrating social conversation
- Demonstrating social understanding
- Recording and sharing ideas
- Expressing self through words and making interests known
- Making viable arguments
- Critiquing others
- Sharing solutions
- Connecting concepts
- Integrating ideas

Look for these key words in the early learning experiences in this chapter, and keep them in mind when working with and assessing the development of collaborative thinking in the young children you are working with.

Strategies for Facilitating Collaborative Thinking

This book presents many strategies for promoting each thinking skill. Here are some key strategies for facilitating collaborative thinking with infants, toddlers, and preschoolers.

1. Consistently develop respectful, responsive, and caring relationships with young children. These caring interactions build attachment, trust, and empathy and are the essential foundation for prosocial behavior.

2. Model collaborating with others to achieve a shared goal. For example, explain to the children a problem you and a coteacher are facing and allow them to hear and see how you work together to find a solution.

3. Provide daily opportunities for small-group activities in which children can work together on a problem, a challenge, or a shared goal. During these activity and choice times, carefully observe children's collaborative efforts and step in to provide coaching, modeling, or other supports for children.

COLLABORATIVE THINKING EXPERIENCE FOR INFANTS

This collaborative thinking experience for infants focuses on supporting the development of positive and trusting relationships with others. Trusting relationships with others are the foundation for the development of collaborative thinking.

Make a "Find Your Friend" Book

Make a classroom book using photographs of children in the class, with photos of at least a few different children on each page. Be sure to use pictures of infants and caregivers in action, expressing emotion, and in caring interactions with friends and loved ones. Laminate the pages so they are sturdy and can be wiped clean if needed.

Materials

- A selection of photographs of children in the class, including groups of children interacting and playing

- Laminator

- Laminating sheets

- Hole punch and metal rings or other material for binding the book

Read the Book Together

Read the book with one or two infants. Search for friends in the book. When an infant points to or recognizes himself or herself or a friend's picture, celebrate the success together: "Hooray, we found Anna!" Model and reinforce that it is fun to be friends and that it is fun to see all your teachers and classmates in the pictures together.

Wonder and Ask Questions

Ask infants if they can find a smiling infant, an infant with a ball, or other emotions or actions depicted in the pictures you placed in the book. For example, you might suggest,

"Let's look for a picture of one of your friends who is smiling. Who has a big smile?" Be sure to celebrate when a smiling infant is found: "Look—you found Mark. He has a *really* big smile—hooray for us! Lonnie is helping Mark get his special blanket. I think that is why he is smiling, do you?"

Extend the Experience

Ask the infants to show the book to their parents or family members at pickup time. Tell the family members about the classroom photograph book and what you all were noticing and saying about it.

Follow the Infant's Lead

This book can be available to infants in the classroom daily. Observe how each infant interacts with the book and the photographs. If you notice that certain features of the book interest one or more children, you might use that observation to guide you in your interactions and extensions of this experience.

Figure 7.1 is a rubric that will help you evaluate how well the infant engaged in the collaborative learning experience. Examples are provided of the information you would record based on the infant's performance on the activity.

Universal Design for Learning Supports for Infants

As a reminder, the suggestions for infants in the text box are aimed at all children but address some needs of infants who have physical or multiple challenges that prevent them

Rubric			
Rate the child's level of participation and understanding on the continuum. Add evidence/descriptions for each child.	Develops secure attachments with trusted adults; reacts to others' emotional expressions; seeks to elicit responses from others	Uses trusted adults as a secure base from which to explore the world; shows concern about the feelings of others; engages in helping, sharing, and turn-taking; has back-and-forth interactions with others	Recognizes basic emotional reactions of others and their causes; notices and accepts that others' feelings about a situation might be different from his or her own; participates cooperatively and constructively in group situations; coordinates actions with others to achieve a common goal; understands perspectives of others
Child 1	Simon saw his own picture on the page, looked up at the teacher, and smiled, pointing at her picture.		
Child 2		Terence found Marijn's picture and took the book over to show him.	
Child 3	Lina climbed into the teacher's lap to see the book as she was reading it.		

Figure 7.1. Infant collaborative thinking experience rubric.

UDL Supports for Infants

- Use hand-over-hand guidance to help infants point. [David]

- Ask infants to match real objects with objects and people in the pictures. [All]

- Offer only two pictures of known friends or caregivers to start and expand book pages used. [All]

- Use a few basic signs to engage infants in the lesson and offer them opportunities to communicate (e.g., MORE, DONE, YES, NO). [Julia]

- Incorporate a switch with a YES, THAT'S MY FRIEND message to support participation in the activity, and consider adding another option with YES, THAT'S MY TEACHER. [All]

- Use a corner sitter or wedge for supported sitting in the group or with an adult. [David]

from independently manipulating the objects around them or from independently coming to engage in an activity. In this collaborative activity, one goal is to use UDL supports to increase interactions with adults and peers.

COLLABORATIVE THINKING EXPERIENCE FOR TODDLERS

This activity is again based on the children's book *One Duck Stuck* by Phyllis Root (1998). In this activity, the duck gets out of the mud with the help of his animal friends and the use of teamwork. After finishing the book, children can learn more about animal sounds and movements, and they can practice being different animals. Toddlers enjoy repeating the common

phrase and imitating the animal movements to help free the duck from the mud.

This activity emphasizes children's collaborative thinking skills—working with others, engaging in social conversation, expressing oneself, observing others, and integrating what you see with your own ideas. Although some of these thinking skills may not seem like they are part of collaboration, for toddlers, skills such as observation and expressing oneself are prerequisite skills to engagement in collaboration in work and in cooperative play. Children learn through parallel play and joint attention with caregivers and peers before or simultaneously to engaging in cooperative play. After reading the story, the children will work together to find toy animals in the mud using tools, clues, and teamwork.

Introducing the Experience

Prior to doing this activity with the children, fill tubs and/or a water/sand table with mud and hide various toys in the mud for the children to find. Teachers can choose to use a set of random small classroom toys to hide or stick more literally to *One Duck Stuck* (Root, 1998) and use sets of small plastic toys that reflect the animals in the book. Provide laminated pictures of all the objects in the tubs and keep track of which items are in which tubs as a UDL support for children. Think about whether it would be better in your classroom to have children working at one big table or at smaller tubs at tables or outside. Because this activity is about collaboration, try to have children work in groups of at least two, or have at least two children negotiating the same workspace so that they can engage with and observe each other.

To start the activity, finish reading the book *One Duck Stuck*. Ask the children questions as you read:

- What do you think will happen next?

- Will [animal] get him unstuck?

- How could he get him unstuck?

- How many animals will it take?

- Why are more animals better?

Depending on the ages of the toddlers, focus on counting the animals or making the animal sounds, the repetitive phrase, animal movements, or the animal pictures and their names. The goal of this activity is to help children remember the names of the animals and discuss how each animal can help the duck with his problem. Providing auditory, visual, and kinesthetic input assists children in making connections with what they are learning and connecting the information to previous information they have learned. For example, when children are looking pictures of the duck, the fish, or the moose, children are more likely to remember the names of the animals and their characteristics if they also move around like the animal and make the sound. Similarly, listening to the word *duck*, repeating *duck*, and physically matching a picture of a duck to a stuffed duck by putting the stuffed duck on the picture will reinforce what the children are learning. In addition, the reflective thinking experience (Chapter 6) focuses on sequencing the animals and story retelling. The whole set of toddler experiences helps build the children's knowledge about animals and mud and the thinking skills necessary for engaging in problem solving.

Mud Excavations

At the mud table or individual mud tubs, arrange children so that they have the opportunity to find two to four toy animals. Set up the mud table with mud; tools used at the beach or in a sand table for digging, such as shovels or spoons; and a space for the found toys. Buckets, cups, scoops, and other small containers are also helpful. At the mud table, prompt children to work together to locate and dig out objects. Encourage the children to brainstorm how they want to locate and dig out toys, and talk through the process with them as they are locating and digging. Some children may engage in trial and error or random digging, whereas others may have a strategy, such as starting from one side of the table and moving systematically to the other. Talk to the children throughout their play in this activity, narrating and extending their actions to provide language for their learning.

Keep pictures of the objects in the mud table next to the table to support the children. As children start to dig out an object, look at the pictures with them and ask them to predict what they are digging out and ask why they think it is that object. Discuss with the children what was found and what tools can be used to find objects and get objects unstuck. Encourage children to use shovels or scoops to move mud. Facilitate by offering suggestions of strategies that are working for others (e.g., "Cindy is really making progress moving mud with the shovel."). Discuss teamwork and working together as friends to find objects. Ask certain children to help others dig out an object. When it is time to stop and/or all toys have been found, ask the children to count how many toys they found with support. Teach children to use new vocabulary from the story by introducing it, discussing its meaning, and providing a picture or context to help children connect the word to a real-life thing or experience. Use picture symbols to support that vocabulary during the activity for all children so that the words adults and children say and write are connected to concepts that children understand. For example, have toy objects or real objects for new vocabulary so that children can learn the word and the characteristics. When they find an object, have them draw and label the object on a piece of paper. Adults can help them write the word and let them draw their representation of the object.

Summarizing the Experience

Use a camera to document the children's work and their experiences. Photographs and videos are helpful for the activity in this series on mud explorations in Chapter 6. After the children finish finding their toys, talk to the whole group about what they did to find the toys and what tools they used. Highlight creative ways that children found the toys and what tools worked best. Ask children to recall what the duck's problem was and how he

Self-Reflection Checklist

- Did I encourage children's enthusiasm to try different tools and strategies?
- Did I ask children to make predictions, and did I document their predictions about the duck's problem?
- Did I model how to make "I wonder if . . ." statements, and did I document children's "I wonder if . . ." statements?
- Did I scaffold children to use their words to describe the digging and the search process and give them new vocabulary, such as *shovel* and *burrow*?
- Did I encourage the children to try their own ideas for finding the toys?
- Did I offer multiple materials to find out what makes it easier or harder to find toys?
- Did I let the children try to manipulate the tools on their own?

Essentials to Remember

- Encourage children to work together and negotiate with their peers.
- Ask children to describe what they did and what they have learned.
- Ask them to identify their tools and objects and relate them to the story.
- Offer multiple opportunities to find objects and to dig.

solved it and what the children's alternative solutions were. Then discuss what problem they had today (i.e., needing to find their hidden toys in mud) and how they solved it. Start to familiarize children with the language involved in the engineering design process by discussing problems and solutions and what they tried that worked and what they tried that did not work. Remind them that engineers have to try many different ideas to find the best solution to a problem.

Universal Design for Learning Supports for Toddlers

This book offers various UDL supports that benefit all children in the classroom, including the specific profile children mentioned. This particular activity continues to use picture symbols to support vocabulary development and speech. It also still uses the picture symbols with words to support brainstorming responses to questions from the book. When reading the book, each child can be responsible for a different animal and have a picture or picture symbol to represent the page that he or she will read. Children who are nonverbal or just starting to speak can use an assistive technology device or a simple talking switch to participate by communicating the book's repeating phrase. A talking switch, often called a "Big Mac," is a large, colored, portable, battery-operated device that can be programmed with one message that is repeated aloud when the child hits the button.

When choosing toys to hide in the mud, assess the needs of your students and the materials available to determine if toys can be used interchangeably or if children are still at a concrete stage where they need to be finding toy animals to go with the story. This may vary depending on the child. Because *One Duck Stuck* has many vocabulary words, such as the animal names and sounds, it is helpful to preteach the words using picture cards to select children who many need more time to learn the words and connect them to prior knowledge. The book can be used at reading centers for more opportunities.

Figure 7.2 provides several UDL supports for this activity in the lesson template that are geared toward the profile children but can also be used with others in the classroom. Jessie benefits from her own individual tray and workspace, but other children may prefer that as well. Because this activity focuses on collaboration, this is a good opportunity to work on Jessie's needs and to support her to work with a peer buddy. Tam can work with a peer buddy for this task, and they can find the objects together and work collaboratively to dig them out. Tam can imitate other children and offer ideas as part of the group. Children who do not like getting dirty should be provided waterproof smocks and gloves and encouraged to try the activity with support.

The picture cards of hidden objects are another example of supports that are helpful for English language learners but also support all children. When using the pictures, children can look at the pictures as clues to predict what they are finding and connect the words to concepts. Picture symbols can also be used with children with physical challenges or linguistic challenges to ask them to choose what tools they want to use. To help scaffold children who may need to use pictures symbols in developing their reading skills, a choice of picture symbols is preferred over giving a choice between two actual tools, but both methods provide choices. The UDL Planning Sheet provides a summary of all the UDL supports used for this toddler unit.

Toddler Experience Planning Template

Problem-solving focus skill	Collaborative thinking
Motivating engineering problem	In the book *One Duck Stuck* by Phyllis Root (1998), the duck goes into a marsh and gets stuck in the mud. Various animal friends try to get the duck out of the mud, but it takes all them working together to free the duck.
Focus of this particular learning experience	In this activity, the children use tools and teamwork to look for hidden objects in the mud table.
Learning objectives for this particular experience	• Children will use tools to find objects in the mud. • Children will ask for help from a peer or adult to find an object. • Children will describe what they are doing to find an object and work with peers.
Materials needed	• Mud table • 1–2 toys (per child) or objects that can be easily hidden in the mud table/tubs of mud • Pictures of the objects hidden in the mud table • Tools (e.g., shovels, buckets, rakes, scoops, cups) • Rubber gloves • Individual tubs • Picture symbols for communication • Grips for use with tools • Individual copies of pictures for children who need their own

Elements of the learning experience		UDL supports
Introduce children to the problem	Finish reading *One Duck Stuck*. Discuss what happened in the book and how the duck was able to get out of the mud.	• Use a big book. • Provide additional copies of the book for the reading center. • Preteach key vocabulary with picture symbols.
Help children understand the problem-solving goal and constraints	Create a mud table or mud tubs and look for objects in the mud. Provide tools for children to use to look for toys hidden in mud. Encourage them to work together to find objects.	• Put children in small groups or offer individual tubs for pairs. • Supply grips for tools as needed for fine motor challenges. • Offer a timer for children who need to know the length of the activity. • Use picture cards to help children find objects.
Support children in demonstrating their thinking	Ask children what they are finding. Ask them how they found it. Encourage children to use a shovel or a scoop to move dirt. Ask them to match their objects to the picture.	• Use peer buddies or a teacher assistant to help children articulate ideas. • Have picture symbols available at mud table/tubs. • Use fading prompts or hand-over-hand guidance to help children find toys.
Provide opportunities for feedback and for trying again	Children need to use the tools provided or ask for other tools that are in the classroom. Provide children with specific feedback on how they are doing in their search, praise them for using the tools well or working together, and suggest other ideas they can try.	• Use fading prompts or hand-over-hand guidance to help children find toys. • Offer tool choices from two pictures or actual objects to encourage participation and choice making.
Help children share and learn from one another	Discuss teamwork and working together as friends to find objects. Ask certain children to help others dig out an object.	• Use peer buddies. • Provide grips and alternative tools for children with fine motor control challenges.

Figure 7.2. Toddler collaborative thinking experience overview and rubric.

(continued)

Figure 7.2.   *(continued)*

Rubric			
Rate the child's level of participation and understanding on the continuum. **Add evidence/ descriptions for each child.**	**Develops secure attachments with trusted adults; reacts to others' emotional expressions** *Does the child seek support and approval from the teachers/adults for his or her efforts?* *Does the child try the task and explore?*	**Uses trusted adults as a secure base from which to explore the world; shows concern about the feelings of others** *Does the child try to show adults his or her work and attempt to explain it in words?* *Does the child engage in parallel or cooperative play?*	**Engages with trusted adults; recognizes basic emotional reactions of others and their causes; notices and accepts that others' feelings about a situation might be different from his or her own** *Does the child engage with others during the task?* *Does the child recognize when it is his or her turn or attempt to solve the conflict with another child?*
Child 1	Holly played in the mud table and tried to find a few toys. She was happy when she found a toy and went over to the teacher to show her.		
Child 2		Victor played at the mud table with Kayla and Lee and showed the teacher how he could scoop the mud with the shovel.	
Child 3			Wanda wanted to use the shovel at the same time as Lee but asked for her turn and waited and used a scoop first instead.

COLLABORATIVE THINKING EXPERIENCE FOR PRESCHOOLERS

This collaborative thinking activity is based on the classic children's story *The Tale of Peter Rabbit* by Beatrix Potter (2002). In this beloved book, Peter Rabbit feasts on vegetables in Mr. McGregor's garden and eats so much that he feels sick. While searching for some parsley to cure his stomachache, Peter is discovered by Mr. McGregor and chased out of the garden. At home, his mother sends him to bed with only chamomile tea. Although the activity could be done with other similar books, we chose this book because it is a high-quality children's book that is readily available and popular in preschool classrooms.

The collaborative thinking skills emphasized in this activity involve recognizing the feelings that different individuals have in different situations. Asking children to think about how both Mr. McGregor and Peter Rabbit feel gives them a chance to practice identifying the emotional reactions of others and identifying the causes of those emotions. Challenging them to use engineering to help Peter Rabbit feel better helps them to see how problem solving can play a role in responding to negative feelings. Teachers can also support collaborative thinking in this activity by helping children work together on their vegetable carriers and by directly talking about how it feels to solve a problem with a friend.

This activity was designed to follow the other four preschool activities in this book. In those activities, children use engineering to pretend to solve a problem for a gardener named Mr. McGreely. If you have carried out those activities, briefly remind the children that previously they were engineers for Mr. McGreely, who wanted to protect his vegetables from bunny rabbits. Now they will use engineering in an opposite way—they will have a chance to solve a problem for a bunny rabbit! (Older preschoolers may appreciate a discussion about the fact that *The Tale of Peter Rabbit* is a fiction book with pretend animals who can talk and move like humans. You are going to ask them to pretend that Peter Rabbit can use his hands to hold the things that the children engineer. But you know that real bunnies cannot use their hands like people.)

Read *The Tale of Peter Rabbit* up until Peter has been chased out of the garden by Mr. McGregor. Ask students how Peter feels when he sneaks into the garden and how Mr. McGregor feels when he discovers Peter. Why do they have such different feelings? After considering the differences in Peter and Mr. McGregor's feelings, say, "Today we will try to make the rabbit feel better."

Ask children to recall the problems that Peter Rabbit faces in the story. You might reread portions of the story to help them with this task. If the children do not mention it, remind them that one of Peter's problems is that he eats so many vegetables that he feels sick. Once you have centered in on this problem, ask the children, "If Peter Rabbit had been able to carry vegetables home with him, instead of eating so many so quickly in the garden, do you think he would have gotten sick?" Tell the children that you are going to challenge them to solve Peter's belly ache problem by building and testing a vegetable carrier. You might ask them, "How will we know if you make a good vegetable carrier?" Children with previous engineering experience might suggest that you "test it," and they might even hone in on strength as the important property of the carrier. One 5-year-old told his teacher, "It has to be strong. We could find out how heavy carrots are to see how strong it has to be." This child led the teacher right to the design goal she had planned to share with the students: The bag needs to be strong enough to hold two pounds of carrots without breaking. At this point, you can ask a child to help you demonstrate the "carrot test"—load a paper bag with two pounds of baby carrots and show how you will lift it up to see if it can hold the load without tearing. When it has handles attached, you will be watching for the handles to stay connected to the bag (see Figures 7.3 and 7.4).

Both to foster their collaborative thinking and to make it easier to accomplish the hands-on task, children should work on this activity in pairs. Having two pairs of hands makes it easier to hold the bag open, hold handle materials in place, and add tape or other fastening materials. You will want to think carefully about how to pair up the children for this activity. If you have been noticing a lot of single-gender play lately, you can use this as an opportunity for boys and girls to work with each other. If you have a group with a large range of fine motor skills, you may want to support children who are still developing

Figure 7.3. The brown-bag vegetable carrier challenge offers an opportunity for this preschool girl to explore different tools used for hole punching.

Figure 7.4. Two preschool boys collaborate on perfecting their brown-bag vegetable carrier design. They asked their teacher if they could keep working together on the task even though their classmates were leaving for an activity in another room.

fine motor control by pairing them with a child who is showing more mastery in that area. You can also have children choose their own partners. This activity presents a wonderful context for the children to think about what friends can do together and to practice the skills of asking a friend to collaborate on a project. When helping children find a partner, think about the previous strengths and needs you have identified and the UDL supports children have utilized to be successful in previous lessons.

Help the children find the partners you have chosen for them, or guide them through a routine for finding a collaborator on their own. Supply the children with small paper lunch bags, tape, and craft materials such as string, straws, pipe cleaners, and cardboard for adding handles to the bags. They will serve as vegetable carriers for Peter Rabbit. Next, help the children test their vegetable carriers by loading them with two pounds of baby carrots and gently lifting them up. If the handles fall off, ask the children what they can try to help the handles stay connected. Take photos as children build and test their vegetable carriers (see Figure 7.5).

At "engineering circle" time, help children share their vegetable carriers or photos of their carriers. Talk about what it felt like to have the help of a friend to build and test the vegetable carriers. Discuss how Peter Rabbit might feel if he had a vegetable carrier to use in the garden. Also talk about how Mr. McGregor would feel if he saw Peter Rabbit using a vegetable carrier! Ask what students might do next. We worked with one excited 4-year-old who wanted to build a new bag at home with wider and bigger straps. He remembered the persistent thinking activity and wanted to improve upon what he had done at school.

Figure 7.6 provides an overview of teacher preparation and facilitation steps for this learning experience.

Figure 7.5. As his teacher offers an outstretched collaborative hand, a preschool child proudly lifts his brown-bag vegetable carrier and discovers it successfully holds 2 pounds of carrots.

"Window into a Classroom" Anecdote

A group of 4- and 5-year-old children were given the vegetable carrier challenge and asked what materials they wanted to use to make handles. Here is how they responded. Notice how Child 3 and Child 5 began collaborating spontaneously:

Child 1:   Cardboard!

Teacher: Okay, we've got some cardboard.

Child 2:   Those pokey things.

Teacher: What are those little pokey things called? These things? Does anyone know what these are called?

Child 3:   Pipe cleaners.

Teacher: Okay, what else?

Child 4:   Um, in the olden days people used some thick straw.

Teacher: Hmm, I don't know if I have straw. But I have string.

Child 4:   That might be okay.

Teacher: Okay, so *you* might have to figure out how to make it thick. What's another thing that you could use?

Child 3:   We could make the handles out of playdough or clay.

Teacher: Okay, what else could we use? There's one more thing that you guys might like. You can decide whether to use it or not. Here's my big roll of tape.

Child 3:   (To Child 5) Let's use pipe cleaners! 'Cuz, like, we could put the pipe cleaners right through the bag.

Child 5:   (To Child 3) Yeah, pipe cleaners: Put 'em through a hole and then tape 'em on so it's strong.

Child 3:   (To Child 5) Yeah, just to be really, really secure. And we can use two different kinds of tape: One on one handle and one on the other.

 ## Self-Reflection Checklist

- Did I ask children to think about the feelings of both Mr. McGregor and Peter Rabbit in the story? Did I prompt further to have children consider the causes of those different feelings?

- For the vegetable carrier challenge, did I think carefully about how to pair up the children or how to teach them a routine for finding their own partner?

- Did I model how to resolve a social conflict about how to build or fix a vegetable carrier?

- Did I model how to test a vegetable carrier with two pounds of carrots?

- Did I encourage children to test their vegetable carrier early and often?

- Did I ask children questions to help them reflect on why their carrier did or did not hold the carrots without breaking?

Preschool Experience Planning Template

Problem-solving focus skill	Collaborative thinking
Motivating engineering problem	In the book *The Tale of Peter Rabbit* by Beatrix Potter (2002), Peter Rabbit sneaks into Mr. McGregor's garden and eats as many vegetables as he can before Mr. McGregor chases him away. He eats so many vegetables that he feels sick. He could solve this problem by using a strong container to carry vegetables home with him.
Focus of this particular learning experience	Whereas *Munchal Munchal Munchal* (Fleming, 2002) is told from the perspective of a gardener who wants to protect his vegetables, *The Tale of Peter Rabbit* is from the point of view of a hungry rabbit. This learning experience is focused on helping children consider the emotional reactions associated with both perspectives and engineering a solution for the rabbit instead of for the gardener.
Learning objectives for this particular experience	• Children will identify the emotional reactions of both Mr. McGregor and Peter Rabbit during the garden chase and explain why they have those reactions. • Children will work with a friend to build and test a vegetable carrier for Peter Rabbit.
Materials needed	• Brown paper lunch bags • Masking tape • String • Paper • Cardboard • Pipe cleaners • Clothespins • 2 lb of baby carrots • *The Tale of Peter Rabbit* by Beatrix Potter • Camera

Elements of the learning experience		UDL supports
Introduce children to the problem	Read *The Tale of Peter Rabbit* until the part where Peter has been chased out of the garden by Mr. McGregor. Ask students how Peter feels when he sneaks into the garden and how Mr. McGregor feels when he discovers Peter. Why do they have such different feelings?	• Provide an opportunity to reread the book in centers or at reading time. • Offer an interactive version of the book. • Allow some students to develop answers ahead of the activity with an adult. • Provide a feelings chart with faces for children to point to the feelings of the characters.
Help children understand the problem-solving goal and constraints	Talk about the problems that Peter Rabbit faces in the story. One problem is that Peter eats so many vegetables that he feels sick. If Peter Rabbit had been able to carry vegetables home with him, rather than eating so many in the garden, he would not have gotten so sick. Children will solve Peter's problem by building and testing a vegetable carrier that is strong enough for 2 pounds of vegetables. They can use a brown paper lunch bag, tape, and craft materials to build their vegetable carrier (i.e., to add strong handles to the lunch bag). Pair each child with a carefully chosen partner, or guide children through a routine to choose their own collaborator for this task.	• Have peer buddies in mixed ability groups. • Offer individual work time with an adult as option. • Offer alternative material options to allow children with fine motor challenges to work independently.
Support children in demonstrating their thinking	Support the children in trying different ways to add handles to a brown paper lunch bag. As the children work, ask them questions about the materials they have chosen, the shape of the handles they are building, and the attachment methods they are trying.	• Use picture symbols for key vocabulary. • Use a communication board or interactive communication device. • Supply easy-cut scissors or lefty scissors. • Offer choices of prepared materials for children who need more cognitive support.

Figure 7.6. Preschool collaborative experience overview and rubric.

(continued)

Figure 7.6. *(continued)*

Provide opportunities for feedback and for trying again	Help the children test their vegetable carriers by loading them with 2 pounds of baby carrots and seeing if the handles stay connected. If the handles fall off, ask the children what they can try to help the handles stay connected.	• Use peer buddies in mixed ability groups. • Offer individual work time with an adult as an option.
Help children share and learn from one another	Take photos as children build and test their vegetable carriers. During a large-group time, share the photos and use them as an entry point to discuss what it felt like to work together with friends and grown-ups to build and test the vegetable carriers. Talk about how Peter Rabbit might feel if he had a vegetable carrier to use in the garden. Also talk about how Mr. McGregor would feel if he saw Peter Rabbit using a vegetable carrier!	• Provide a feelings chart with faces for children to point to the feelings of the characters. • Offer a smaller group discussion option.

Rubric			
Rate the child's level of participation and understanding on the continuum. Add evidence/ descriptions for each child.	Demonstrates turn-taking while working on the vegetable-carrier task; shows concern about the feelings of others	Interacts with peers while working on the vegetable-carrier task; recognizes basic emotional reactions of others and their causes; notices and accepts that others' feelings about a situation might be different from his or her own	Communicates thinking about vegetable carrier to peers; interacts with peers to plan, coordinate roles, and cooperate on the vegetable-carrier task; negotiates to resolve social conflicts about the task
Child 1			Eamon described his idea for pipe cleaner handles to another child and suggested that he bend the pipe cleaners while she makes the holes for them. When she said, "No," Eamon asked her, "Well, how else could we do it?"
Child 2		After listening to the story, Jordan said that Mr. McGregor probably felt like Mr. Greeley: frustrated that a bunny was taking his vegetables. When asked to work with Harvey on a vegetable carrier, Jordan held his hand and walked with him to the materials box.	
Child 3	Sarita and Andy were paired by the teacher. They did not talk with each other but took turns adding materials to their paper bag. Sarita taped a piece of string, then Andy added a cardboard strip, then Sarita taped more string, and so forth.		

Essentials to Remember

- Because the main goal of this activity is fostering collaborative thinking, adult support in this activity should be focused on helping children interact with each other as they work.

- Although children should feel successful with the engineering task of building and testing a vegetable carrier, it is more important in this activity to encourage their productive interactions with peers.

- Acknowledge and encourage turn-taking. When a child suggests that her partner take a turn with the building, reinforce that action with specific praise: "I noticed that you asked Lisa to tape on the second piece of string! Great job. Engineers solve problems better when they work together like that."

- Ask children to share ideas with each other as the primary audience rather than an adult. When a bag's handles fall off during testing, ask both children in the pair to share ideas with each other for next steps: "Hmm. What happened to the handle here? Miguel, can you tell Adele your ideas for fixing it? Adele, can you share some ideas for Miguel to think about?"

- Offer resources for children to communicate their ideas to each other through modes other than talking. Perhaps they can act out the Peter Rabbit story in the dramatic play area first. Or they might be more successful interacting with the physical materials if they each draw a picture first and then describe their pictures to each other.

Universal Design for Learning Supports for Preschoolers

In the overview, a variety of UDL supports are suggested for all children for different aspects of the collaborative thinking activity. This activity encourages children to create a vegetable carrier by adding handles in a way that is strong enough to support the carrots. For some children with spatial or cognitive challenges, this activity may be a struggle. As in other activities, Brandon would benefit from working with a partner who can help him put materials together and be patient as he expresses himself. Partners should build on each other's strengths and weaknesses. Both Brandon and José will need additional support in expressing their thoughts and could benefit from practice with the vocabulary and time to formulate their responses for engineering circle ahead of time with an adult. To avoid frustration, encourage children to try not to worry about finding a correct answer; rather, they should try different solutions and learn from others. Focus on supporting children like Brandon and José to be able to verbalize their reasoning behind their designs with pictures, picture symbols, or words. Have some preprepared materials for handles ready for children who might succeed with less frustration by first making the carrier from some options, as opposed to generating the ideas completely on their own.

RESOURCES

Developmental Trajectory and Key Standards and Guidelines

Dichtelmiller, M.L. (2001). *Omnibus guidelines: Preschool through third grade.* Ann Arbor, MI: Rebus Planning Assoc.

Head Start Child Development and Early Learning Frameworks. (2010). *Social & emotional development: Cooperation.* Retrieved from http://eclkc.ohs.acf.hhs.gov/hslc/hs/sr/approach/cdelf/se_dev.html

High/Scope Press & High/Scope Educational Research Foundation. (2003). *Preschool Child Observation Record.* Ypsilanti, MI: Authors.

Ohio Department of Education. (2012). *Ohio early learning and development standards.* Retrieved from http://education.ohio.gov/getattachment/Topics/Early-Learning/Early-Learning-Content-Standards/ELDS-Social-Emotional-FINAL-October-2012.pdf.aspx

PBS Kids. (2014). *Child development tracker: Approaches to learning.* Retrieved from http://www.pbs.org/parents/childdevelopmenttracker/five/approachestolearning.html

Publications

Bodrova, E., & Leong, D.J. (2003). Chopsticks and counting sticks: Do play and foundational skills need to compete for the teacher's attention in an early childhood classroom? *Young Children, 58*(3). Retrieved from http://www.naeyc.org/files/yc/file/200305/Chopsticks_Bodrova.pdf

Cartwright, S. (1995, May). Block play: Experiences in cooperative living and learning. *Child Care Information Exchange,* 30–41.

Hirsch, E.S. (Ed.). (1996). *The block book* (3rd ed.). Washington, DC: NAEYC.

Lau, P.N. (2009). The effects of cooperative learning on preschoolers' mathematics problem solving abilities. *Educational Studies in Mathematics, 72*(3), 307–324.

Leong, D.J., & Bodrova, E. (2012). Assessing and scaffolding make-believe play. *Young Children, 67*(1), 28–34. Retrieved from http://www.naeyc.org/files/yc/file/201201/Leong_Make_Believe_Play_Jan2012.pdf

Ostrosky, M., & Meadan, H. (2010). Helping children play and learn together. *Young Children, 65*(1), 104–110. Retrieved from http://www.naeyc.org/files/yc/file/201001/OstroskyWeb0110.pdf

Rogers, D.L. (1987). Fostering social development through block play. *Day Care and Early Learning.* Retrieved from http://www.imaginationplayground.com/images/content/2/9/2976/Fostering-Social-Development-Through-Block-Play.pdf

Sandall, S. (2003, May). Play modifications for children with disabilities. *Beyond the Journal.* Retrieved from https://www.naeyc.org/files/yc/file/200305/PlayModifications_Sandall_1.pdf

Additional Suggestions for Encouraging Collaborative Thinking

- Encourage open-ended play in all the areas of the environment: blocks, dramatic play, art, music, outside, and so forth.

- Even in circle time, provide opportunities for children to talk to one other child to answer a simple question.

- Group games support children in interacting with rules.

8

Curious, Persistent, Flexible, Reflective, and Collaborative Teachers

This book has focused on two big ideas. The first is that young children can be emergent engineers. As described, preschoolers, toddlers, and even infants exhibit many of the foundational skills used in the complex problem-solving activity of engineering design. Furthermore, teachers and caregivers can support and foster the development of young children's problem-solving skills. The second big idea in this book is that children's emergent engineering activities can further develop their higher order thinking skills and at the same time provide an exciting context for integrated STEM learning in the early years. Previous chapters presented strategies for teaching curious, persistent, flexible, reflective, and collaborative thinking with very young children using a universal design approach. We have shown how applying this problem-solving framework promotes STEM learning and development among all young children and also enhances learning across the curriculum in areas such as language and literacy, approaches to learning, and the domain of social and emotional development.

This final chapter deepens the potential impact of these engineering design experiences by applying our framework and the five higher order thinking skills to the adults and the broader classroom or early learning context. Most of this book has focused on children's thinking. Implementing early learning experiences such as those presented in this book provides rich opportunities for young children to develop their emerging engineering and higher order thinking skills. Now the approach is extended to focus on adult thinking. It is not enough to just plan discrete activities for children to develop their thinking skills. Adults must continually develop and model their use of higher order thinking skills and do so in ways that are visible to children.

Research shows that children's learning can be greatly enhanced when the overall learning environment and the adults in this environment reflect, model, and demonstrate higher order thinking skills in everyday routines and interactions. This chapter examines *teachers'* curious, persistent, flexible, reflective, and collaborative thinking and suggests concrete strategies for incorporating, extending, and modeling these higher order thinking skills in classrooms and other early learning environments.

The five thinking skills presented in this book are important professional competencies for educators. The widely used Classroom Assessment Scoring System (CLASS) identifies each of these skills as key components of high-quality teaching (Pianta, La Paro, & Hamre, 2008). For example, asking questions, wondering (curiosity), and being persistent are identified as high-quality teaching behaviors that promote young children's concept

development. The code of ethics of both the NAEYC and the DEC of the Council for Exceptional Children call for educators to establish and maintain collaborative relationships and to consistently engage in reflective practices (Division for Early Childhood, 2009; Feeney, Freeman, & Pizzolongo, 2012).

Curiosity, persistence, flexibility, reflection, and collaboration can also be thought of as teaching dispositions. A *disposition* is a "value, commitment, or an ethic that is internally held and externally demonstrated" (Cudahy, Finnan, Jarusiewicz, & McCarty, 2002). Dispositions are often defined as habits of mind and action. Together, these thinking skills and habits represent a professional disposition toward lifelong learning. Many consider lifelong learning to be a core component of professionalism in teaching (Stremmel, 2007). Educators of young children learn with and from children in a joint process of inquiry. Their curiosity about how children learn and make sense of the world guides them to carefully observe and record children's behaviors. They reflect on these observations and explore ways to extend each child's learning and development through intentional and deliberate teaching practices and interactions. When they encounter challenges, they do not give up—on themselves, their colleagues, children, or families. They persist in seeking new solutions to ensure that all children and families have opportunities for growth, learning, and joy. Educators know that collaboration with families and colleagues is essential to their ability to be effective in this process.

This cycle of professional practice reflects an inquiry stance and a commitment to lifelong learning. It is important to nurture and support this curiosity, persistence, flexibility, reflection, and collaboration professionally and among co-workers for two primary reasons:

1. *To solve teaching challenges* by strengthening themselves as lifelong learners and problem solvers who are equipped to support the development of all young children

2. *To model problem-solving* in order to support and deepen the development of children's thinking skills

Next, each thinking skill is described and applied to adults in the context of teaching young children from birth to age 5. Then the final section of this chapter illustrates strategies teachers can use in applying this problem-solving framework to everyday problems they face.

CURIOUS TEACHERS

We have learned that curiosity fuels learning and exploration among children and is an essential foundation for cognitive development and science learning. Curious thinking is just as important for teachers. A curious teacher is best defined as a teacher who asks

Curious Teachers . . .

- Wonder aloud
- Ask open-ended questions
- Talk with excitement about learning and exploring

questions and wonders. Curiosity fuels effective teaching by motivating us to ask questions and seek new solutions. Professor Andrew Stremmel writes, "Teaching is a process involving continual inquiry and renewal, and a teacher, among other things, is first and foremost a questioner" (2007, p. 1).

When teachers demonstrate and model curiosity, they create learning environments that value and nurture children's curiosity. These are learning environments filled with excitement, exploration, and imagination. In high-quality classrooms, teachers consistently demonstrate curious thinking by asking open-ended questions and wondering. Research affirms that these practices support children's thinking and concept development (Pianta, La Paro, & Hamre, 2008).

PERSISTENT TEACHERS

Persistence is an essential disposition for early educators, especially when working with children with special needs or challenging behaviors. Educators know that teaching young children is complex and that one approach or strategy will not work with every child. Persistent educators hold high expectations for all children. They do not give up when their first strategy for engaging a child does not work. They stick with it and keep trying new strategies until they are successful. When teachers of young children use persistence, they engage with a child "in a sustained back and forth exchange with the intention of helping him or her really understand ideas or get to the correct answer. The teacher persists in these efforts rather than just stopping with one clarifying comment" (Pianta, La Paro, & Hamre, 2008, p. 73). This is the essence of persistence and of high-quality teaching practices.

When teachers model persistence, take risks, and try a new approach in the face of a challenge, they foster the development of persistent thinking. Teachers can model several key lessons about persistence; for example, 1) persistence means trying again and often trying a new or different approach, and 2) persistence can result in improvement and success. Persistence also relies heavily on another thinking skill in our problem-solving framework: reflection. Persistence and reflection go hand in hand. When teachers try again and again, they do not just repeat the same approach over and over. They reflect on their approach to inform their next attempt.

 Persistent Teachers . . .

- Do not give up
- Believe they can succeed and believe every child can succeed
- Seek out alternative approaches and solutions
- Learn from prior attempts

Flexible Teachers . . .

- Are open-minded
- Consider new and different ideas
- Change direction or course as needed
- Are willing to take a risk

FLEXIBLE TEACHERS

Flexible thinking is the hallmark of effective early childhood educators. They must adapt and improve daily when their best planning and intentions get disrupted by the unexpected. An outdoor drama activity must suddenly get moved indoors when a storm arrives. An elaborate cooking activity must be adapted when the oven decides to quit. Another dimension of flexible thinking is the awareness that there is almost always more than one way to solve a given problem.

So how can educators model this flexible thinking in ways that enhance children's thinking? One way that teachers model flexibility is by thinking out loud as they adapt a planned outdoor activity to an indoor one. When a teacher says what he or she is doing or thinking, this is sometimes referred to as "self-talk," a high-quality teaching practice described by Pianta, La Paro, and Hamre (2008) as a strategy for modeling and promoting language development. Another way that teachers demonstrate flexible thinking is by allowing children to suggest many possible responses to a question or a problem rather than looking for just one answer.

REFLECTIVE TEACHERS

Reflection means that teachers must step back from their practice and make time to ask questions and wonder. Reflective thinking can be considered on three levels: reflection *on* action, reflection *in* action, and reflection *for* action (Killion & Todnem, 1991; Schön, 1983, 1987). Teachers reflect *on* their practices when they think about and talk about why an interaction or a lesson did or did not go as planned. They reflect *in* action when they take a moment to think during a situation or interaction with children. When they do this and then adapt or modify their actions to get the response they want from children, they are reflecting in action (Thomas & Packer, 2013). Teachers reflect *for* action when they think and talk about how to prepare for an action or interaction. Reflection is the process that informs how educators differentiate and adapt their teaching for individual learners. In diverse and inclusive classrooms, differentiated instruction and implementation of UDL supports are essential for engaging and supporting each individual learner.

 Reflective Teachers . . .

- Take time to pause and think about their teaching practices
- Observe and take notes
- Wonder why an activity or interaction did or did not go as planned
- Notice and adapt based on prior experiences

Teachers reflect regularly. Reflection can come to be a natural part of the teaching process. Yet often they reflect in private or only with other adults. Children often do not know how or when their teachers reflect. How can teachers make reflection more visible to children in ways that model this thinking process? One way is to think and wonder out loud, as suggested for flexible thinking. For example, share with children that you noticed how much they liked the book you read yesterday about fire engines. Now you are wondering if they might be interested in visiting the local fire station or inviting a firefighter to visit the class. When a teacher takes notes about an experience to refer to later when evaluating the experience, he or she can share this reflective process with children, making it visible to them.

COLLABORATIVE TEACHERS

When teachers think collaboratively, they engage with others to achieve a shared goal. Therefore, the foundation for collaboration is the presence or development of a shared goal. In the complex work of teaching, collaboration with colleagues enables teachers to reflect and inquire together about problems and challenges in order to develop new approaches and solutions. Sometimes this collaboration involves multidisciplinary teams coming together to share, reflect, and
plan for how to support an individual child. Other times, members of a teaching team meet to think together about how children are learning in their classrooms and how to modify, adapt, and expand their teaching to extend that learning.

Research confirms that these teacher collaboration processes are associated with teacher learning and improved teaching practices (Hord, 1997; Nelson & Slavit, 2008). Learning together with other teachers about how to improve teaching can be one of the most rewarding and professionally enriching aspects of our work.

APPLYING THINKING SKILLS TO PRACTICE

The problem-solving framework, with its five thinking skills, will now be applied to two teaching scenarios. This use of the problem-solving framework is demonstrated for two purposes: first, to solve a teaching challenge, and second, to model problem-solving thinking for children.

1. *Solving a teaching challenge:* A typical teaching problem illustrates how a teacher applies these thinking skills to his or her practice.

❋ Collaborative Teachers . . .

- Make time to talk, share, and learn with others
- Establish shared goals with others
- Demonstrate respect for differing perspectives and ideas
- Value collaborative problem solving

Mariela, a preschool teacher, has noticed that 3-year-old Cassie consistently avoids drawing and writing. Mariela is concerned that Cassie's resistance to drawing will interfere with her development of important school readiness skills. How can Mariela use the five problem-solving skills as a teacher to figure out how to support Cassie's learning?

During this school year, Mariela has tried several different approaches she previously used with other children to engage Cassie in drawing activities. Despite these repeated attempts, Cassie still refuses to participate in any drawing or writing activities. When pushed, Cassie becomes upset and refuses to talk or participate in any activity for a period of time.

Mariela becomes curious—she wonders why Cassie avoids drawing. All the other children in the class regularly engage in these kinds of activities and seem to enjoy them. They "sign" their names on the white board upon arrival in the morning and sit at the writing center table drawing pictures during activity times.

Mariela reflects on what Cassie chooses to do most often and how Cassie has responded in the past when encouraged to use drawing materials. Mariela shares her concerns at a collaborative teaching team meeting. The teachers all decide to keep observational notes this week in response to the questions about Cassie. One of the teachers suggests they ask Cassie's family about her drawing experiences at home, and they all agree this will be helpful information.

At the next week's meeting, the teachers share their notes. They are fascinated to learn that Cassie in fact did engage in a writing activity that week. Cassie spent most of her time playing dress-up in the dramatic play area. Another child brought a pad of paper and markers to the area to make a shopping list that week, and Cassie started writing a list of her own. However, Cassie's parents reported that she does not seem to have an interest in drawing at home.

Teachers brought Cassie's shopping list to their meeting. They reflected collaboratively on Cassie's writing. One teacher suggested that Cassie might be more motivated to write when she is with peers in the context of an activity that is meaningful. They then generated a list of new strategies for engaging Cassie in drawing and writing, all building on Cassie's demonstrated interest in writing in the context of dramatic play activities. Table 8.1 summarizes how Mariela applied the five thinking skills to solve a problem in her practice.

2. *Modeling problem-solving for children:* The second scenario illustrates how teachers can model the problem-solving process and make it visible to children.

    Pierre, a teacher of toddlers, is confronted by a problem on the playground one day. One of the three tricycles has a broken wheel, and he has a class of eight toddlers who all want

Table 8.1. How Mariela used problem-solving skills: The case of Cassie's writing

Curious	Persistent	Flexible	Reflective	Collaborative
• Wondered about Cassie's behavior • Wondered how Cassie was at home	• Tried multiple strategies to engage Cassie • Believed that Cassie could succeed	• Was open to generating new approaches to try • Was willing to follow Cassie's lead	• Took observational notes • Reviewed and evaluated prior efforts to engage Cassie	• Met with the team to discuss • Pooled knowledge and insights with the team • Learned that Cassie was writing with her peers

to ride the tricycles today. How can Pierre model his use of the five problem-solving skills in ways that are visible to the children?

Pierre wants to get the broken tricycle fixed and back into use as soon as possible, but he also sees an opportunity to model critical problem-solving skills with the toddlers. With the toddlers all standing around inspecting the broken tricycle, Pierre calls to his coteacher, Amanda, to show her the problem. He asks her if they have a screwdriver to reattach the wheel to the tricycle. Amanda replies that the screwdriver has recently gone missing. The children look worried.

Pierre promises the children that he will not give up. He wonders aloud: "How can we fix the wheel without a screwdriver?" He says he thinks maybe a quarter would work. He pulls one out of his pocket and tries to use it to turn the screw, but the quarter is too thick. He explains that he will need to adapt his approach and try something else. He asks Amanda and the children if they can think of any other items that might work similarly to a screwdriver, with a hard, straight, thin edge. They generate several different ideas: a dime, a small pair of scissors, or a key. Pierre thinks out loud: "So we have a couple of possible other tools we can try. Let's try one at a time and figure out if any of them will work to screw this wheel back on."

They gather the other possible tools, and after several attempts, the dime works to screw the wheel back on securely. Pierre reflects aloud: "I wasn't sure if we were going to be able to fix this without the screwdriver. But we kept trying until we fixed it with the dime. You all really know how to help solve a problem." Table 8.2 summarizes how Pierre applied the thinking skills in this scenario.

These two problem-solving scenarios illustrate how individual teachers applied the problem-solving framework. However, creating a problem-solving culture in early childhood programs requires the involvement of not only individual teachers but also program leaders and the community of teachers. Early childhood programs can create an organizational culture that supports and fosters teachers'—and children's—problem solving. Research shows that the organizational context in which teachers work (i.e., the classroom, program, or school) influences teachers' behaviors and practices (Douglass, 2011; Nelson & Slavit, 2008). Think about a work environment in which new ideas are welcomed, teachers feel safe asking questions and wondering with colleagues and supervisors about teaching challenges, and leaders actively support and reward these inquiry processes. This is an environment that supports collaborative problem solving, creating a safe space for inquiry, reflection, and adaptation of teaching practices to achieve desired outcomes. This chapter can be used in staff training as a tool for dialogue about how to support an inquiry approach to teaching in your own program or school.

Table 8.2. How Pierre demonstrated the problem-solving skills: The case of the broken tricycle

Curious	Persistent	Flexible	Reflective	Collaborative
• Wondered aloud what other tools might substitute for a screwdriver	• Did not give up • Believed that they could find a solution to the problem	• Asked for help • Tried different new ideas	• Thought out loud about each attempt • Explained his thinking process and how it resulted in success	• Asked for ideas and suggestions • Shared joy at their collective success

CONCLUSION

Children's learning of the thinking skills needed for problem solving and engineering design can be maximized by applying a problem-solving framework to teaching. Through enriching and inclusive learning experiences and modeling of our own problem-solving processes, all children can develop as curious, persistent, flexible, reflective, and collaborative learners. Often teachers draw upon these thinking skills when responding to challenges they face as teachers. This chapter identifies specific ways teachers can apply the problem-solving framework to problems they face. Furthermore, this chapter argues that teachers must make these thinking processes visible to children so that they model the use of higher order thinking skills in ways that can extend children's learning.

The problem-solving framework presented in this book is a powerful resource for promoting higher order thinking skills. Both adults and children, including infants, develop and practice these thinking skills in the context of supportive learning environments and relationships. Teachers plan learning experiences, such as those described in this book, that engage children's curiosity and foster their thinking processes. In addition, teachers look for opportunities in their day-to-day work to model their own use of problem-solving skills when encountering challenges. In doing so, they create an environment that stimulates and nurtures young children as problem solvers and emerging engineers.

References

ABC News (Producer). (1999, February 9). The deep dive: One company's secret weapon for innovation. *Nightline* [Television broadcast]. New York, NY: American Broadcasting Company. Available from Films Media Group at http://www.films.com/ecTitleDetail.aspx?TitleID=11160&r=SR

ABET. (2012). *Criteria for accrediting engineering programs, 2012–2013.* Retrieved from http://www.abet.org/DisplayTemplates/DocsHandbook.aspx?id=3143

Adi-Japha, E., Berberich-Artzi, J., & Libnawe, A. (2010). Cognitive flexibility in drawings of bilingual children. *Child Development, 81*(5), 1356–1366.

Ahmed, S., Wallace, K.M., & Blessing, L. (2003). Understanding the differences between how novice and experienced designers approach design tasks. *Research in Engineering Design, 14*, 1–11.

Ainsworth, M.S. (1979). Infant–mother attachment. *American Psychologist, 34*(10), 932.

Atman, C.J., Adams, R.S., Mosborg, S., Cardella, M.E., Turns, J., & Saleem, J. (2007). Engineering design processes: A comparison of students and expert practitioners. *Journal of Engineering Education, 96*(4), 359–379.

Atman, C.J., Kilgore, D., & McKenna, A. (2008). Characterizing design learning: A mixed-methods study of engineering designers' use of language. *Journal of Engineering Education, 97*, 309–326.

Atman, C.J., Yasuhara, K., Adams, R.S., Barker, T.J., Turns, J., & Rhone, E. (2008). Breadth in problem scoping: A comparison of freshman and senior engineering students. *International Journal of Engineering Education, 24*(2), 234–245.

Banerjee, P.N., & Tamis-LeMonda, C.S. (2007). Infants' persistence and mothers' teaching as predictors of toddlers' cognitive development. *Infant Behavior and Development, 30*, 479–491.

Barrett, T.M., Davis, E.F., & Needham, A. (2007). Learning about tools in infancy. *Developmental Psychology, 43*(2), 352–368.

Basham, J.D., & Marino, M.T. (2013). Understanding STEM education and supporting students through universal design for learning. *Teaching Exceptional Children, 45*(4), 8–15.

Beck, S.R., Apperly, I.A., Chappell, J.M., Guthrie, C., & Cutting, N. (2011). Making tools isn't child's play. *Cognition, 119*, 301–306.

Belsky, J., Friedman, S.L., & Hsieh, K.H. (2001). Testing a core emotion-regulation prediction: Does early attentional persistence moderate the effect of infant negative emotionality on later development? *Child Development, 72*(1), 123–133.

Bers, M.U. (2008). *Blocks to robots: Learning with technology in the early childhood classroom.* New York, NY: Teachers College Press.

Bers, M.U., & Resnick, M. (2014). *About Scratch Jr.* Retrieved from http://www.scratchjr.org

Beswick, D.G., & Tallmadge, G.K. (1971). Reexamination of two learning style studies in the light of the cognitive process theory of curiosity. *Journal of Educational Psychology, 62*(6), 456–462. Retrieved from http://dx.doi.org/10.1037/h0031817

Blagojevic, B., Twomey, D., & Labas, L. (2002). *Universal design for learning: From the start.* Retrieved from http://www.ccids.umaine.edu/facts/facts6/udl.htm

Borrego, M., Karlin, J., McNair, L.D., & Beddoes, K. (2013). Team effectiveness theory from industrial and organizational psychology applied to engineering student project teams: A research review. *Journal of Engineering Education, 102*(4), 472–512.

Brewer, C.A., & Smith, D. (Eds.). (2011). *Vision and change: A call to action.* Retrieved from http://visionandchange.org/files/2011/03/Revised-Vision-and-Change-Final-Report.pdf

Browder, D.M., Spooner, F., Wakeman, S., Trela, K., & Baker, J.N. (2006). Aligning instruction with academic content standards: Finding the link. *Research and Practice for Persons with Severe Disabilities, 31*(4), 309–321.

Brownell, C.A., Ramani, G.B., & Zerwas, S. (2006). Becoming a social partner with peers: Cooperation and social understanding in one- and two-year-olds. *Child Development, 77*(4), 803–821. doi:10.1111/j.1467-8624.2006.t01-1-.x-i1

Bucciarelli, L. (1994). *Designing engineers.* Cambridge, MA: MIT Press.

Butera, G., Mihai, A., Clay, J., Vaiouli, P., Friesen, A., Horn, E., . . . Butler, C. (2012, October 30). *Initiating and sustaining a meaningful teacher-researcher collaboration in a preschool curriculum design.* Presentation handout, Division for Early Childhood Conference, Minneapolis, MN.

Butler, L.P., & Walton, G.M. (2013). The opportunity to collaborate increases preschoolers' motivation for challenging tasks. *Journal of Experimental Child Psychology, 116*(4), 953–961. doi:http://dx.doi.org/10.1016/j.jecp.2013.06.007

Buysse, V., & Hollingsworth, H.L. (2009). Program quality and early childhood inclusion recommendations for professional development. *Topics in Early Childhood Special Education, 29*(2), 119–128.

California Department of Education (2010). *California Preschool Curriculum Framework.* Retrieved from http://www.cde.ca.gov/sp/cd/re/documents/psframework-kvol1.pdf

Capobianco, B.M., Diefes-Dux, H.A., & Mena, I.B. (2011). Elementary school teachers' attempts at integrating engineering design: Transformation or assimilation? *Proceedings of the Annual Conference of the American Society for Engineering Education* (AC 2011-495), Vancouver, BC, June 26–29, 2011. Retrieved from http://www.asee.org/public/conferences/1/papers/495/view

Cardella, M.E., Atman, C.J., Turns, J., Adams, R.S. (2008). Students with differing design processes as freshmen: Case studies on change. *International Journal of Engineering Education, 24*(2), 246–259.

Carle, E. (2009). *Have you seen my cat?* New York, NY: Little Simon.

Cartwright, K.B. (2012). Insights from cognitive neuroscience: The importance of executive function for early reading development and education. *Early Education and Development, 23*(1), 24–36.

Center for Applied Special Technology. (2012a). *Research evidence: National design on universal design for learning.* Retrieved from http://www.udlcenter.org/research/researchevidence

Center for Applied Special Technology. (2012b). *UDL guidelines 2.0: National design on universal design for learning.* Retrieved from http://www.udlcenter.org/aboutudl/udlguidelines

Center for Child and Family Studies. (2010). *Desired results for children and families.* Retrieved from http://www.desiredresults.us

Chalufour, I., & Worth, K. (2003). *Discovering nature with young children.* Portsmouth, NH: Prentice Hall.

Chalufour, I., & Worth, K. (2004). *Building structures with young children.* Portsmouth, NH: Prentice Hall.

Chalufour, I., & Worth, K. (2005). *Exploring water with young children.* Portsmouth, NH: Prentice Hall.

Chen, Z., & Siegler, R.S. (2000). Across the great divide: Bridging the gap between understanding of toddlers' and older children's thinking. *Monographs of the Society for Research in Child Development, 65*(2), 1–96.

Clements, D., & Sarama, J. (2003, April). Building blocks of early childhood mathematics. *Teaching Children Mathematics,* 480–485.

Conezio, K., & French, L. (2002a, September). Capitalizing on children's fascination with the everyday world to foster language and literacy development. *Beyond the Journal.* Retrieved from http://www.naeyc.org/files/yc/file/200209/ScienceInThePreschoolClassroom.pdf

Conezio, K., & French, L. (2002b). Science in the preschool classroom. *Young Children, 57*(5), 12–18.

Conn-Powers, M., Cross, A.F., Traub, E.K., & Hutter-Pishgahi, L. (2006, September). The universal design of early education: Moving forward for all children. *Young Children.* Retrieved from http://www.naeyc.org/files/yc/file/200609/ConnPowersBTJ.pdf

Crismond, D.P., & Adams, R.S. (2012). The informed design teaching and learning matrix. *Journal of Engineering Education, 101*(4), 738–797.

Cross, N. (2003). The expertise of exceptional designers. In N. Cross & E. Edmonds (Eds.), *Expertise in design* (pp. 25–35). Sydney, Australia: Creativity and Cognition Press at the University of Technology.

Cross, N. (2004). Expertise in design: An overview. *Design Studies, 25*(5), 427–441.

Cudahy, D., Finnan, C., Jarusiewicz, C., & McCarty, B. (2002). *Seeing dispositions: Translating our shared values into observable behavior.* Retrieved from http://mynkuhelp.nku.edu/content/dam/coehs/docs/dispositions/symposium_2002/day2/seeingdispositions.ppt

Cunconan-Lahr, R.L., & Stifel, S. (2007). *Questions to consider in UDL observations of early childhood environments.* Retrieved from http://www.northampton.edu/Documents/Departments/ECE/Checklist%20and%20Questions.pdf

Cunconan-Lahr, R.L., & Stifel, S. (2013). *Universal design for learning (UDL) checklist for early childhood environments.* Retrieved from http://www.northampton.edu/Documents/Departments/ece/checklist%20and%20Questions.pdf

Cutting, N., Apperly, I.A., & Beck, S.R. (2011). Why do children lack the flexibility to innovate tools? *Journal of Experimental Child Psychology, 109,* 497–511.

DK Publishing. (2006). *Baby says peekaboo!* New York, NY: Dorling Kindersley.

Daehler, M.W. (2000). A key bridge to understanding the development of thinking and problem solving. *Monographs of the Society for Research in Child Development, 65*(2), 97–105.

Daly, S.R., Adams, R.S., & Bodner, G.M. (2012). What does it mean to design? A qualitative investigation of design professionals' experiences. *Journal of Engineering Education, 101*(2), 187–219.

Darling, A.L., & Dannels, D.P. (2010). Practicing engineers talk about the importance of talk: A report on the role of oral communication in the workplace. *Communication Education, 52*(1), 1–16.

Davis, L.A., & Gibbin, R.D. (Eds.). (2002). *Raising public awareness of engineering.* Washington, DC: National Academies Press.

Dehaene, S. (1997). *The number sense: How the mind creates mathematics.* Oxford, England: Oxford University Press.

DeLoache, J.S., Cassidy, D.J., & Brown, A.L. (1985). Precursors of mnemonic strategies in very young children's memory. *Child Development, 56,* 125–137.

DeVries, R., & Sales, C. (2011). *Ramps and pathways: A constructivist approach to physics with young children.* Washington, DC: National Center for the Education of Young Children.

Division for Early Childhood. (2009). *Code of ethics.* Missoula, MT: Division for Early Childhood. Retrieved from http://dec.membershipsoftware.org/files/Position%20Statement%20and%20Papers/Member%20Code%20of%20Ethics.pdf

Division for Early Childhood National Association for the Education of Young Children. (2009). *Early childhood inclusion: A joint position statement of the Division for Early Childhood (DEC) and the National Association for the Education of Young Children (NAEYC).* Chapel Hill: University of North Carolina, FPG Child Development Institute.

Douglass, A. (2011). Improving family engagement: The organizational context and its influence on partnering with parents in formal child care settings. *Early Childhood Research and Practice, 13*(2). Retrieved from http://ecrp.uiuc.edu/v13n2/douglass.html

Drake, K., Belsky, J., & Fearon, R.M.P. (2013, May 6). From early attachment to engagement with learning in school: The role of self-regulation and persistence. *Developmental Psychology.* Advance online publication. doi:10.1037/a0032779. Retrieved from http://www.ncbi.nlm.nih.gov/pubmed/23647414

Dym, C.L. (1994). *Engineering: A synthesis of views.* New York, NY: Cambridge University Press.

Dym, C.L., & Little, P. (2004). *Engineering design: A project-based introduction.* New York, NY: Wiley.

Eisenberg, N., Smith, C.L., & Spinrad, T.L. (2010). Effortful control: Relations with emotion regulation, adjustment, and socialization in childhood. In K.D. Vohs & R.F. Baumeister (Eds.), *Self-regulation: Research, theory, and applications* (2nd ed., pp. 263–283). New York, NY: Guilford.

Ellis, A.E., & Oakes, L.M. (2006). Infants flexibly use different dimensions to categorize objects. *Developmental Psychology, 42,* 1000–1011.

Epstein, A.S. (2003, September). How planning and reflection develop young children's thinking skills. *Beyond the Journal.* Retrieved from http://www.naeyc.org/files/yc/file/200309/Planning&Reflection.pdf

Feeney, S., Freeman, N., & Pizzolongo, P. (2012). *Ethics and the early childhood educator: Using the NAEYC code.* Washington, DC: NAEYC.

Fischer, K.W., Bullock, D.H., Rotenberg, E.J., & Raya, P. (1993). The dynamics of competence: How context contributes directly to skill. In R. Wozniak & K.W. Fischer (Eds.), *Development in context: Acting and thinking in specific environments* (pp. 93–117). Hillsdale, NJ: Erlbaum.

Fleming, C. (2002). *Muncha! Muncha! Muncha!* New York, NY: Atheneum Books.

Fontanelle, S.A., Kahrs, B.A., Neal, S.A., Newton, A.T., & Lockman, J.J. (2007). Infant manual exploration of composite substrates. *Journal of Experimental Child Psychology, 98*(3), 153–167.

Fortus, D., Dershimer, R.C., Krajcik, J.S., Marx, R.W., & Mamlok-Naaman, R. (2004). Design-based science and student learning. *Journal of Research in Science Teaching, 41*(10), 1081–1110.

Frodi, A., Bridges, L., & Grolnick, W. (1985). Correlates of mastery-related behavior: A short-term longitudinal study of infants in their second year. *Child Development, 56,* 1291–1298.

Galinsky, E. (2011). *Give the gift of curiosity for the holidays—lessons from Laura Shulz.* Retrieved from http://www.huffingtonpost.com/ellen-galinsky/give-the-gift-of-curiosit_1_b_1157991.html

Gelman, R., & Brenneman, K. (2004). Science learning pathways for young children. *Early Childhood Research Quarterly, 19,* 150–158.

Gelman, R., Brenneman, K., Macdonald, G., & Roman, M. (2009). *Preschool Pathways to Science (PrePS™): Facilitating scientific ways of thinking, talking, doing, and understanding.* Baltimore, MD: Paul H. Brookes Publishing Co.

Gibson, J.E., Scherer, W.T., & Gibson, W.F. (2007). *How to do a systems analysis.* New York, NY: Wiley Interscience.

Gillis, A., Luthin, K., Parette, H.P., & Blum, C. (2012). Using VoiceThread to create meaningful receptive expressive learning activities for young children. *Early Childhood Education Journal, 40,* 203–211.

Gonzalez, M. (2014, March). App evaluation: UDL tool 1.0. *Society for Information Technology & Teacher Education International Conference, 2014*(1), 1809–1811.

Gopnik, A. (2012). Scientific thinking in young children: Theoretical advances, empirical research, and policy implications. *Science, 337,* 1623.

Gopnik, A., Glymour, C., Sobel, D.M., Schulz, L.E., Kushnir, T., & Danks, D. (2004). A theory of causal learning in children: Causal maps and Bayes nets. *Psychological review, 111*(1), 3–32.

Grolnick, W.S., & Ryan, R.M. (1989). Parent styles associated with children's self-regulation and competence in school. *Journal of Educational Psychology, 81*(2), 143.

Guernsey, L. (2007). *Into the minds of babes: How screen time affects children from birth to age five.* New York, NY: Basic Books.

Hauser-Cram, P., Bronson, M.B., & Upshur, C.C. (1993). The effects of the classroom environment on the social and mastery behavior of preschool children with disabilities. *Early Childhood Research Quarterly, 8,* 479–497.

Henderson, A.M.E., Wang, Y., Matz, L.E., & Woodward, A.L. (2013). Active experience shapes 10-month-old infants' understanding of collaborative goals. *Infancy, 18*(1), 10–39. doi:10.1111/j.1532–7078.2012.00126.x

Hespos, S.J., & Baillargeon, R. (2008). Young infants' actions reveal their developing knowledge of support variables: Converging evidence for violation-of-expectation findings. *Cognition, 107*(1), 304–316.

Hess, R.D., Holloway, S.D., Dickson, W.P., & Price, G.G. (1984). Maternal variables as predictors of children's school readiness and later achievement in vocabulary and mathematics in sixth grade. *Child Development, 55*(5), 1902–1912.

Hill, E. (2003). *Where's Spot?* New York, NY: Putnam.

Hord, S.M. (1997). *Professional learning communities: Communities of continuous inquiry and improvement.* Austin, TX: Southwest Educational Development Laboratory. Retrieved from http://www.sedl.org/pubs/change34/plc-cha34.pdf

Horn, E., & Banerjee, R. (2009). Understanding curriculum modifications and embedded learning opportunities in the context of supporting all children's success. *Language, Speech, and Hearing Services in Schools, 40*(4), 406–415.

Howes, C. (1999). Attachment relationships in the context of multiple caregivers. In J. Cassidy & P.R. Shaver (Eds.), *Handbook of attachment theory and research* (pp. 671–687). New York, NY: Guilford.

Howland, A.A., Baird, K.A., Pocock, A., Coy, S., & Arbuckle, C. (2013). *Supporting language acquisition and content-specific science access: Universal design for learning using LEGO WeDos to teach simple machines.* Paper presented at Hawaii University International Conferences, Honolulu, HI.

Intrater, R.G. (1997). *Baby faces peekaboo!* New York, NY: Scholastic.

Jirout, J., & Klahr, D. (2012). Children's scientific curiosity: In search of an operational definition of an elusive concept. *Developmental Review, 32*(2), 125–160.

Kagan, S.L., Moore, E., & Bredekamp, S. (Eds.). (1998). *Reconsidering children's early development and learning toward common views and vocabulary: National Education Goals Panel.* Darby, PA: DIANE.

Karmiloff-Smith, A. (1990). Constraints on representational change: Evidence from children's drawing. *Cognition, 34,* 57–83.

Kelley, S.A., Brownell, C.A., & Campbell, S.B. (2000). Mastery motivation and self-evaluative affect in toddlers: Longitudinal relations with maternal behavior. *Child Development, 71*(4), 1061–1071.

Kelley, S.A., & Jennings, K.D. (2003). Putting the pieces together: Maternal depression, maternal behavior, and toddler helplessness. *Infant Mental Health Journal, 24*(1), 74–90.

Kelley, T., & Littman, J. (2001). *The art of innovation: Lessons in creativity from IDEO, America's leading design firm.* New York, NY: Random House.

Killion, J.P., & Todnem, G. (1991). A process of personal theory building. *Educational Leadership, 48*(6), 14–16.

La Paro, K.M., & Pianta, R.C. (2000). Predicting children's competence in the early school years: A meta-analytic review. *Review of Educational Research, 70*(4), 443–484. doi:10.3102/00346543070004443

Larkina, M., Guler, O.E., Kleinknecht, E., & Bauer, P.J. (2008). Maternal provision of structure in a deliberate memory task in relation to their preschool children's recall. *Journal of Experimental Child Psychology, 100,* 235–251.

Lawson, B. (1997). *How designers think: The design process demystified* (3rd ed.). Boston, MA: Architectural Press.

Lieber, J., Horn, E., Palmer, S., & Fleming, K. (2008). Access to the general education curriculum for preschoolers with disabilities: Children's school success. *Exceptionality, 16*(1), 18–32.

Li-Grining, C.P., Votruba-Drzal, E., Maldonado-Carreño, C., & Haas, K. (2010). Children's early approaches to learning and academic trajectories through fifth grade. *Developmental Psychology, 46*(5), 1062.

Loewenstein, G. (1994). The psychology of curiosity: A review and reinterpretation. *Psychological bulletin, 116*(1), 75.

Lucas, C.G., Bridgers, S., Griffiths, T.L., & Gopnik, A. (2014). When children are better (or at least more open-minded) learners than adults: Developmental differences in learning the forms of causal relationships. *Cognition, 131,* 284–299.

Maass, R. (1998). *Garden.* Markham, ON, Canada: Henry Holt and Company.

Marcovitch, S., Jacques, S., Boseovski, J.J., & Zelazo, P.D. (2008). Self-reflection and the cognitive control of behavior: Implications for learning. *Mind, Brain, and Education, 2*(3), 136–141.

Martin, A., Ryan, R.M., & Brooks-Gunn, J. (2013). Longitudinal associations among interest, persistence, supportive parenting, and achievement in early childhood. *Early Childhood Research Quarterly, 28*(4), 658–667.

Massachusetts Department of Early Education and Care. (2011). *Massachusetts early learning guidelines for infants and toddlers.* Retrieved from http://www.eec.state.ma.us/docs1/Workforce_Dev/Layout.pdf

Massachusetts Department of Education. (2003). *Guidelines for Preschool Learning Experiences.* Retrieved from http://fcsn.org/pti/topics/earlychildhood/preschool_learning_eec.pdf

Massachusetts Department of Elementary and Secondary Education. (2014) *Pre-K Science, Technology, and Engineering Standards.* Retrieved from http://www.mass.gov/edu/docs/eec/2013/20131009-pk-sci-tech-standards.pdf

McClelland, M.M., Acock, A.C., & Morrison, F.J. (2006). The impact of kindergarten learning-related skills on academic trajectories at the end of elementary school. *Early Childhood Research Quarterly, 21*(4), 471–490.

McCormack, T., & Atance, C.M. (2011). Planning in young children: A review and synthesis. *Developmental Review, 31*(1), 1–31.

Messer, D. (1995). Mastery motivation: Past, present and future. In R.H. MacTurk & G. Morgan (Eds.), *Mastery motivation: Origins, conceptualizations, and applications* (pp. 293–316). Norwood, NJ: Ablex.

Mokrova, I., O'Brien, M., Calkins, S.D., Leerkes, E.M., & Marcovitch, S. (2013). The role of persistence at preschool age in academic skills at kindergarten. *European Journal of Psychology of Education, 28*(4), 1495–1503. doi:10.1007/s10212-013-0177-2

Moore, T. (2008). *Beyond the evidence: Building universal early childhood services from the ground up.* Paper presented at the 8th National Conference, Centre for Child Community Health, Sydney, Australia.

National Association for the Education of Young Children. (2014). *NAEYC early childhood program standards and accreditation criteria & guidance for assessment.* Washington, DC: Author. Retrieved from http://www.naeyc.org/files/academy/file/AllCriteriaDocument.pdf

National Center for the Education of Young Children & The Fred Rogers Center. (2012). *Technology and interactive media as tools in early childhood programs serving children from birth through age 8: A joint position statement of the National Association for the Education of Young Children and the Fred Rogers Center for Early Learning and Children's Media at Saint Vincent College.* Retrieved from http://www.naeyc.org/files/naeyc/file/positions/PS_technology_WEB2.pdf

National Education Goals Panel (1993). *The national education goals report. Volume one: The national report.* Washington, DC: U.S. Government Printing Office.

National Governors Association Center for Best Practices & Council of Chief State School Officers. (2010). *Common Core State Standards for mathematics.* Washington, DC: Authors.

National Research Council. (2012). *A framework for K–12 science education: Practices, crosscutting concepts, and core ideas.* Washington, DC: National Academies Press.

Neitzel, C., & Stright, A.D. (2003). Mothers' scaffolding of children's problem solving: Establishing a foundation of academic self-regulatory competence. *Journal of Family Psychology, 17*(1), 147–159. doi:10.1037/0893-3200.17.1.147

Nelson, G. (2007). *Math at their own pace: Child-directed activities for developing early number sense.* St. Paul, MN: Redleaf Press.

Nelson, T.H., & Slavit, D. (2008). Supported teacher collaborative inquiry. *Teacher Education Quarterly, 35*(1), 99–116.

Next Generation Science Standards Lead States. (2013). *Next Generation Science Standards: For states, by states.* Washington, DC: National Academies Press. Retrieved from http://www.nextgenscience.org/next-generation-science-standards

Nuner, J. (2007). Foster creativity that will last a lifetime. *Texas Child Care Quarterly, 31*(2), 16–21. Retrieved from http://www.childcarequarterly.com/pdf/fall07_creativity.pdf

Odom, S.L., Buysse, V., & Soukakou, E. (2011). Inclusion for young children with disabilities: A quarter century of research perspectives. *Journal of Early Intervention, 33*(4), 344–357. doi:10.1177/1053815111430094

Office of Head Start. (2010). *Head Start child development and early learning frameworks: Promoting positive outcomes in early childhood programs serving children 3–5 years old (2010).* Washington, DC: U.S. Department of Health and Human Services. Retrieved from https://eclkc.ohs.acf.hhs.gov/hslc/tta-system/teaching/eecd/Assessment/Child%20Outcomes/HS_Revised_Child_Outcomes_Framework(rev-Sept2011).pdf

Office of Head Start. (2011). *The Head Start Child Development and Learning Framework: Promoting Positive Outcomes in Early Childhood Programs Serving Children 3–5 Years Old.* Retrieved from https://eclkc.ohs.acf.hhs.gov/hslc/tta-system/teaching/eecd/Assessment/Child%20Outcomes/HS_Revised_Child_Outcomes_Framework(rev-Sept2011).pdf

Ogu, U., & Schmidt, S.R. (2009, March). Investigating rocks and sand: Addressing multiple learning styles through an inquiry-based approach. *Beyond the Journal.* Retrieved from http://www.naeyc.org/files/yc/file/200903/BTJSchmidt_Ogu_Expanded.pdf

Ohio Department of Education. (2012). *Ohio Early Learning and Development Standards.* Retrieved from http://education.ohio.gov/Topics/Early-Learning/Early-Learning-Content-Standards/The-Standards

Papert, S. (1980). *Mindstorms: Children, computers, and powerful ideas.* New York, NY: Basic Books.

Parette, H.P., Blum, C., & Luthin, K. (2013). Pedagogy and use of apps for early literacy: Making connections in planned classroom activities. In J. Whittingham, S. Huffman, W. Rickman, & C. Wiedmaier (Eds.), *Technological tools for the literacy classroom* (pp. 180–195). Hershey, PA: Information Science Reference. doi:10.4018/978-1-4666-3974-4.ch011

Parlakian, R. (2001). *Look, listen, and learn: Reflective supervision and relationship-based work.* Washington, DC: ZERO TO THREE.

Perry, B. (n.d.) Why young children are curious. *Early Childhood Today.* Retrieved from http://www.scholastic.com/teachers/article/why-young-children-are-curious

Perry, B. (2001). *Curiosity: The fuel of development.* Retrieved from http://teacher.scholastic.com/professional/bruceperry/curiosity.htm

Petroski, H. (1996). *Invention by design: How engineers get from thought to thing.* Cambridge, MA: Harvard University Press.

Piaget, J. (1954). *The construction of reality in the child.* New York, NY: Basic Books.

Piaget, J. (1969). *The psychology of intelligence.* Totowa, NJ: Littlefield, Adams.

Piaget, J., & Inhelder, B. (1966). *The psychology of the child.* New York, NY: Basic Books.

Pianta, R.C., La Paro, K.M., & Hamre, B.K. (2008). *Classroom Assessment Scoring System® (CLASS™) manual, Pre-K.* Baltimore, MD: Paul H. Brookes Publishing Co.

Pianta, R.C., Smith, N., & Reeve, R.E. (1991). Observing mother and child behavior in a problem-solving situation at school entry: Relations with classroom adjustment. *School Psychology Quarterly, 6*(1), 1.

Portsmore, M.D. (2010). *Exploring how experience with planning impacts first grade students' planning and solutions to engineering design problems.* Doctoral dissertation, Tufts University, Medford, MA.

Potter, B. (2002/1902). *The tale of Peter Rabbit.* London, England: Warne.

Rakison, D.H., & Poulin-Dubois, D. (2001). Developmental origin of the animate-inanimate distinction. *Psychological Bulletin, 127*(2), 209–228.

Ratner, H.H. (1980). The role of social context in memory development. In M. Perlmutter (Ed.), *Children's memory: New directions for child development* (pp. 49–68). San Francisco, CA: Jossey-Bass.

Razza, R.A., Martin, A., & Brooks-Gunn, J. (2010). Associations among family environment, sustained attention, and school readiness for low-income children. *Developmental Psychology, 46*(6), 1528.

Razza, R.A., Martin, A., & Brooks-Gunn, J. (2012). The implications of early attentional regulation for school success among low-income children. *Journal of Applied Developmental Psychology, 33*(6), 311–319.

Richards, C.A., & Sanderson, J.A. (1999). The role of imagination in facilitating deductive reasoning in 2-, 3-, and 4-year-olds. *Cognition, 72*(2), B1–B9.

Richardson, S. (Writer). (2010). Reaching and engaging all learners through technology. In Laureate Education Inc. (Producer), *Universal design for learning* [video]. Baltimore, MD.

Rimm-Kaufman, S.E., Pianta, R.C., & Cox, M.J. (2000). Teachers' judgments of problems in the transition to kindergarten. *Early Childhood Research Quarterly, 15*(2), 147–166.

Robson, S., & Rowe, V. (2012). Observing young children's creative thinking: Engagement, involvement and persistence. *International Journal of Early Years Education, 20*(4), 349–364. doi:10.1080/09669760.2012.743098

Rogoff, B., Mistry, J., Göncü, A., Mosier, C., Chavajay, P., & Heath, S.B. (1993). Guided participation in cultural activity by toddlers and caregivers. *Monographs of the Society for Research in Child Development*, 1–174.

Root, P. (1998). *One duck stuck*. Cambridge, MA: Candlewick Press.

Roth, C. (1999). *Ten dirty pigs, ten clean pigs*. New York, NY: North-South Books.

Rothbart, M.K., & Bates, J.E. (2006). Temperament. In N. Eisenberg, W. Damon, & R.M. Lerner (Eds.), *Handbook of child psychology*, Vol. 3: *Social, emotional, and personality development* (6th ed., pp. 99–166). New York, NY: Wiley.

Rous, B., & Hyson, M. (2007, March). Promoting positive outcomes for children with disabilities: Recommendations for curriculum, assessment, and program evaluation. *Division for Early Childhood, Council for Exceptional Children*. Retrieved from http://dec.membershipsoftware.org/files/Position%20Statement%20and%20Papers/Prmtg_Pos_Outcomes_Companion_Paper.pdf

Salmon, A.K. (2010). Tools to enhance young children's thinking. *Young Children, 65*(5), 26–31.

Sandall, S.R., & Schwartz, I.S. (2008). *Building blocks for teaching preschoolers with special needs* (2nd ed.). Baltimore, MD: Paul H. Brookes Publishing Co.

Schaefer, B.A., & McDermott, P.A. (1999). Learning behavior and intelligence as explanations for children's scholastic achievement. *Journal of School Psychology, 37*(3), 299–313.

Schön, D.A. (1983). *The reflective practitioner: How professionals think in action*. New York, NY: Basic Books.

Schön, D.A. (1987). *Educating the reflective practitioner toward a new design for teaching and learning in the professions*. Jossey-Bass higher education series. San Francisco, CA: Jossey-Bass.

Schraw, G. (1994). The effect of metacognitive knowledge on local and global monitoring. *Contemporary Educational Psychology, 19*(2), 143–154.

Schulz, L., Bonawitz, E.B., & Griffiths, T.L. (2007). Can being scared give you a tummy ache? Naive theories, ambiguous evidence and preschoolers' causal inferences. *Developmental Psychology, 43*(5), 1124–1139.

Schulz, L.E., & Sommerville, J. (2006). God does not play dice: Causal determinism and preschoolers' causal inferences. *Child Development, 77*(2), 427–442.

Science Buddies. (2014). *Engineering design project guide*. Retrieved from http://www.sciencebuddies.org/engineering-design-process/engineering-design-notebook.shtml

Seizt, H.J. (2006, March). The plan: Building on children's interests. *Beyond the Journal*. Retrieved from http://www.naeyc.org/files/yc/file/200603/SeitzBTJ.pdf

Shaffer, L., Hall, E., & Lynch, M. (2009). Toddlers' scientific explorations: Encounters with insects. *Young Children, 64*(6), 18–23.

Sharp, C. (2004). Developing young children's creativity: What can we learn from research? *Topic, 32*, 5–12.

Shutts, K., Banaji, M.R., & Spelke, E.S. (2010). Social categories guide young children's preferences for novel objects. *Developmental Science, 13*(4), 599–610.

Simon, H.A. (1996). *The sciences of the artificial* (2nd ed.). Cambridge, MA: MIT Press.

Sloutsky, V., & Robinson, C.W. (2013). Redundancy matters: Flexible learning of multiple contingencies in infants. *Cognition, 126*(2), 156–164.

Spooner, F., Baker, J.N., Harris, A.A., Ahlgrim-Delzell, L., & Browder, D.M. (2007). Effects of training in universal design for learning on lesson plan development. *Remedial and Special Education, 28*(2), 108–116.

Sternberg, R.J. (2003). Creative thinking in the classroom. *Scandinavian Journal of Educational Research, 47*(3), 325–338.

Stone-MacDonald, A., Bartolini, V.L., Douglass, A., Love, M.L. (2011). *Focusing a new lens: STEM professional development for early education and care educators and programs*. Retrieved from http://www.communityinclusion.org/ecs/stem

Stremmel, A.J. (2007). The value of teacher research: Nurturing professional and personal growth through inquiry. *Voices of Practitioners*. Retrieved from http://journal.naeyc.org/btj/vp/pdf/Voices-Stremmel.pdf

Stright, A.D., Neitzel, C., Sears, K.G., & Hoke-Sinex, L. (2001). Instruction begins in the home: Relations between parental instruction and children's self-regulation in the classroom. *Journal of Educational Psychology, 93*(3), 456.

Sylva, K. (1992). Conversations in the nursery: How they contribute to aspirations and plans. *Language and Education, 6*(2–4), 147–148.

Texas Child Care. (2014). Science and discovery. *Texas Child CareQuarterly, 34*(4). Retrieved from http://www.childcarequarterly.com/pdf/spring14_basics.pdf

The Thomas Edison Papers. (2012). *Document sampler*. Retrieved from http://edison.rutgers.edu/docsamp.htm

Thomas, S.B., & Packer, D. (2013). A reflective teaching road map for pre-service and novice early childhood educators. *International Journal of Early Childhood Special Education, 5*(1), 1–14.

Thompson, R.A., & Haskins, R. (2014). Early stress gets under the skin: Promising initiatives to help children facing chronic adversity. *Future of Children, 24*(1).

Tinker, R., Zucker, A., & Staudt, C. (2009). *Preliminary research on universal design for learning (UDL) in grades 3–6 science education*. Paper presented at the National Association for Research in Science Teaching (NARST), Garden Grove, CA. Retrieved from http://concord.org/sites/default/files/pdf/UDL_NARST_2009_rev.pdf

Trudeau, K., & Harle, A.Z. (2006). Using reflection to increase children's learning in kindergarten. *Young Children, 61*(4), 101–104.

U.S. Department of Health and Human Services, Administration on Children, Youth and Families, Head Start Bureau. (2003). *The Head Start leaders guide to positive child outcomes*. Washington, DC: Author. Retrieved from http://eclkc.ohs.acf.hhs.gov/hslc/hs/resources/ECLKC_Bookstore/PDFs/HeadStartGuidePositiveChildOutcomes.pdf

Vygotsky, L.S. (1962). The development of scientific concepts in childhood. In L.S. Vygotsky, *Thought and language* (pp. 82–118). Cambridge, MA: MIT Press.

Vygotsky, L.S., & Cole, M. (1978). *Mind in society: The development of higher psychological processes*. Cambridge, MA: Harvard University Press.

Watkins, J., Spencer, K., & Hammer, D. (2014). Examining young students' problem scoping in engineering design. *Journal of Pre-College Engineering Education Research, 4*(1), 43–53.

WGBH Educational Foundation. (2011). *Design squad nation: Parents and educators online workshop.* Retrieved from http://pbskids.org/designsquad/pdf/parentseducators/workshop/designprocess_poster.pdf

Wheatley, K.F. (n.d.). *Teacher persistence: A crucial disposition, with implications for teacher education.* Retrieved from http://www.usca.edu/essays/vol32002/wheatley.pdf

Wigfield, A., Eccles, J.S., Schiefele, U., Roeser, R.W., & Davis-Kean, P. (2006). Development of achievement motivation. In N. Eisenberg, W. Damon, & R.M. Lerner (Eds.), *Handbook of child psychology*, Vol. 3: *Social, emotional, and personality development* (6th ed., pp. 933–1002). New York, NY: Wiley.

Willingham, T. (2011, February 11). Celebrating and inspiring curiosity as a key component in learning. *TED Conversations.* Retrieved from http://www.ted.com/conversations/145/celebrating_and_inspiring_curi.html

Worth, K. (2010). Science in EC classrooms. *Early Childhood Research and Practice.* Retrieved from http://ecrp.uiuc.edu/beyond/seed/worth.html

Worth, K., & Grollman, S. (2003). *Worms, shadows, and whirlpools: Science in the early childhood classroom.* Portsmouth, NH: Heinemann.

Wulf, W. (1998, Winter). The image of engineering. *Issues in Science and Technology.* Retrieved from http://www.issues.org/15.2/wulf.htm

Yarrow, L.J., Morgan, G.A., Jennings, K.D., Harmon, R.J., & Gaiter, J.L. (1982). Infants' persistence at tasks: Relationships to cognitive functioning and early experience. *Infant Behavior and Development, 5*(2–4), 131–141. doi:http://dx.doi.org/10.1016/S0163-6383(82)80023-4

ZERO TO THREE. (2012). *Tips on nurturing your child's curiosity.* Retrieved from http://www.zerotothree.org/child-development/social-emotional-development/tips-on-nurturing-your-childs-curiosity.html

Appendixes

APPENDIX A

Early Childhood UDL Planning Sheet

Infants (Sample)

Age group: _Infant_   Teacher: _Ms. G_   Activity: _Peekaboo games_

[All] = UDL suggestion for all students who need additional scaffolding; [Name] = UDL suggestion geared toward specific student based on strength/need; [Other] = UDL suggestion for children who have other needs, such as fine or gross motor challenges

UDL guidelines

Representation (What are they learning?)		Action and expression (How do they learn and show what they know?)		Engagement (Why do they want to participate and be engaged?)	
Materials	**Multisensory opportunities**	**Activities**	**Multimodal assessment**	**Environment**	**Preferences**
Add picture symbols to the book to support infants who will learn communication using picture symbols. [All] Use supportive seating options such as a corner sitter or a wedge for children with low muscle tone. [David] Use mirrors to show the infants their features and faces. [All] Provide scarves with different levels of opaqueness and different textures that make various sounds (e.g., crunchy fabric, soft fabric that whooshes together). [Julia]	Provide a plush dog that looks like Spot to touch and hold for added sensory input during the activity. [Julia] Use hand-over-hand guidance to help infants point, touch, and lift the flaps or grab the scarves. [David] Provide objects of different textures that make various sounds (e.g., crunchy fabric, soft fabric that whooshes together; boxes). [All]	Use the same pictures in this activity as are used in other activities to create continuity and greater recognition possibilities for infants. [All] Incorporate a switch with a YES, THAT'S MY FRIEND message to support participation in the activity, and consider another option with YES, THAT'S MY TEACHER. [All]	Use a few basic signs to engage infants in the lesson and offer them opportunities to communicate (e.g., MORE, DONE, YES, NO). [Julia] Offer only two pictures of known friends or caregivers to start and expand. [All] Incorporate a switch with YES to give the infants another way to respond. [All]	Ask infants to match real objects with objects and people in the pictures. [All] Offer only two pictures of known friends or caregivers to start and expand the book pages used. [All] Limit distractions in the room or play soft music without words to help focus the infants. [All]	Use cats of various sizes to promote different challenge levels to infants. [David] Hide the stuffed cat in a soft-object obstacle course where the infants can crawl around independently looking for the cat. [Julia]

Engaging Young Engineers: Teaching Problem-Solving Skills Through STEM by Angi Stone-MacDonald, Kristen Wendell, Anne Douglass, and Mary Lu Love. Copyright © 2015 by Paul H. Brookes Publishing Co., Inc. All rights reserved.

Early Childhood UDL Planning Sheet
Toddlers (Sample)

Age group: Toddlers   **Teacher:** Ms. S   **Activity:** Mud explorations

[All] = UDL suggestion for all students who need additional scaffolding; [Name] = UDL suggestion geared toward specific student based on strength/need; [Other] = UDL suggestion for children who have other needs, such as fine or gross motor challenges

UDL guidelines

Representation (What are they learning?)		Action and expression (How do they learn and show what they know?)		Engagement (Why do they want to participate and be engaged?)	
Materials	**Multisensory opportunities**	**Activities**	**Multimodal assessment**	**Environment**	**Preferences**
Different size blocks [All]	Bristle Blocks [Tam]	Have child build individually [Jessie]	Drawing [All]	Individual material sets for each child [Jessie]	Choice of building materials [All]
Material picture labels [Tam]	Sensory puzzle blocks [Tam]	Have child tell other child how to build using words [Tam]	Photos [All]	Group play areas and individual work mats [Jessie, All]	Choice of assessment options [All]
Different kinds of blocks [All]	Grips for tools [Other]	Offer peer or teacher support [All]	Video [All]	Large block area or table workspaces [All]	Counting manipulatives and number symbols [All]
Electronic version of book [Tam, Jessie]	Timer [Jessie]	Offer more or fewer choices based on child's level for this activity and thinking skill [All]	Share with one adult or with the class [Tam, Jessie]	Picture directions for cleaning [Tam]	
Big book [All]		Provide fading prompts or hand-over-hand physical support [Other]	Share orally or show a product (including a video) [All]	Individual tubs for children who do not want to work at the water table [Jessie]	
Additional copies of book for reading center [All]		Preteach key animals/vocabulary [Tam, Jessie]	Provide prepared sentence strips with possible answers and matching picture symbols [Other]		
Grips for markers [Other]		Model digging and excavating an object [All]			
Picture symbols for key vocabulary [Tam]					
Sequence board [All]					
Multiple felt/story boards for children to use in centers [All]					
Glue sticks (or paintbrushes to apply glue to paper) [Other]					
Picture cards [Other]					
Gloves [Other]					
Individual trays/bags for children [Jessie]					

Early Childhood UDL Planning Sheet

Preschoolers (Sample)

Age group: Preschoolers   **Teacher:** Ms. T   **Activity:** Munchal Munchal Munchal book/activity

[All] = UDL suggestion for all students who need additional scaffolding; [Name] = UDL suggestion geared toward specific student based on strength/need; [Other] = UDL suggestion for children who have other needs, such as fine or gross motor challenges

UDL guidelines

Representation (What are they learning?)		Action and expression (How do they learn and show what they know?)		Engagement (Why do they want to participate and be engaged?)	
Materials	**Multisensory opportunities**	**Activities**	**Multimodal assessment**	**Environment**	**Preferences**
Bristle Blocks [Brandon, All] Magnetic blocks [Brandon] Individual sticky work mats [José] Picture labels for materials (English and Spanish) [José] Communication board and story on iPad or tablet computer [Brandon] Feelings chart with faces for children to point to the feelings of the characters [Brandon] Easy cut and lefty scissors [Other] Sticky or nonslip surface [Other]	Bristle Blocks [Brandon, All] Time Timer during storytime [José] Audio or interactive version of book on tablet [All] Talking stick [All] Computer for drawing design plans [All, Other]	Have child tell other child how to build using communication device or words [Brandon, José] Provide picture directions and picture list of materials [Brandon, José] Preteach key vocabulary [José] Multiple testing opportunities [All] Provide precut shapes to use in drawing plans [All] Allow children to touch and move building materials while making plans [All] Review engineering vocabulary [José]	Photographs [All] Explanation to students of steps and solution [Brandon] Explanation in Spanish and English [José] Group presentation answers developed ahead of time with adult [Brandon, José] Oral Journaling [Brandon, José] Computer/iPad/tablet computer journaling program [Brandon, José]	Turn-taking stick [José] Adult or peer supports [Brandon, José, Other] Felt or magnet board for picture display [All] Picture symbols for key vocabulary for journaling [All] Help signal/card [All]	Choice of building materials [All] Choice of assessment options [All] Small-group or large-group discussion for engineering circle [All]

Early Childhood UDL Planning Sheet

Age group: _____   Teacher: _____   Activity: _____

[All] = UDL suggestion for all students who need additional scaffolding; [Name] = UDL suggestion geared toward specific student based on strength/need; [Other] = UDL suggestion for children who have other needs, such as fine or gross motor challenges

UDL guidelines

Representation (What are they learning?)		Action and expression (How do they learn and show what they know?)		Engagement (Why do they want to participate and be engaged?)	
Materials	Multisensory opportunities	Activities	Multimodal assessment	Environment	Preferences

Engaging Young Engineers: Teaching Problem-Solving Skills Through STEM by Angi Stone-MacDonald, Kristen Wendell, Anne Douglass, and Mary Lu Love. Copyright © 2015 by Paul H. Brookes Publishing Co., Inc. All rights reserved.

Infant Experience Planning Template

Planning steps	Description
Focus What is the problem-solving focus skill? (curious, persistent, flexible, reflective, and/or collaborative)	
Specific Learning Objective(s) What will the infants know or be able to do or say as a result of this experience?	
Materials What materials are needed to implement this experience?	
Steps What are the steps for implementing this experience?	
Promoting Thinking How will adults help the infants think about what they are doing? For example, how will adults apply each strategy for this experience?	
Explain and Discuss the Problem How will adults talk about and/or demonstrate the problem?	
Narrate Your Actions How will adults narrate their actions to provide language modeling?	
Wonder and Ask Questions What questions will adults ask?	
Extend and Modify the Experience How might this experience be extended or modified for each infant and also over time?	
Follow the Infant's Lead How will adults assess the infants' responses during the experience? How will they apply that information to guide their interactions with each infant?	

Toddler Experience Planning Template

Problem-solving focus skill	_____ thinking
Motivating engineering problem	
Focus of this particular learning experience	
Learning objectives for this particular experience	
Materials needed	

Elements of the learning experience	UDL supports
Introduce children to the problem	
Help children understand the problem-solving goal and constraints	
Support children in demonstrating their thinking	
Provide opportunities for feedback and for trying again	
Help children share and learn from one another	

Rubric			
Rate the child's level of participation and understanding on the continuum. Add evidence/descriptions for each child.	Developmental skill Skills demonstrated in this activity related to skill	Developmental skill Skills demonstrated in this activity related to skill	Developmental skill Skills demonstrated in this activity related to skill
Child 1			
Child 2			
Child 3			

Preschool Experience Planning Template

Problem-solving focus skill	_____ thinking	
Motivating engineering problem		
Focus of this particular learning experience		
Learning objectives for this particular experience		
Materials needed		

Elements of the learning experience		UDL supports
Introduce children to the problem		
Help children understand the problem-solving goal and constraints		
Support children in demonstrating their thinking		
Provide opportunities for feedback and for trying again		
Help children share and learn from one another		

Rubric			
Rate the child's level of participation and understanding on the continuum. Add evidence/descriptions for each child.	Developmental skill Skills demonstrated in this activity related to skill	Developmental skill Skills demonstrated in this activity related to skill	Developmental skill Skills demonstrated in this activity related to skill
Child 1			
Child 2			
Child 3			

Index

Note: The letters *f* and *t* indicate that the entry refers to a page's figure or table, respectively.